T0298815

Global Linkages and Economic Rebalancing in East Asia

Global Linkages and Economic Rebalancing in East Asia

Edited by

Takuji Kinkyo
Yoichi Matsubayashi
Shigeyuki Hamori

Kobe University, Japan

 World Scientific

NEW JERSEY · LONDON · SINGAPORE · BEIJING · SHANGHAI · HONG KONG · TAIPEI · CHENNAI

Published by

World Scientific Publishing Co. Pte. Ltd.

5 Toh Tuck Link, Singapore 596224

USA office: 27 Warren Street, Suite 401-402, Hackensack, NJ 07601

UK office: 57 Shelton Street, Covent Garden, London WC2H 9HE

Library of Congress Cataloging-in-Publication Data
Kinkyo, Takuji, author.
    Global linkages and economic rebalancing in East Asia / by Takuji Kinkyo,
Yoichi Matsubayashi & Shigeyuki Hamori (Kobe University, Japan).
    p. cm.
    Includes bibliographical references and index.
    ISBN 978-9814412841
    1. East Asia--Economic conditions--21st century. 2. East Asia--Foreign economic relations.
3. East Asia--Economic policy. I. Matsubayashi, Yoichi, author. II. Hamori, Shigeyuki, 1959–
III. Title.
    HC460.5.K576 2013
    337.95--dc23

    2012033630

British Library Cataloguing-in-Publication Data
A catalogue record for this book is available from the British Library.

First published 2013 (Hardcover)
Reprinted 2017 (in paperback edition)
ISBN 978-981-3224-83-4

Copyright © 2013 by World Scientific Publishing Co. Pte. Ltd.

In-house Editors: Lum Pui Yee/Dipasri Sardar

Typeset by Stallion Press
Email: enquiries@stallionpress.com

Printed in Singapore.

CONTENTS

ABOUT THE EDITORS

Dr. Takuji Kinkyo is a Professor of Economics at Kobe University in Japan. He received his Ph.D. from University of London. He previously worked as Director, International Department at Ministry of Finance Japan, and was Visiting Lecturer at School of Oriental and African Studies, University of London. His research interests include emerging market financial crises, finance and development, and Asian economic integration. His work has been published in leading academic journals, including Cambridge Journal of Economics and World Development.

Dr. Yoichi MATSUBAYASHI is a Professor of Economics at Kobe University in Japan. He received his Ph.D. from Kobe University. His main concern is international macroeconomics, especially external imbalances in the recent world economy. He has published many papers in refereed journals, such as Japanese economic Review, Japan and the World economy.

Dr. Shigeyuki HAMORI is a Professor of Economics at Kobe University in Japan. He received his Ph.D. from Duke University and has published many papers in refereed journals. He is the author of *An Empirical Investigation of Stock markets: the CCF Approach* (Kluwer Academic Publishers, 2003). He is also the co-author of *Hidden Markov Models: Applications to Financial Economics* (Springer, 2004), *Empirical Techniques in Finance* (Springer, 2005), and *Introduction of the Euro and the Monetary Policy of the European Central Bank* (World Scientific, 2009).

INTRODUCTION

Takuji Kinkyo*, Yoichi Matsubayashi†
and Shigeyuki Hamori‡

Faculty of Economics, Kobe University
2-1, Rokkodai, Nada-Ku, Kobe 657-8501, Japan
*Kinkyo@econ.kobe-u.ac.jp
†myoichi@econb.kobe-u.ac.jp
‡hamori@econ.kobe-u.ac.jp

Post-war economic achievement in East Asia, which includes Greater China (Mainland China, Hong Kong and Taiwan), Japan, South Korea, and Association of Southeast Asian Nations (ASEAN), was remarkable. According to Spence (2011), only thirteen economies maintained an average growth rate of more than 7% for more than twenty-five years during the post-war period. Nine out of these thirteen economies are located in East Asia.

East Asia's sustained high economic growth was driven primarily by an outward-oriented growth strategy (Commission on Growth and Development, 2008; IMF, 2011). The region's economies successfully took advantage of comparative advantages and economies of scale by opening up the market to the global economy. East Asia's exports in the world market have expanded dramatically, currently accounting for approximately 30% of the total world exports.

In comparison with other regions, economic growth in East Asia is heavily dependent on exports when compared with other regions (IMF, 2011). East Asia's dependence on exports became even stronger after the Asian financial crisis of 1997–1998. Following the crisis, domestic demand, particularly investment contracted and economic recovery was led mainly by exports in the region. Although China was not seriously affected by the Asian crisis, it has actively pursued an export-oriented growth strategy by keeping the exchange rate undervalued. East Asia's export-led growth pattern led to a surge in current account surplus and a large stock of accumulated foreign reserves in the region.

However, East Asia's heavy dependence on exports rendered the region's economies vulnerable to external demand shocks. Indeed, East Asian economies were significantly affected by the global financial crisis of 2008–2009 despite the limited exposure of their banks to subprime mortgage securities (Kinkyo, 2012). As the crisis spread beyond the U.S. markets, the overly optimistic view held that the impacts of the U.S.-originated crisis on East Asia would be minimal due to Asia's decoupling from U.S. business cycles. The deepening of regional economic integration was considered to have weakened the correlation of business cycles between the United States and other extra-regional economies and those of East Asia (IMF, 2007). In reality, however, the sudden drop in exports to the United States and Europe inevitably led to economic downturns in the region, indicating strong economic linkages between East Asia and advanced economies.

Economic integration in East Asia has been led by foreign trade over the past several decades. A notable feature of the area's intra-regional trade is the high proportion of vertical intra-industry trade in intermediate goods (Fukao *et al.*, 2003), which reflects the fragmentation of production processes and the expansion of vertically integrated supply chains across the region. However, the demand for the final goods made from these intermediate goods is heavily dependent on an extra-region, such as the United States or Europe. In East Asia, the share of final goods is larger in extra-regional trade, whereas the share of intermediate goods is larger in intra-regional trade. Accordingly, the global financial crisis caused not only a sharp reduction in East Asia's exports of final goods to the United States but also a contraction in the intra-regional trade of intermediate goods.

Given the prospect of weaker economic growth in the United States and Europe after the global financial crisis, the sustainability of East Asia's export-oriented growth strategy is called into question. East Asia's rebalancing demand towards both domestic and intra-regional sources is important to build a stronger foundation for the region's sustainable growth and to buttress global economic expansion.

It should also be emphasized that economic rebalancing in East Asia is the key to rectifying current account imbalances between the

United States and East Asia, particularly China. From the mid-2000s, China's current surplus expanded rapidly, reaching 10% of the GDP on the eve of the global financial crisis. Underlying this trend was the secular decline in the share of household consumption in the GDP (Bergsten *et al.*, 2009). Although the level of investment remained high, domestic saving surpassed it, generating a large current account surplus in China. Arguably, the combination of current account imbalances and financial instability due to inadequate policies, regulations and market practices caused and exacerbated the global financial crisis (Spence, 2011).

Although the imbalances have been reduced largely due to global slowdown in the wake of the global crisis, it is not certain at this moment whether the observed reduction is a sustainable trend or a temporary cyclical adjustment (IMF, 2011). Rectifying current account imbalances, which continues to be a key topic on the agenda of the Group of Twenty (G20), is important to prevent another major financial crisis.

Against the background outlined above, this book discusses East Asia's challenges in seeking to promote economic integration and rebalancing demand in the region. More specifically, the following questions are addressed: To what extent are the business cycles in East Asian economies synchronized with the rest of the world? How do the policy and institutional changes in these economies affect the pattern and degree of their business cycle synchronization? What are the major challenges for China in achieving economic rebalancing and sustainable growth? A brief overview of the content of each chapter is provided below.

Part 1. Business Cycle Synchronization

Chapter 1, by Hiroshi Tsubouchi and Hideaki Matsuoka, is titled "Decoupling: A Re-examination." This chapter examines the degree to which East Asia's business cycles have decoupled from the rest of the world. Using a time-varying parameter vector auto regression (VAR) model, the authors find that the impact on Asia of extra-regional shocks originating from the United States and the European Union (EU) became stronger after China joined the World Trade Organization (WTO) in 2001. The authors also find that the impact of extra-regional shocks on Asia have become weaker since the onset of the global financial crisis, indicating that the degree of decoupling has increased in the region. However, the authors note that their estimation sample covers only a short period after the global financial crisis and that further studies are necessary to draw more robust conclusions.

Chapter 2, by Fumihide Takeuchi, is titled "Business Cycle Synchronization and Production Fragmentation in East Asia". This chapter employs the structural factor-augmented vector autoregression (FAVAR) method to analyze factors affecting the business cycles of East Asia and major advanced economies. Business cycle synchronization across these countries has increased since the Asian crisis of 1997–1998. A comparison of the extracted shocks with empirically observed financial, productivity and natural resource price shocks reveals that the business cycles of East Asia and the major advanced economies are largely affected by common factors, whereas those of the Euro zone countries are not. In East Asia, the observed business cycle synchronization appears to reflect the accumulation of technology embodied in capital goods that are traded actively in the region. The author argues that the supply-side factors, such as trade structures, industrial structures and productivity shocks, are important elements in determining the extent of business cycle synchronization.

Chapter 3, by Kyosuke Shiotani and Yoichi Matsubayashi, is titled "Financial Market Linkage in East Asian Countries." This chapter quantitatively examines how stock price shocks originating in the United States were transmitted to East Asia by using a technique that has recently attracted attention, the Bayesian network. The authors find that the channel by which U.S.-originating shocks were transmitted to East Asia has changed over time. For example, during the early 2000s, U.S.-originating shocks were observed to impact South Korea and China first and to affect Japan indirectly via these countries. By contrast, during the global financial crisis, U.S.-originating shocks were observed to impact Japan first and then to affect other Asian economies indirectly via Japan. The authors contend that the transmission channel of U.S.-originating shocks to East Asia has become complex due to the recent strengthening of intra-regional trade linkages in East Asia.

Part 2. Effects of Policy and Institutional Changes

Chapter 4, by Hikari Ban, is titled "The Impact of East Asian FTAs on the Structure of Demand". This chapter analyzes the impact of East Asian FTAs on the structure of demand by combining a static computable general equilibrium (CGE) analysis and an input–output (I–O) analysis. The findings suggest that FTAs (Free Trade Agreements) increase international trade and deepen production networks inside East Asia. This chapter also shows that although the share of production induced from final demand in the United States and the EU declines with the presence of FTAs, the magnitude of this decline is relatively small, and the degree of dependence on the United States and the EU remains relatively high. The author argues that this result appears to relate to the size of the U.S. and EU economies and to the fact that the decrease in the share of production is largely caused by domestic final demand.

Chapter 5, by Takeshi Inoue, Yuki Toyoshima and Shigeyuki Hamori, is titled "Inflation Targeting in South Korea, Indonesia, the Philippines and Thailand: The Impact on Business Cycle Synchronization between Each Country and the World". In this chapter, the authors analyze the extent to which the adoption of inflation targeting in four Asian countries (South Korea, Indonesia, the Philippines and Thailand) has affected their business cycle synchronization with the rest of the world. To this end, they apply the dynamic conditional correlation (DCC) model developed by Engle (2002). This is a relatively novel approach because the surveyed literature indicates that empirical studies tend to characterize inflation targeting by estimating the monetary reaction function for each country. The authors' empirical evidence indicates that the adoption of IT in Asia has little impact on business cycle synchronization with the rest of the world and that the effect is positive in some of the countries, if any. This finding is consistent with the finding of Flood and Rose (2010) despite the different methodologies applied.

Chapter 6, by Fengbao Yin and Shigeyuki Hamori, is titled "Globalization and Economic Growth in East Asia". This chapter analyzes the relationship between globalization and economic growth in the East Asian region. One of the distinct features of recent developments in the global economy has been the simultaneous progress of globalization and regionalization. A typical example is East Asia, where the region's original diversity and non-systemic integration have engendered a complex intertwining of regionalism and globalization. Using the index of globalization developed by KOF Swiss Economic Institute, the authors empirically examine the effect of globalization on economic growth in East Asia. The results indicate that although globalization has a positive effect on East Asia's economic growth, the marginal gain from further globalization has diminished since the Asian crisis of 1997–1998. The authors argue that a system-based approach is needed to promote deeper intra-regional integration in East Asia.

Chapter 7, by Shigesaburo Kabe, is titled "Can South–South Trade Be a Driving Force for Future Economic Growth?" This chapter discusses the importance of South–South trade as an alternative source of economic growth in East Asia. After reviewing the current state and future potential of South–South trade, the author identifies four key areas that require particular attention for the promotion of South–South trade: liberalizing trade by reducing tariffs and non-trade barriers; promoting service trade by removing restrictions, such as those for factor mobility; strengthening regional cooperation as a tool to promote trade by improving infrastructure and institutions; and deepening socio-cultural understanding to avoid trade frictions. The author concludes by emphasizing that a continuous, cumulative effort to create a better environment for trade is important for the further development of South–South trade.

Part 3. Challenges to China's Rebalancing and Sustainable Growth

Chapter 8, by Guifu Chen, is titled "An Empirical Analysis of the Determinants of Household Saving (Consumption) in China: A Panel Analysis of Provincial Data, 1995–2010". This chapter empirically examines the determinants of the household saving rate in China using panel provincial data for 1995–2010. Following Horioka and Wan (2006), the author estimates a system generalized method of momentum (GMM) model, which includes standard determinants of saving rates, such as the per capita income growth rate, the real interest rate, the demographic structure and the inflation rate. The estimation results are broadly consistent with those of Horioka and Wan (2006) and support the life-cycle hypothesis. Based on these findings, the author suggests that the Chinese government should adopt proactive policies to further increase household income levels and improve social security systems, which would contribute to an increase of household consumption in China.

Chapter 9, by Long Ke, is titled "Financing Infrastructure Construction in China". This chapter analyzes the role of government and the sources of funds for infrastructure development in China. The author argues that although the government and state-owned enterprises (SOEs) will continue to play a key role, China will need to rely more on private and foreign sources of funds to meet the growing demand for infrastructure construction. The author also identifies four areas that should be given priority in promoting private and foreign investment: improving the administration system for infrastructure projects, enhancing the transparency of the bidding system, privatizing SOEs to promote competition with private companies and increasing the efficiency of the operation system.

Chapter 10, by Takuji Kinkyo, is titled "Is the Renminbi Appreciating Fast Enough?" This chapter examines whether the Chinese renminbi is appreciating fast enough to match the pace of changes in underlying fundamentals. To address this question, the renminbi's equilibrium exchange rate is estimated using Clark and MacDonald's (1999) BEER (Behavioral Equilibrium Exchange Rate) approach. It is shown that the renminbi is not appreciating fast enough to match the pace of changes in underlying fundamentals, notably the Balassa–Samuelson effect and net foreign asset accumulation. The findings suggest that the fundamental cause of the renminbi's persistent undervaluation is the lack of flexibility in China's exchange rate regime. The author argues that greater exchange rate flexibility would help China to achieve economic rebalancing by allowing real exchange rates to appreciate and facilitating further interest rate liberalization.

Acknowledgment

The authors are grateful to Dr. Soji Kurimoto, Distinguished Professor at Osaka Medical School for his generous funding support for our research projects. We are also grateful to Ms. Pui Yee Lum and Ms. Dipasri Sardar for their excellent editorial work.

References

Bergsten, CF, C Freeman, NR Lardy and DJ Mitchell (2009). *China's rise: Challenges and opportunities*. Peterson Institute for International Economics and Center for Strategic and International Studies, Washington DC.

Clark, P and R MacDonald (1999). Exchange Rates and Economic Fundamentals: A Methodological Comparison of BEERs and FEERs. In *Equilibrium Exchange Rates*, J Stein and R MacDonald (eds.), pp. 285–322. Boston: Kluwer.

Commission on Growth and Development (2008). *The Growth Report: Strategies for Sustained Growth and Inclusive Development*. World Bank, Washington DC.

Engle, RF (2002). Dynamic conditional correlation: A simple class of multivariate generalized autoregressive conditional heteroskedasticity models. *Journal of Business and Economic Statistics*, 20, 339–350.

Flood, RP and AK Rose (2010). Inflation targeting and business cycle synchronization. *Journal of International Money and Finance*, 29, 704–727.

Fukao, K, H Ishido and K Ito (2003). Vertical intra-industry trade and foreign direct investment in East Asia. *Journal of the Japanese and International Economies*, 17(4), 468–506.

IMF (2007). World Economic Outlook. IMF, Washington DC, April.

IMF (2011). Rebalancing growth in Asia: Economic dimensions for China. IMF, Washington DC.

Kinkyo, T (2012). *Policy Response, in Two Asias: The Emerging Postcrisis Divide.* S Rosefielde, M Kuboniwa and S Mizobata (eds.), pp. 155–176. Singapore: World Scientific Publishing.

Spence, M (2011). *The Next Convergence: The Future of Economic Growth in a Multispeed World.* New York: Farrar, Straus and Giroux.

CHAPTER 1

DECOUPLING — A RE-EXAMINATION

Hiroshi Tsubouchi* and Hideaki Matsuoka†

Japan Center for Economic Research Nikkei Bldg. 11F,
1-3-7 Otemachi Chiyoda-Ku, Tokyo 100-8066, Japan
*tsubouchi@jcer.or.jp
†h-matsuoka@jcer.or.jp

1. Introduction

After 2002, observers spoke of the decoupling of Asian economies as emerging economies in Asia and elsewhere developed rapidly and increased their weight in the world economy. Some argued that decoupled economies would be insulated from recession in Western economies and might instead help drive the world economy.[1]

---

[1] Tonoki *et al.* (2008) examined co-movements of business cycles in Japan and in Asian countries based on the Composite Indexes (CI) of business indicators, including monthly data and data on Japanese imports from and exports to Asian countries in Foreign Trade Statistics of the Ministry of Finance. As a result of the analysis of total imports and exports as well as imports and exports by goods, they found certain co-movements. Takeuchi (2011) **analyzed** factors affecting the business cycles of sixteen economies, including those of the seven major developed nations and nine East Asian countries, and found that all countries have been affected by soaring energy prices, especially in the 2000s. He also found that the business cycles of East Asian economies are affected to a large extent by common factors, while those of the Euro zone countries are not.

Such views persisted even after the summer of 2007 as non-performing loans began to pile up in the United States. They only fell silent after Lehman Brothers collapsed and the impact of the world financial crisis spread worldwide. Economies of BRICs and Asian countries were affected by the financial crisis and either fell into recession or slowed. Many observers concluded that decoupling was not taking place after all in Asian economies.[2]

We believe that such a conclusion may be premature. It should not be strange that Asian economies were affected even if they had decoupled to some extent because, owing to globalization, no country would have been completely insulated from the impact of a global recession accompanied by enormous shocks originating elsewhere in the world. Rather, it might be that Asian economies have steadily become more autonomous and for precisely that reason were less impacted by the recent financial crisis in the West than they would otherwise have been. Like the United States, European and Japanese economies, Asian economies did slow considerably, but they rebounded quickly. If Asian economies further increase their autonomy, they should be able to insulate their economic activities from any shock originating in the West.

Using a time-varying parameter vector autoregressive (TVP-VAR) model, this chapter analyzes changes in the way the American economy influences other economies and examines the extent to which the Chinese and other Asian economies have increased their autonomy.

2. Looking Back at the World Economy Since 1990s

Before presenting our main arguments, we will outline the world economy as it has developed since the 1990s (Figs. 1, 2 and 3). We will review economic conditions in Japan, the United States, the European Union (EU), China and other Asian economies by dividing the time span into three periods: the 1990s (before the Asian financial crisis), the first half of the 2000s (before the global financial crisis) and the latter half of the 2000s (after the global financial crisis).

---

[2] Cabinet Office (2011) explains the background of this discussion in detail.

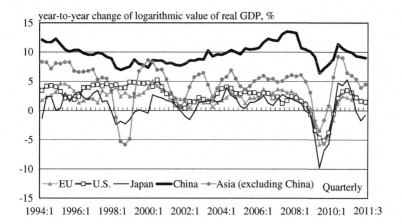

Fig. 1. Economic growth in major countries/regions.

Note: Asia consists of China, Hong Kong, South Korea, Taiwan, Singapore, Indonesia, Malaysia, Philippines and Thailand.
Source: CEIC.

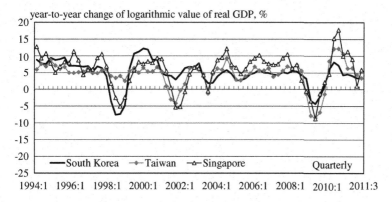

Fig. 2. Economic growth in some Asian economies.
Source: CEIC.

2.1. *1990s — Before the Asian financial crisis*

In the first half of the 1990s, the collapse of the bubble in stock and land prices resulted in a large amount of debt for the corporate and household sector in Japan. The number of business failures and personal

year-to-year change of logarithmic value of real GDP, %

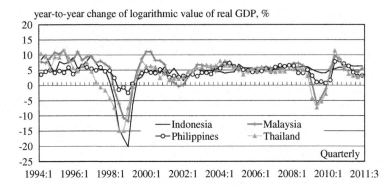

Fig. 3.   Economic growth in other Asian economies.

Source: CEIC.

bankruptcies rose sharply and the financial positions of Japanese banks were grievously impaired, ushering in a "lost decade".

On the other hand, economic expansion continued for about ten years in the United States from 1991. Personal consumption, which accounts for approximately 70% of U.S. GDP, was supported by the wealth effect arising from strong personal income and surging stock prices. Vigorous investment in high technology also contributed to rapid growth. European economies stagnated in the first half of 1990s as consolidation followed the boom associated with German unification and an economic downturn followed tight monetary policy in the United Kingdom. European economies were nevertheless able to recover as economic expansion in the United States and Asia fueled rising exports.

However, the Asian crisis originating in Thailand with the financial collapse of the baht in 1997 had enormously negative repercussions for all Asian economies, including Indonesia and South Korea. At the same time, the Japanese economy faced more serious problems as a string of financial institutions went bankrupt. In contrast, China experienced no economic turmoil partly because international capital flows into Chinese financial markets were regulated.

2.2. First half of the 2000s — Before the global financial crisis

In the United States, the dot-com bubble which had inflated during the 1990s began collapsing in March of 2001. This adversely impacted the

Japanese and Asian economies, which had been recovering on the expansion of demand for information technology. In addition to the Federal Reserve's accommodative stance on interest rates, foreign currency reserves in Asian countries which went to purchase U.S. Treasuries caused long-term interest rates to decline.

This decline in interest rates was one of the factors driving the boom in housing and real estate. The resulting surge in asset prices boosted personal consumption in the United States and European countries. In addition, China joined WTO (World Trade Organization) in 2001 and joined the global market. This began to affect each country's economy in a positive way. Thanks to exports to the booming economies of the West and Asia, the Japanese economy was able to stage a recovery which, though gradual, ultimately became the longest in the post-war period.

From the summer in 2007, rising defaults on subprime loans to lower income households created huge losses for financial institutions in the United States. Because financial institutions in European countries purchased large amounts of securitized subprime mortgage-backed securities, the loss caused a crisis first in the financial sector and then in the European and global economies. In September of 2008, as the bankruptcy of Lehman Brothers triggered a freeze-up of the financial system, economic activity in each country suddenly plummeted. Japan, South Korea, Taiwan, Singapore and Germany, which had enjoyed export-led expansion, abruptly faced a painful recession. Even China's real growth rate dropped to 6.5% in the first quarter of 2009 after having been in the double digits.

2.3. The latter half of the 2000s — After the global financial crisis

Although the global financial crisis brought stagnation all over the world, the process of recovery varied from country to country and was described as a "Multi-speed recovery".[3] Governments of the G20 Group of Twenty Finance Ministers and Central Bank Governors agreed to implement large fiscal expenditures. The world economy then gradually started to recover, but the upturn in the emerging economies of China and other Asian nations turned out to be even stronger than those seen in the advanced

---

[3] IMF *World Economic Outlook*, January 2010.

economies of the United States, the EU and Japan. While developed countries suffered from high unemployment, turmoil in housing markets and large fiscal deficits, Asian countries enjoyed strong fiscal balances and were therefore in a position to rapidly implement fiscal stimulus measures of considerable size.[4]

3. Factors Affecting Decoupling

Before examining whether decoupling is in fact taking place in Asian economies, we will first define the term and discuss the factors which affect it.

For present purposes, we define decoupling as the tendency for short term fluctuations in the growth rate of a given economy to arise from endogenous rather than exogenous factors. Because different economies are linked with each other through trade and investment, the impact of a given shock will extend not only the economy where it originates but to other economies as well through trade and investment (Fig. 4). We can therefore divide those factors which affect the growth rate of a given economy into (1) endogenous factors or shocks originating in that economy

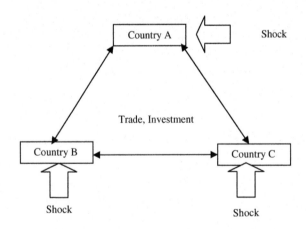

Fig. 4. Interdependence of economies.

---

[4]According to the IMF publication "Update on Fiscal Stimulus and Financial Sector Measures, April 26, 2009", the size of fiscal stimulus compared to nominal GDP in 2009 was 3.1% in China, 3.9% in South Korea and 2.4% in Japan.

itself and (2) exogenous factors or shocks originating in other economies. We can then assume that decoupling is in progress when the proportion of such endogenous factors is increasing.

The bigger an economy is and the higher the proportion of imports to its GDP, the more that economy influences other economies. On the other hand, the bigger an economy is and the lower the share of exports in total demand, the less the economy is exposed to exogenous shocks. In other words, if the share of domestic demand (in the form of consumption and investment) in total demand increases while the share of exports decreases, decoupling will proceed. This mechanism is not offset by growing world trade and strengthening connections among different economies. Even if exports increase, so long as the share of those exports in total demand decreases, the impact of exogenous shocks will diminish relative to the size of the economy, and decoupling will proceed.

For example, consider the share of the American, European, Japanese, Chinese and other Asian economies in the world economy (Fig. 5). It can be observed that the shares of the Chinese and other Asian economies are increasing. This trend suggests that the autonomy of these economies is increasing.

On the other hand, when we look at the share of exports in total demand (Fig. 6), we observe that these shares are increasing in the

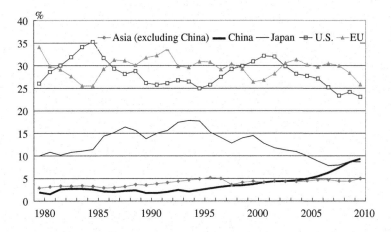

Fig. 5. Share of each economies' nominal GDP in the world economy.
Source: IMF World Economic Outlook.

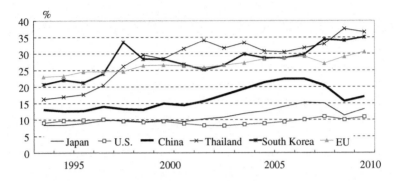

Fig. 6. Share of exports in total demand.

Source: CEIC.

Chinese and other Asian economies. This implies that the autonomy of these economies is decreasing.

4. Methodology

In this section, we analyze the interdependence among the United States, European, Japanese, Chinese and other Asian economies using a VAR model. Since interdependency may have changed throughout the time period we considered in the previous section, we will use a time-varying parameter vector autoregressive (TVP-VAR) model instead of the conventional VAR model.[5]

While we estimate the parameters of the conventional VAR model under the assumption that the magnitude of the influence of one economy on other economies is constant over time, we estimate the parameters of the TVP-VAR model under the assumption that the magnitude of this influence can change. This means that the conventional VAR model implicitly assumes that the structure of the relationship among economies is stable while the TVP-VAR model allows for the possibility of changes in this relationship over time. These

---

[5] We will discuss the details of the methods of TVP-VAR model in the supplementary discussion.

characteristics have made the TVP-VAR a popular model in recent analysis.[6]

The model we formulated is represented by Eq. (1), where the growth rate of each economy is explained in terms of its own and other economies' growth rates in the previous period.

$$
\begin{aligned}
US_t &= \beta_{11}US_{t-1} + \beta_{12}EU_{t-1} + \beta_{13}JP_{t-1} + \beta_{14}China_{t-1} + \beta_{15}Asia_{t-1} + e_{us\_t} \\
EU_t &= \beta_{21}US_{t-1} + \beta_{22}EU_{t-1} + \beta_{23}JP_{t-1} + \beta_{24}China_{t-1} + \beta_{25}Asia_{t-1} + e_{eu\_t} \\
JP_t &= \beta_{31}US_{t-1} + \beta_{32}EU_{t-1} + \beta_{33}JP_{t-1} + \beta_{34}China_{t-1} + \beta_{35}Asia_{t-1} + e_{jp\_t} \\
China_t &= \beta_{41}US_{t-1} + \beta_{42}EU_{t-1} + \beta_{43}JP_{t-1} + \beta_{44}China_{t-1} + \beta_{45}Asia_{t-1} + e_{China\_t} \\
Asia_t &= \beta_{51}US_{t-1} + \beta_{52}EU_{t-1} + \beta_{53}JP_{t-1} + \beta_{54}China_{t-1} + \beta_{55}Asia_{t-1} + e_{Asia\_t}
\end{aligned}
\tag{1}
$$

US_t, EU_t, JP_t, $China_t$ and $Asia_t$ stand for real growth rates of the corresponding economies. β_{ij} stands for the influence of the previous-period growth rate of the economy j to the growth rate of the economy i. These parameters stand for the direct influence between economies. The number 1 represents the United States, 2 the EU, 3 Japan, 4 China and 5 other Asian economies. We assume that the parameters follow a random-walk process.

The disturbance $e_{i,t}$ of Eq. (1) stands for the current shock in economy i. In conventional VAR model analysis, we assume that this disturbance consists of a mutually independent shock and we identify it by the Cholesky decomposition. For example, by assuming that disturbance is more

---

[6]Using the TVP-VAR model, Shiratsuka *et al.* (2010) **analyzed** the effect of the policy commitment by the Bank of Japan to a zero interest rate. Nakajima *et al.* (2011) **analyzed** the relationship between the Japanese economy and monetary policy by using the same technique. Endo and Hirakata (2010) **analyzed** the influence changes in the world economy on exports and production in Japan using TVP-VAR model. They concluded that the world economic structure may have been changed by global financial shocks and the emergence of newly **industrialized** countries such as China, India, Russia, Brazil, Indonesia and South Africa. They found that the upturn in exports and production in Japan from 2007 to 2008 and their subsequent downturn can be explained for the most part by factors common worldwide and that the influence of newly **industrialized** economies on developed economies has increased throughout the 2000s.

independent in the United States, Europe, Japan, China and other Asian economies, in descending order, we can estimate mutually independent disturbance u_{i_t} of Eq. (2).

$$
\left.
\begin{aligned}
e_{us\_t} &= u_{us\_t} \\
e_{eu\_t} &= b_{21}u_{us\_t} + u_{eu\_t} \\
e_{jp\_t} &= b_{31}u_{us\_t} + b_{32}u_{eu\_t} + u_{jp\_t} \\
e_{China\_t} &= b_{41}u_{us\_t} + b_{42}u_{eu\_t} + b_{43}u_{jp\_t} + u_{China\_t} \\
e_{Asia\_t} &= b_{51}u_{us\_t} + b_{52}u_{eu\_t} + b_{53}u_{jp\_t} + b_{54}u_{China\_t} + u_{Asia\_t}
\end{aligned}
\right\}
\qquad (2)
$$

In the conventional VAR model analysis we estimate b_{ij}, which stands for the influence of current shocks originating in economy j on economy i with the assumption that b_{ij} is constant. We assume that each b_{ij} also fluctuates and follows a random-walk process, and estimate Eqs. (1) and (2) simultaneously.

Both β_{ij} and b_{ij} show interdependency among economies. As for their characteristics, as we discussed in Sec. 3, the bigger economy j is and the higher the proportion of imports in economy j, the more a shock originating in economy j will affect economy i, i.e., the bigger β_{ij} and b_{ij}, become. On the other hand, the bigger the size of economy i and the lower the share of exports in total demand, the less affected economy i will be by shocks originating in economy j, i.e., the smaller β_{ij} and b_{ij}, become.

We next analyze the interdependence among economies and the change of that interdependence over time by using the data for growth rates[7] discussed in Sec. 2. While we treat the United States, the EU, Japan and China independently, we have aggregated the GDP of other seven Asian economies[8] because the sample period is short and the size of each Asian economy is small compared to the other economies. The estimation period starts from the second quarter of 1994 and ends at the third quarter of 2011. That is, the number of the sample is 70 quarters.

---

[7] We used the year-to-year difference in the logarithmic value of real GDP rather than growth rate itself.

[8] We selected South Korea, Taiwan, Singapore, Indonesia, Malaysia, the Philippines and Thailand and used the nominal GDP-weighted average of the year-to-year change in the logarithmic values of real GDP for these countries.

5. Decomposition of the Forecast Variance

As discussed above, we define "decoupling" as the tendency for short term fluctuations in the growth rate of a given economy to arise from endogenous rather than exogenous factors.

In this section, among the various analytical methods used in employing the VAR model, we adopt the "decomposition of the forecast variance" method in order to estimate the extent to which fluctuations in growth rate can be attributed to endogenous shocks as opposed to exogenous shocks. Decomposition of the forecast variance is an analytical method to show the contribution of disturbance $u_{i,t}$ to forecast errors of growth rates of each economy in Eq. (1). Concretely, the contribution of a shock in a given economy to changes in its own growth rate and those of other economies is calculated by using the estimated parameters of Eqs. (1) and (2) and the variance of the mutually independent shock in each economy.

In this kind of analysis, the focus is usually on the sequence of the contribution rate under the estimated constant parameters. In the present analysis, however, we are interested in changes in the contribution under the estimated varying parameters. We therefore select the contribution rate for a certain period, say two quarters, after the shock and then observe its change in order to determine the extent to which decoupling has taken place.

The results are presented in Figs. 7, 8, 9, 10 and 11. The contribution of an endogenous shock is always large, as we would expect. Other results are as follows:

U.S.: On average, 80% of the fluctuation in the growth rate was attributed to endogenous shocks and there was almost no impact from exogenous shocks originating in other economies. After the global financial crisis, exogenous shocks originating in the European economy had an impact.

EU: While fluctuations in the growth rate were attributed to endogenous shocks, the impact of shocks originating in the United States grew over time. They peaked around the time of the global financial crisis, but the impact of endogenous shock subsequently grew once more.

Japan: While fluctuations in Japan's growth rate were also attributed to endogenous shocks, the impact of shocks originating in the United States and other Asian economies became more prominent. Although we had expected the influence of shocks originating in the

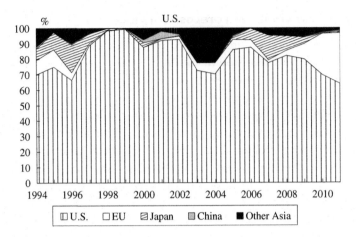

Fig. 7. Decomposition of the forecast variance (contribution rate): the United States.

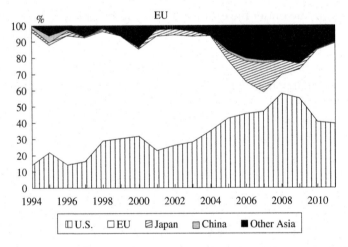

Fig. 8. Decomposition of the forecast variance (contribution rate): EU.

Chinese economy to become stronger, this was not observed. This may be because the Japanese economy is affected by U.S. shocks indirectly through the Chinese economy.

China: While fluctuations in the growth rate were attributed to endogenous shocks, the impact of Japanese and American shocks became stronger after China joined the WTO in 2001. Most recently, the impact of

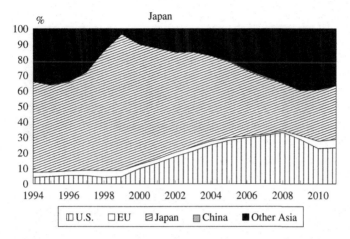

Fig. 9. Decomposition of the forecast variance (contribution rate): Japan.

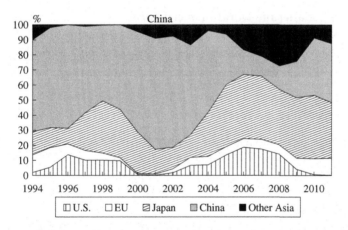

Fig. 10. Decomposition of the forecast variance (contribution rate): China.

shocks originating in the European economy has become more significant than that of shocks originating in the United States. The influence of shocks in other Asian economies gradually rose and became strongest around the time of the global financial crisis but has diminished since that time.

Other Asian economies: On average, 70% of the fluctuations in the growth rate are attributed to endogenous shocks, followed by shocks in the United States and Japan. The influence of endogenous shocks became

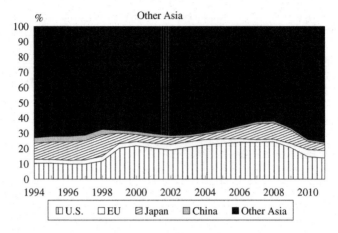

Fig. 11. Decomposition of the forecast variance (contribution rate): Other Asia.

even stronger after the world financial crisis. While we expected that the impact of shocks originating in the Chinese economy would grow in strength, this was not observed. The reasons are likely to be the same as those that apply to Japan.

6. Conclusion

This chapter has examined the degree to which decoupling has taken place in the economies of China and other Asian nations by analyzing changes in interdependence among the United States, European, Japanese, Chinese and other Asian economies. We have used a time-varying parameter VAR model for the analysis.

We have found that the impact of the U.S. economy on the European and Japanese economies increased, but this is not the case for Asian economies. We also found that the influence of the European economy on the U.S. economy has increased, but this is not the case for Japan and other Asian economies.

The Chinese economy initially possessed autonomy, but after joining the WTO in 2001, the impact on Chinese economy of shocks originating from the Japanese and U.S. economies became stronger, although the impact of shocks from the European economy has recently increased relative to that from the U.S. economy. On the other hand, the impact on other Asian economies of extra-regional shocks has become weaker since the onset of global financial crisis, indicating that the degree of decoupling has increased in such countries.

However, there is little data for the period following the global financial crisis, though it is now accumulating so further studies will be necessary.

7. Supplementary Discussion — Why is a Time-varying Parameter Model Used?

This section will provide a supplementary explanation on the time-varying parameter model used in Sec. 4. Ordinary least squares (OLS) is often used to show interdependency among variables. The estimated parameters indicate the average relationship in the past. However, there are many cases in which parameters are not constant and change over time. In this chapter, the relationship among each country's growth rate could change because of the change in the structure of trade.

For instance, let us compare the estimated impact on the Japanese growth rate from the U.S. growth rate (β_{31} of Eq. (1) in Sec. 4) with that by ordinary least squares. As β_{31} varies stochastically in a time-varying parameter model, it can be noted as β_{31t}. The estimated model is as follows:

$$JP_t = \beta_{31t}US_{t-1} + \beta_{32t}EU_{t-1} + \beta_{33t}JP_{t-1} + \beta_{34t}China_{t-1} + \beta_{35t}Asia_{t-1} + e_{jp\_t}$$

$$\beta_{31t} = \beta_{31t-1} + \varepsilon_{31t}.$$

We used Kalman filtering for estimation. Figure 12 shows the estimated parameters of β_{31}. The constant one is estimated by OLS and the fluctuating one is estimated as a time-varying parameter.

While the constant parameter is roughly 0.25 through the period, the time-varying parameter continued to increase since 1990s and peaked around the time of the global financial crisis. It subsequently declined and remained at approximately 0.5 as of the third quarter of 2011.

A possible explanation of the change is as follows: First, the parameter continued to increase from the 1990s because the growth rate of U.S. imports was higher than that of GDP thanks to strong domestic demand in the form of consumption (Fig. 13), and that supported Japanese exports significantly. Second, the parameter decreased after the global financial crisis because the share of the United States in Japanese exports decreased (Fig. 14).

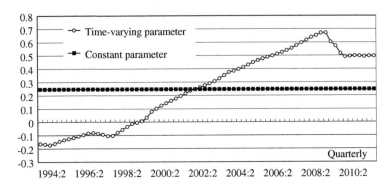

Fig. 12. Time-varying parameter and constant parameter.

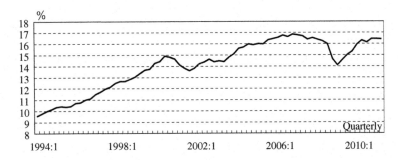

Fig. 13. Propensity of imports in the United States (= real imports/real GDP).
Source: U.S. Bureau of Economic Analysis "NIPA" Tables.

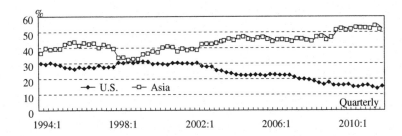

Fig. 14. Share of Japanese exports to the United States and Asian countries.

Note: Asia consists of China, Hong Kong, South Korea, Taiwan, Singapore, Indonesia, Malaysia, the Philippines and Thailand.
Source: Ministry of Finance "Trade Statistics".

Because the interdependency among economies could vary over time according to the change in the structure of trade, a time-varying parameter model is a useful tool for analysis.

Acknowledgments

The authors would like to thank K. Asako, T. Miyagawa, N. Iiduka and H. Iiboshi for valuable comments on earlier drafts. Viewpoints expressed in this chapter remain our own.

References

Cabinet Office (2011). World economic trends. The Autumn Report in 2009. (in Japanese)

Endo, S and N Hirakata (2010). Fluctuation of Japanese production: Global financial shocks and structural change of the world economy. *Bank of Japan Review*, 2010-J-05, Bank of Japan. (in Japanese)

Nakajima, J, M Kasuya and T Watanabe (2011). Bayesian analysis of time-varying parameter vector autoregressive model for the Japanese economy and monetary policy. *Journal of the Japanese and International Economies*, 25, 225–245.

Shiratsuka, S, Y Teranishi and J Nakajima (2010). Effect of commitment in monetary policy: Experience of Japan. *Monetary and Economic Studies*, 29, 239–266, Bank of Japan. (in Japanese)

Tonoki, Y, K Ochiai and K Asako (2008). Business cycles in Japan and in Asian countries — Tests of co-movements between CI and trade statistics. *Financial Review*, 90, 55–72, Ministry of Finance, Japan. (in Japanese)

Takeuchi, F (2011). A decomposition of global business cycles using structural FAVAR. *The Economic Analysis*, No.184, Economic and Social Research Institute, Cabinet Office. (in Japanese)

CHAPTER 2

BUSINESS CYCLE SYNCHRONIZATION AND PRODUCTION FRAGMENTATION IN EAST ASIA

Fumihide Takeuchi

Institute of General Education, Japan Advanced Institute of Science and Technology
1-1, Asahidai, Nomi, Ishikawa, 923-1292, Japan
ftake@jaist.ac.jp

1. Introduction

Are business cycles in countries around the world becoming increasingly synchronized? Many would answer in the affirmative if they saw the impact of the 2008 financial crisis and economic slowdown in the United States on economies around the world. This global slowdown, however, is due less to the global synchronization of business cycles than to the extraordinary magnitude of the United States financial crisis. In fact, the international business cycle literature suggests that, from a longer-term perspective, the global synchronization of business cycles is becoming less important, while the importance of regional synchronization among the highly integrated economies, North America, Western Europe and emergent Asia, appears to be increasing.[1]

With regard to Asia, recent research, including a study by the Asian Development Bank (ADB, 2007), has shown that business cycles in East Asia

---

[1] See, for example, International Monetary Fund (IMF) (2007).

and the major developed economies have become increasingly synchronized. Takeuchi (2011c) uses a two-country Dynamic General Equilibrium (DGE) model to analyze factors contributing to the observed increase in international business cycle synchronization between eight East Asian developing countries and the major developed economies, Japan and the United States. The model focuses on the role of production fragmentation among these countries. Model simulations are conducted for two periods (1993–1997 and 1999–2005), one before and one after the Asian financial crisis, and show that the increase in business cycle synchronization can be attributed mainly to the growing fragmentation of production activities.

In this chapter, the structural FAVAR (structural factor-augmented vector autoregression) method used in Takeuchi (2011a) is employed to analyze factors affecting the business cycles of thirteen economies, including six major developed countries and seven East Asian countries. This VAR approach can identify several kinds of structural shocks that affect selected countries during the same period as well as spillovers that occur with time lags. Comparing these extracted shocks with empirically observed financial, productivity and natural resource price shocks reveals that the business cycles of East Asian economies, Japan and the United States are all affected to a large extent by common factors, while those of the European countries are not. In the former countries, the observed business cycle synchronization appears to reflect the accumulation of technology (investment-specific technological change) embodied in capital goods that are then traded vigorously for production fragmentation.

With regard to the factors underlying international business cycles, the role of the trade in goods and of capital flows between the concerned countries have been widely discussed. However, the mechanisms through which this synchronization occurs have never been clarified, especially with regard to pairs of countries that include a developing economy. This chapter argues that supply-side factors, including trade and industrial structures and productivity shocks, are important elements in this difference and that the structure of trade, rather than total trade volume (demand-side factors), is key in determining the extent of business cycle synchronization.

The remainder of this chapter is organized as follows. Section 2 summarizes the preceding studies. Section 3 provides an empirical analysis of business cycle co-movements and the fragmentation of production activity in the sample countries. Section 4 presents the structural FAVAR model and the estimation results, and Sec. 5 concludes.

2. Related Literature

With respect to developed countries, Frankel and Rose (1998) and Clark and van Wincoop (2001) showed that the extent of co-movements in the business cycle was positively correlated with trade intensity. Meanwhile, Miyagawa and Imamura (2003) arrived at a similar conclusion for developed economies (excluding Japan) based on a survey of the existing literature and their own analyses on the relationship between trade and international business cycles in the Asia-Pacific region. However, they found that trade could not explain the business cycle correlation between Asian developing countries and Japan or the United States. Crosby (2003), also covering the Asia-Pacific region, arrived at results similar to those of Miyagawa and Imamura (2003) after conducting a regression analysis using the coefficient of correlation of business cycles as the dependent variable and the trade intensity index as the independent variable. What these various studies show is that pairs of developed countries closely linked by trade have a tendency to show a large degree of business cycle correlation, while pairs of developing countries do not. These findings raise the question of why the impact of trade on international business cycles differs so significantly for developed and developing economies.[2]

This chapter argues that the structure of trade is an important element in this difference and, more so than total trade volume, is key in determining the extent of business cycle synchronization, particularly within a group of trading partners that includes developing economies. Preceding studies focusing on the influence of trade structure in business cycle synchronization include Shin and Wang (2004), Fidrmuc (2004), Kumamura (2006), Calderón *et al.* (2007), Ng (2010) and Takeuchi (2011a, 2011c). Among them, Shin and Wang (2004), Calderón *et al.* (2007), Kumamura (2006) and Takeuchi (2011a, 2011c) focus on the role of trade/industrial structures in the synchronizing of the business cycles of developing countries.

Studies focusing on the role of production fragmentation on business cycles include Ng (2010) and Takeuchi (2011a, 2011c). Ng (2010) examines whether pairs of countries with more extensive bilateral production fragmentation arrangements tend to have more closely correlated business cycles and found that bilateral production fragmentation has a positive

---

[2]The trade intensity index is calculated as the share of bilateral trade out of the total trade divided by the share of the two countries' total trade out of the world total trade.

effect on synchronization while the standard bilateral trade intensity index has a negative effect. Kumamura (2006) and Calderón *et al.* (2007) show that differences in the responsiveness of business cycle synchronization to trade intensities are explained by differences in the patterns of industrial structure specialization and bilateral trade. According to their results, for trading partners who have a specialized industrial structure, growing trade leads to less synchronized cycles. These are important findings that highlight the need to incorporate into the analysis not only demand-side but also supply-side factors, such as intra-industry trade, and by extension, the role of production networks that are responsible for a large part of intra-industry trade.

In East Asia, production networks have been formed through foreign direct investment by multinational enterprises (MNEs). MNEs divide production into discrete steps located in different countries, resulting in the fragmentation of production. Within these networks, each country specializes in a particular stage of the production process, and intermediate and capital goods are actively traded. This new type of trade may engender an international transmission of demand and technology in a manner quite different from the traditional Heckscher–Ohlin framework, where different kinds of final goods are traded according to the comparative advantages of each country.

Unlike Takeuchi (2011a), which employs a structural FAVAR, this chapter separately analyzes the background factors for business cycle synchronization in East Asia and major developed economies for two periods, 1993–1997 and 1999–2007. The results show that increases in business cycle synchronization can be attributed mainly to the growing fragmentation of production activities, which is due to the fact that East Asian economic environments changed significantly after the Asian financial crisis of 1997–1998.

3. The Correlation of Business Cycles and Fragmentation

3.1. *Business cycle synchronization in East Asia and in major advanced countries*

The purpose of this section is to examine developments in business cycle synchronization between, and the fragmentation of production in, East Asia and major advanced countries. To analyze business cycle synchronization, output co-movements are measured by collecting monthly data on seasonally adjusted production for the six major developed (Japan, the United States, Germany, France, Italy and the United Kingdom) and seven East Asian countries (China, Taiwan, South Korea, Malaysia, Thailand, Singapore and the Philippines). Business cycles are extracted using the Hodrick–Prescott (HP) filter. The correlation of business cycles for the seventy-eight pairs of countries is calculated for the periods from January 1999 to December 2007 and from January 1993 to June 1997. The two periods, omitting the period from July 1997 to December 1998, were selected to eliminate possible distortion of the results due to the irregular shock of the Asian financial crisis.

Table 1 shows different groups' averaged correlations. The correlations increase significantly for almost all of the observations except in the cases of European countries, as shown in the relationships between columns (1) and (2). This finding indicates that business cycle synchronization is not restricted to some specific groups but is a common trend in the sample countries.

When examined more closely, however, Table 1 reveals some differences in the degree of business cycle correlation depending on the countries and areas concerned: (1) correlation of coefficients between European countries and others is lower than that found in the pairs involving East Asia, Japan and the United States and among European countries only; (2) correlation of coefficients in the pairs that include China is lower than in others. Table 1 shows the results of the significance testing performed on the differences between correlations of coefficients. The difference between a correlation coefficient of 0.5227 for pairs between East Asia, Japan and the United States (excluding China) and 0.3767 for pairs between the former set of countries and Euro countries is significant at the 1% level. The same results are found even if China is included and/or Euro countries are restricted to European Union member countries.

Compared to the average correlation coefficient of pairs excluding China (0.4421), the average correlation between China and the other twelve countries (0.2052) is lower by a statistically significant margin. It is possible that this difference is due to the fact that the business cycle of China is mainly affected by East Asia's averaged Total Factor Productivity (TFP) shock, which is calculated using each country's real GDP as a weight. The business cycles of other East Asian economies, however, are influenced mainly by investment-specific technological change. This interpretation is based on the empirical results of the structural FAVAR, as explained later.

Table 1. Average correlations in different groups.

No.	Group	(1) Mean value of correlation coefficients (1999–2007)	H_0	t-values		(2) Mean value of correlation coefficients (1993–1997)	H_0	t-values	
1	East Asia, Japan, U.S.	0.4572				0.0906	(1)=(2)	7.9002	***
2	East Asia, Japan, U.S. (excl. China)	0.5227				0.0599	(1)=(2)	10.1005	***
3	EU with East Asia-Japan-U.S.	0.3468	1=3	2.7664	**	0.1590	(1)=(2)	5.0025	***
4	EU with East Asia-Japan-U.S. (excl. China)	0.3703	2=4	4.1386	***	0.1744	(1)=(2)	5.0517	***
5	Euro with East Asia-Japan-U.S.	0.3567	1=5	2.3826	*	0.1534	(1)=(2)	4.4921	***
6	Euro with East Asia-Japan-U.S. (excl. China)	0.3767	2=6	3.6535	***	0.1681	(1)=(2)	4.3594	***
7	China with others	0.2052				0.1441	(1)=(2)	0.9001	
8	Among pairs excl. China	0.4421	7=8	5.9659	***	0.1429	(1)=(2)	8.4852	***
9	China with East Asia-Japan-U.S.	0.2282	2=9	5.8686	***	0.1982	(1)=(2)	0.3279	
10	EU zone	0.4488	2=10	0.7123		0.3623	(1)=(2)	0.6666	
11	Euro zone	0.4609	2=11	0.4339		0.3643	(1)=(2)	0.6849	

Note: *significant at the 100% level, **significant at the 5% level, ***significant at the 1% level.

3.2. Fragmentation of production in East Asia and Japan/the United States

The observed increase in co-movements between business cycles in East Asia, Japan and the United States raises the question of which factors are responsible for this correlation. The argument presented here suggests that the fragmentation of production plays a major role. It is therefore useful to look at fragmentation in greater detail.

In this context, the state of fragmentation is represented by the trade in capital and intermediate goods.[3] Figure 1(a) depicts the trade share of capital goods out of the total trade for East Asia, Japan and the United States.[4] Two line graphs are shown: one is the share of the intra-group trade, and the other is the share of the inter-group trade with the rest of the world. The graph shows that the trade share of capital goods increases within the group but decreases in the case of inter-group trade in the early 2000s. In other words, the capital goods trade intensified within the group. Figure 1(b) presents the ratio of intra- and inter-group trade of capital goods to GDP, showing that the intra-group trade-GDP ratio increases in the early 2000s much more than the inter-trade GDP ratio does. These two graphs show the aggregated data for East Asia, Japan and the United States, but the same trends can be observed in almost all countries in the group. In the case of intermediate goods trade, the same trends can be confirmed.

3.3. Changes in the economic environment after the Asian financial crisis

As shown in the above section, business cycle correlation has increased significantly in East Asia, Japan and the United States since the late 1990s. During the same period, trade in capital goods began to intensify in these countries as well. The purpose here is to explore what effects the 1997–1998 Asian financial crisis had on changes in the production process.

Devereux and Sutherland (2009) point out that "financial globaliza-tion", or the simultaneous increase in stocks of gross external assets

---

[3] The data are from UN Comtrade. Trade values of capital and intermediate goods on an annual basis can be obtained by using the Broad Economic Categories (BEC), a special trade classification of the UN trade database.

[4] Taiwan is excluded due to data limitations.

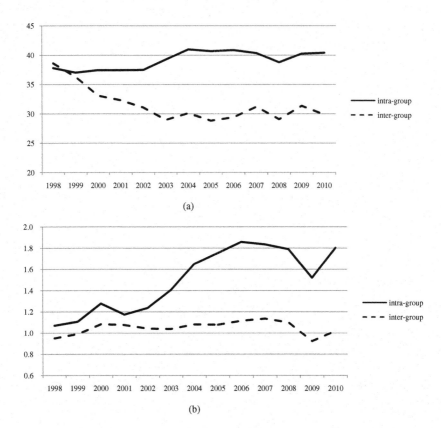

Fig. 1. (a) The inter- and intra-group trade share (%) of capital goods out of the total trade for East Asia, Japan and the United States (above); (b) The ratios (%) of inter- and intra-group capital goods trade to GDP for East Asia, Japan and the United States (below). The data back to 1998 (UN Comtrade).

and liabilities in emerging economies, including East Asia, dates back to the crisis. In particular, East Asian countries have been accumulating large stocks of U.S. treasury bills in their official reserve assets while receiving large inflows of foreign direct investment (FDI) and portfolio equity investments. With respect to official reserve assets, Aizenman and Marion (2003) and Aizenman and Lee (2007) reveal that the financial crisis in East Asia led to profound changes in the demand for such reserves because Asian countries began regarding them as a precautionary adjustment, reflecting their desire for self-insurance against exposure to sudden stops.[5]

---

[5]The IMF (2008) conducted an empirical analysis to explain the determinants of the current account balances (a flow of net external assets) of East Asian countries.

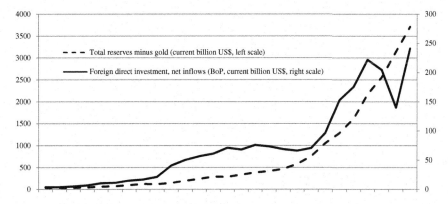

Fig. 2. Total reserves minus gold and net inflow of FDI in East Asian countries. *Source*: International Financial Statistics.

The build-up of large, positive net external positions as well as large reserve assets instilled considerable confidence in the investment potential of these economies, helping trigger a large increase in the inflow of FDI in the 2000s. Figure 2 shows the values of foreign exchange reserve and net inflow of FDI in the sampled seven East Asian countries. It is evident that the two show a similar increase, especially after 2000. This large FDI inflow from Japan, the United States and other advanced countries account for the expansion in production fragmentation networks in East Asia.

4. Structural FAVAR

4.1. Model

This section explains the basis of the structural FAVAR method employed to analyze the factors affecting the business cycles of thirteen economies, including six major developed and seven East Asian countries. This VAR approach can identify several kinds of structural shocks that affect the selected countries within the same period as well as spillovers that are

---

The study concluded that a large part of these external balances were explained by the countries' experience of the financial crisis and not by the standard factors that have been highlighted in the literature, such as the government balance, youth and old-age dependency ratios, growth opportunities, initial income level etc.

assumed to happen with time lags. Estimation procedures consist of two steps. First, we estimate the structural FAVAR. Second, the extracted shocks are compared with empirically observed financial, productivity and natural resource price shocks.

In this chapter, the estimation of the structural FAVAR is based on Stock and Watson (2005) and Takeuchi (2011a) as follows.

Let Y_t be the vector of detrended GDP growth rates of n countries. First, the reduced form VAR is estimated as:

$$Y_t = A(L)Y_{t-1} + v_t \sim N(0, \Sigma_v), \tag{1}$$

where the diagonal elements of the matrix lag polynomial $A(L)$ have a degree of p, and the off-diagonal elements have a degree of q. Denote the resulting (restricted) VAR by VAR (p, q).

Next, we consider the structural FAVAR model consisting of the VAR model (1) with errors that have the factor structure

$$v_t = \lambda f_t + \varepsilon_t, \tag{2}$$

where $E(f_t f_t) = diag\,(\sigma_{f_1}, ..., \sigma_{f_k})$ and $E(\varepsilon_t \varepsilon_t) = diag\,(\sigma_{\varepsilon_1}, ..., \sigma_{\varepsilon_n})$ and f_t are the common international factors, λ is the $n \times k$ matrix of factor loadings, and ε_t are the country-specific, or idiosyncratic, shocks. From (2), it follows that the business cycle of each country is affected by the spillover effects from other countries, common international shocks, and the country's own idiosyncratic shocks.[6] The Eq. (2) is estimated using the EM algorithm, a useful method for estimating unknown parameters.[7]

4.2. Data and model selection

The monthly data on seasonally adjusted production for the six major developed countries (Japan, the United States, Germany, France, Italy and

---

[6] The definition of what constitutes a common international shock depends on the frequency of the data. For example, a financial crisis that starts in one country but spills over into other countries within days would be identified in the structural FAVAR as a common international shock and not as a spillover effect.

[7] The EM algorithm is an iterative optimization method used to estimate unknown parameters with given measurement data. See Dempster *et al.* (1977).

the United Kingdom) and the seven East Asian countries (China, Taiwan, South Korea, Malaysia, Thailand, Singapore and the Philippines) are from the IMF's International Financial Statistics (IFS) database. Business cycles are extracted using the HP filter. These extracted data are the same as those in Sec. 3.1.

With the structural changes caused by the Asian financial crisis in mind, determinants of the business cycles were specified separately for two periods: before and after the crisis. Thus, the estimation period is from January 1993 to June 1997 and January 1999 to December 2007. The two periods, omitting the years 1997–1998 and the years after 2008, were selected to eliminate a possible distortion of the results due to the irregular shock of the Asian financial crisis and of the recent worldwide recession.

First, the AIC and BIC computed for the two subsamples point to a VAR (2,1) specification for the Eq. (1). Next, the structural FAVAR specification (2) is overidentified, so likelihood ratio tests of the overidentifying restrictions can be performed on the number of factors k. In the first subsample, a hypothesis of $k = 6$ is accepted against the unrestricted alternative (i.e., against Σ_v with full rank), and in the second subsample, a hypothesis of $k = 5$ is accepted.

In the first period, however, the obtained p-value of the likelihood ratio test is small (0.035), indicating that factors could not be identified as clearly as in the case of the second period (p-value = 0.1638). This result is consistent with the correlation of coefficients shown in Table 1 where the coefficients in the first period are much lower than those in the second period.

Several candidates for factors simultaneously affecting the business cycles of the selected countries are as follows: (1) world factor; (2) advanced countries factor; (3) Euro/European Union (EU) member factor; (4) East Asian factor; (5) East Asia–United States factor representing the fluctuation in the exchange rate of the Japanese yen against the US dollar; (6) production fragmentation factor affecting East Asia–Japan–United States.

With regard to the third factor, we adopt the EU factor (for Germany, France, Italy and the United Kingdom) for the first period and the Euro factor (for Germany, France and Italy) for the second period. This is due to the fact that during the first year of the second period, 1999, the euro was introduced to world financial markets as an accounting currency, replacing the former European Currency Unit (ECU). The fifth factor is adopted only in the first period as many East Asian countries attempted to maintain relative stability of their currencies with respect to the U.S. dollar in the first half period. In the case where the relative stability of their currencies against the U.S. dollar is maintained, any changes in the value of the Japanese yen against the U.S. currency directly translate into changes in the competitiveness of their exports to Japanese exports (Moneta and Rüffer, 2009).

The fact that the fifth factor stopped influencing the above countries during the second period is consistent with the change in the behavior of East Asian countries' exchange rates against the U.S. dollar. In the 2000s, East Asian countries' exchange rates against the U.S. dollar became volatile and no longer represented their competitiveness against Japanese exports.

4.3. Empirical results

4.3.1. Variance decomposition

Through variance decomposition, the business cycle in each country is decomposed into a total of eight different factors (seven in the latter half period): the effects of six different factors (five in the latter half period) simultaneously had an international impact on the relevant countries, a spillover effect and an internal shock.

Table 2 shows the results of the variance decomposition for the second half period.[8] Seven factors are shown in the top row of the Table. Vertically, the impact ratio of each factor is displayed for three time periods: the current term during which a shock occurred, half a year (6 months) later and one year (12 months) later. The sum of the factors'

---

[8] As described previously, factors could not be identified clearly in the likelihood ratio test of the overidentifying restrictions for the first half period. Thus, Table 2 shows the results of the variance decomposition only of the second period. In line with the variance decomposition of the first period, the following results can be observed: (1) the degree of the impact made by the production fragmentation factor varies by country. Countries that are relatively greatly impacted are limited to South Korea, Malaysia, and Japan; (2) the only countries continuously and relatively strongly impacted by the East Asian factor are Taiwan and China. The East Asian factor does not strongly impact the entire East Asian region; (3) the European factor has a relatively large impact on each country.

Table 2. Variance decomposition based on the structural FAVAR.

		World	East Asia	Fragmentation	Advanced	Euro	Spillover	Own
Korea	1	0.15	0.08	0.16			0.00	0.61
	6	0.07	0.02	0.30			0.16	0.45
	12	0.05	0.02	0.33			0.26	0.34
Malaysia	1	0.15	0.04	0.29			0.00	0.52
	6	0.10	0.00	0.48			0.15	0.27
	12	0.06	0.00	0.51			0.27	0.16
Thailand	1	0.18	0.00	0.25			0.00	0.57
	6	0.08	0.00	0.47			0.24	0.21
	12	0.04	0.00	0.47			0.38	0.11
Taiwan	1	0.00	0.00	0.21			0.00	0.79
	6	0.00	0.04	0.25			0.09	0.62
	12	0.00	0.04	0.26			0.14	0.56
Singapore	1	0.02	0.03	0.08			0.00	0.87
	6	0.03	0.01	0.25			0.20	0.51
	12	0.03	0.00	0.34			0.32	0.31
Philippines	1	0.00	0.00	0.07			0.00	0.93
	6	0.00	0.00	0.25			0.10	0.65
	12	0.01	0.00	0.37			0.20	0.42
China	1	0.00	0.98	0.00			0.00	0.02
	6	0.00	0.82	0.01			0.15	0.02
	12	0.00	0.66	0.06			0.27	0.01
Japan	1	0.36		0.04	0.04		0.00	0.56
	6	0.14		0.35	0.02		0.23	0.26
	12	0.08		0.44	0.01		0.39	0.08
U.S.	1	0.00		0.43	0.01		0.00	0.56
	6	0.01		0.47	0.01		0.09	0.42
	12	0.01		0.47	0.01		0.15	0.36

(*Continued*)

Table 2. (*Continued*)

		World	East Asia	Fragmentation	Advanced	Euro	Spillover	Own
France	1	0.46			0.07	0.03	0.00	0.44
	6	0.26			0.03	0.03	0.26	0.42
	12	0.21			0.02	0.02	0.44	0.31
Germany	1	0.00			0.04	0.54	0.00	0.42
	6	0.05			0.09	0.34	0.29	0.23
	12	0.05			0.08	0.20	0.54	0.13
Italy	1	0.09			0.58	0.08	0.00	0.25
	6	0.09			0.35	0.15	0.30	0.11
	12	0.08			0.24	0.10	0.51	0.07
U.K.	1	0.96			0.03		0.00	0.01
	6	0.69			0.01		0.29	0.01
	12	0.47			0.00		0.52	0.01

contribution ratios in the row is 1. In the impulse response, the variance decomposition results after half a year or one year are the amplified shocks brought to its own country half a year or one year ago, as in the case of structural shocks and internal shocks. The other results are considered spillover effects.

The following observations can be made from Table 2. The first and most important one is that the production fragmentation factor has a large impact on the relevant countries almost without exception. The degree of the impact grows from month to month. Furthermore, this impact is observed not only in East Asia but also in Japan and the United States, which were originally capital goods providers. This result is in line with the analysis by Takeuchi (2011c). Since the 2000s, as foreign direct investments and their local production progressed, and production fragmentation expanded, capital goods produced in East Asia began to be exported to Japan and the United States and incorporated into capital stock, supporting their production activities.

In addition to the points mentioned above, the important results from the variance decomposition in the latter half period are as follows: (1) The East Asian factor has made a large impact on China's business cycles; (2) the contributions of the Euro bloc factor are smaller than those of the production fragmentation factor.[9]

Unlike the other East Asian countries, China has been strongly impacted by TFP and not by investment-specific technological change, which has a close relationship with trade (import/export of capital goods). One reason for this may be the fact that China is a large country with a large domestic market and, until recent years, had been relatively unaffected by trade compared with the surrounding countries.

The other potential reasons are (1) China's capital coefficient has been higher than that of other countries, and thus, capital goods imports may have a smaller marginal effect on production in China,[10] and (2) if the value added in Chinese industrial sectors producing tradable goods is limited, then the aggregate economic impact of export growth will be smaller than it might appear. The second reason was discussed in Gangnes and Assche's (2010) study of the Chinese electronics sector where a considerable and rising portion of the sector's trade involves cross-hauling parts and components, sometimes with limited value added created before re-export.

4.3.2. Examination of the factors

It was found that the increased linkage of business cycles in East Asia, Japan and the United States in the 2000s is mainly driven by the production fragmentation factor. What type of observable data are related to the production fragmentation factor? Is it possible to confirm the expected correlation with empirical data related to production fragmentation?

As mentioned earlier, investment-specific technological change is considered as data related to production fragmentation. Investment-specific technological change refers to technologies embodied in capital goods. It is expected that East Asia, through production fragmentation, has a more active trade in capital goods, with a bigger contribution to the macro economy, than other regions.[11] Said technologies are considered to

---

[9] The common currency euro is likely to contribute to changes in the industrial structure of member countries that lead to productivity differentials among the countries and that make international business cycles less synchronized. See Takeuchi (2011b).

[10] See Ministry of Economy, Trade and Industry, Japan (2005).

[11] See Ando *et al.* (2006).

be the source of corporate competitiveness in East Asia, and these are not seen in the other regions (ADB, 2003). Kwack and Sun (2005), conducting an empirical analysis on South Korea, which has a large degree of dependence on import of these capital goods, conclude that the majority of the country's TFP growth rate during 1969–2000 can be explained by the transfer of technologies embodied in imported capital goods.

The method used to measure investment-specific technological change in this chapter is based on the model presented by Greenwood *et al.* (1997, 2000). This method considers the technologies embodied in machinery and equipment (capital goods) as distinct from TFP-related technological progress, unlike the approach of Kwack and Sun (2005).[12]

When capital stock is designated as K, the machinery and equipment (investment) incorporated into capital stock as I and the depreciation rate of capital stock as δ, the investment-specific technological change (q) is incorporated into the capital stock transition equation as follows:

$$K_{t+1} = (1-\delta)K_t + q_t I_t. \tag{3}$$

Unlike TFP, which has a direct impact on production, investment-specific technological change influences the economy through investment activities, as shown in the above equation.

In the model, a representative agent makes a consumption or investment choice using the agent's income. Therefore, production expansion through investment-specific technological change is consequently accompanied by changes in the ratio of the price of consumption goods to effective investment (qI) (lowered relative price of effective investment). In contrast, production expansion caused by rising TFP does not change the relative price. In other words, the movements of investment-specific technological change (q) are expressed as the ratio of the price of consumption

---

[12] Investment-specific technology was investigated first using the closed model adopted by Greenwood *et al.* (1997, 2000). Afterward, Boileau (2002) and Takeuchi (2011c) introduced this concept into the international business cycle model. Greenwood *et al.* (1997, 2000) investigated the role of technology in generating growth in the United States during the post-war period. The technology was represented by the decline in the relative price of capital goods and the increase in the capital goods production-GDP ratio observed during the same period. They argued that this type of technology should be distinguished from the traditional Hicks-neutral form of technology.

goods to effective investment price (relative price increase in consumption goods = relative price decrease in effective investment = growth in investment-specific technological change). In this chapter, to obtain q, the private consumption deflator of SNA is divided by the machinery and equipment deflator from the same SNA's gross fixed capital formation deflators.

Except for specific East Asian countries, the investment-specific technological changes indicate upward trends. These upward trends were similarly confirmed in the preceding studies covering developed countries. In addition, a comparison with East Asia suggests that the growth in investment-specific technological change in each NIES country generally exceeds that of each ASEAN (Association of Southeast Asian Nations) country. Investment-specific technological changes necessary for comparisons with the fragmentation factors were aggregated using each country's real GDP from the year 2000 as a weight.

From the investment-specific technological changes, calculated as shown above, the cyclical components are extracted through the HP filter to calculate the correlation coefficient between the production fragmentation factor obtained by structural FAVAR and the cycles. The results were 0.1512 in the first half period (1993–1997) and 0.3798 in the latter half period (1999–2007). In the latter, a clear positive correlation was observed (significance level at 5%).[13] The analysis results shown above indicated that the technologies embodied in capital goods traded internationally through production fragmentation have a strong correlation with the production fragmentation factor in the latter half period. Additionally, the results show that such technologies have a large impact on business cycles in the relevant countries.

Table 3 shows the calculated correlation coefficients between factors and observable shocks.

Empirical data considered in addition to investment-specific technology include the following: (1) the prices of energy (crude oil, coal and natural gas), the average prices of other primary commodities excluding energy (such as food and iron ore) and all-inclusive international commodity prices; (2) financial shocks; (3) the nominal yen-dollar exchange rate; and (4) TFP. In all of the data, cyclical components were calculated in a similar way to that previously described [a seasonally adjusted series

---

[13] To compare with observable shocks calculated using quarterly SNA data (Nos. 4, 5, 7 and 8 in Table 3), the extracted monthly factors are converted into quarterly data using a simple arithmetic average.

Table 3. Correlations between international factors and observable shocks.

International factors	Observable shocks	1999–2007 Correlation coefficients	*T*-test for correlation
1 world	— fuel price	−0.2630	**
2 world	— non-fuel price	−0.2547	**
3 world	— commodity price	−0.2944	**
4 East Asia	— TFP	0.2986	**
5 fragmentation	— investment-specific technology	0.3798	**
6 Euro	— TFP	−0.2685	*
7 advanced	— financial shock	−0.3282	**
		1993–1997	
1 world	— fuel price	−0.1215	
2 world	— non-fuel price	0.0912	
3 world	— commodity price	−0.0556	
4 East Asia	— TFP	0.1497	
5 fragmentation	— investment-specific technology	0.1512	
6 East Asia-U.S.	— yen/U.S. dollar	−0.0593	
7 EU	— TFP	−0.1536	
8 advanced	— financial shock	−0.2801	**

Note: The correlations between world factors and three commodity price shocks in the second period are for 2004–2007. *significant at the 10% level, **significant at the 5% level.

was used for (1)] to calculate the correlation coefficients with each factor, excluding spillover effects and each country's internal shocks. In preparing these data, IMF's International Financial Statistics (IFS), DRI International Economic and Financial Database (Global Insight Inc.), CEIC databases (CEIC Data Company Ltd.) and Penn World Table (Version 6.2) were used.

Variable (1) serves as a proxy variable for resource price shocks; the data were obtained from IFS. This chapter based the financial shocks in

(2) on the methodology developed by Christiano *et al.* (1997). When a monetary policy target is designated as R_t, and the information held by a monetary authority is Θ_t, the financial shock ε_t can be derived from $R_t = g(\Theta_t) + \varepsilon_t$. $g(\Theta_t)$ represents a linear function. The financial shock ε_t has no serial correlation, and the assumption can thus be made that ε_t has no correlation with Θ_t.

The financial shock was derived using data from the United States and modeled by a structural VAR composed of simultaneous equations, including this monetary policy function. Financial shocks in the United States are treated as international financial shocks, consistent with Stock and Watson (2005). This approach is justified by the United States' status as a key-currency country.

As mentioned earlier, appreciation (rate decrease) of the yen–dollar rate (yen/U.S. dollar) in (3) leads to an increase in East Asian countries' export competitiveness (over Japan), moving in tandem with the dollar, and depreciation (rate increase) leads to a decrease in said competitiveness. The relationship between the change in the yen–dollar rate and the East Asia–United States factor is expected to be inversely correlated.

The TFP in (4) was obtained by referring to Backus *et al.* (1992, 1994) and Glick and Rogoff (1995) and by calculating the Solow residual using the Cobb–Douglas production function of $\ln(Y_t) - \pi\ln(L_t)$ (where Y_t represents real GDP, L_t, the number of employees and π, the labor share). As discussed in Backus *et al.* (1992), the absence of capital stock data due to data constraints is not a serious problem. This is because the short-run volatility of capital stock is small and can be assumed to be orthogonal to the cycle. In contrast, it is usually desirable to use the data on labor hours for L_t, but in this calculation, the number of employees was used, because data on labor hours by quarter and/or month are difficult to obtain. As a result, the Solow residual may include business cycle movements and cannot be regarded as purely representing technological change. In consideration of this issue, the HP filter was used to extract trend components from the Solow residual to obtain TFP. To observe the correlation with factors, the averaged TFP values are calculated using the real GDP from the year 2000 as a weight.

From Table 3, significant correlation could be confirmed in (1) energy, other primary commodities and general commodity prices, and the world factor in the latter half period; (2) East Asia's TFP and the East Asian factor in the latter half period; (3) investment-specific technological change and the production fragmentation factor in the latter half period; (4) Euro bloc's TFP and the Euro bloc factor in the latter half period; and (5) financial shock and the developed countries factor in the first and latter half periods. Table 4 only lists items in which significant correlation could be confirmed in one of the two estimation periods, except in the relationship between the East Asia–United States factor and the yen–dollar rate, which is analyzed and listed only in the first half period.

Several points to be noted are summarized below. First, with regard to the relationship between commodity prices and the world factor, a significant negative correlation was observed after 2004 in the latter half period. During this year, commodities, such as crude oil, exhibited a marked upward trend. Second, as discussed above, a negative correlation was expected between the East-Asia–United States factor and the yen–dollar rate. Although the sign condition was satisfied, the correlation was not significant.

Third, between the Euro bloc TFP and the Euro bloc factor, a negative correlation was found in the latter half period. Determining whether the productivity shock is procyclical or countercyclical requires further investigation. On the one hand, there are studies supporting the procyclical interpretation (e.g., Basu and Fernald, 2001; Inklaar, 2007) that insist that procyclical productivity is consistent with real business cycle (RBC) theory and can be empirically confirmed using long-term data.

On the other hand, other studies have shown that productivity has become acyclical or countercyclical since the late 1980s (e.g., Berger, 2011). The reason for a possible countercyclical productivity shock is that companies tend to be excessively burdened with production factors during economic booms and tend to carry out restructuring during bust periods. The tendency to curtail employment continues even during the ensuing economic recovery. Berger (2011), using data and simulating the theoretical model simultaneously, clarified the mechanism of countercyclical productivity.

This chapter's analysis confirmed the presence of countercyclical productivity in the Euro bloc and procyclical productivity in East Asia. Although not shown in Table 3, the correlation coefficient was negative, if not significant, between the advanced countries factor and their TFP. Future analysis should focus on whether the relationship between productivity shocks and business cycles is different in advanced and developing countries.

Fourth, a negative correlation between the monetary policy shock and the advanced countries factor was confirmed as expected. However, this correlation was observed only in advanced countries, with no correlation observed in East Asian countries. This result is similar to that of Takeuchi (2011a). The degree of financial deepening is greater in advanced countries than in East Asian countries, making the result that the effects of the financial shock are limited to the former, reasonable.

5. Conclusion

This chapter employs the structural FAVAR method to analyze factors affecting the business cycles of East Asia, Japan and the United States. Business cycle synchronization across these countries has been increasing since the Asian financial crisis of 1997–1998. Comparing the extracted shocks with empirically observed financial, productivity and natural resource price shocks reveals that the business cycles of East Asia and the major advanced economies are affected to a large extent by common factors, while those of the Euro zone countries are not. In East Asia, the observed business cycle synchronization appears to reflect the accumulation of technology (investment-specific technological change) embodied in capital goods that are traded vigorously in the region.

Regarding the factors underlying international business cycles, the role of the trade in goods and of capital flows between the countries concerned has been widely discussed. However, the mechanisms through which this synchronization occurs have never been clarified, especially for pairs of countries that include a developing economy. This chapter argues that the supply-side factors, including trade, industrial structures and productivity shocks, are important elements in this difference and that the structure of trade rather than total trade volume (demand-side factors) is key in determining the extent of business cycle synchronization.

The analysis of investment-specific technology in this chapter reveals that the trade of capital goods, which embodies that technology, has, in recent years, been gradually shifting weight from exchanges between East Asia and the major developed economies of Japan and the United States to trade among East Asian countries. If this trend progresses any further in the future, the regional characteristics of East Asia's business cycles are expected to become more distinct. As they go through the "global rebalancing of demand", which mainly affects the United States–East Asia trade imbalance, East Asian countries are more likely to explore the possibility of pursuing policy coordination and of introducing more common economic policies than ever before. If this becomes the case, it will become important to ascertain how the above-mentioned supply-side factors, which promote business cycle linkage across countries in the region, will change.

References

Aizenman, J and N Marion (2003). The high demand for international reserves in the Far East: What is going on? *Journal of the Japanese and International Economies*, 17, 370–400.

Aizenman, J and J Lee (2007). International reserves: Precautionary versus mercantilist views, theory and evidence. *Open Economies Review*, 18, 191–214.

Ando, M, S Arndt and F Kimura (2006). Production networks in East Asia: Strategic behavior by Japanese and U.S. firms. *Japan Center for Economic Research (JCER) Discussion Paper 103*.

Asian Development Bank (ADB) (2003). Asian Development Outlook 2003. 205–272.

Asian Development Bank (ADB) (2007). Asian Development Outlook 2007. 66–81.

Backus, D, P Kehoe and F Kydland (1992). International real business cycles. *The Journal of Political Economy*, 100, 745–775.

Backus, D, P Kehoe and F Kydland (1994). Dynamics of the trade balance and the terms of trade: The J-curve? *The American Economic Review*, 84, 84–103.

Basu, S and JG Fernald (2001). Why is productivity procyclical? Why do we care? In *New Developments in Productivity Analysis*, CR Hulten, ER Dean, Dean and MJ Harper (eds.), pp. 225–301. Chicago, IL: University of Chicago Press.

Berger, D (2011). *Countercyclical Restructuring and Jobless Recoveries*. Mimeo.

Boileau, M (2002). Trade in capital goods and investment-specific technical change. *Journal of Economic Dynamics & Control*, 26, 964–984.

Calderón, C, A Chong and E Stein (2007). Trade intensity and business cycle synchronization: Are developing countries any different? *Journal of International Economics*, 71, 2–21.

Christiano, LJ, M Eichenbaum and CL Evans (1997). Sticky price and limited participation models of money: A comparison. *European Economic Review*, 41, 1201–1249.

Clark, TE and E van Wincoop (2001). Borders and business cycles. *Journal of International Economies*, 55, 59–85.

Crosby, M (2003). Business cycle correlations in Asia-Pacific. *Economic Letters*, 80, 36–44.

Dempster, AP, NM Laird and DB Rubin (1977). Maximum likelihood from incomplete data via the EM algorithm. *Journal of the Royal Statistical Society. Series B (Methodological)*, 39, 1–38.

Devereux, MB and A Sutherland (2009). A portfolio model of capital flows to emerging markets. *Journal of Development Economics*, 89, 181–193.

Fidrmuc, J (2004). The endogeneity of the optimum currency area criteria, intra-industry trade and EMU enlargement. *Contemporary Economic Policy*, 22, 1–12.

Frankel, J and A Rose (1998). The endogeneity of the optimum currency area criteria. *Economic Journal*, 108, 1009–1025.

Gangnes, B and AV Assche (2010). Global production networks in electronics and intra-Asian trade. University of Hawaii at Manoa, Department of Economics Working paper No. 10-4.

Glick, R and K Rogoff (1995). Global versus country-specific productivity shocks and the current account. *Journal of Monetary Economics*, 35, 159–192.

Greenwood, J, Z Hercowitz and P Krusell (1997). Long-run implications of investment-specific technological change. *The American Economic Review*, 87, 342–362.

Greenwood, J, Z Hercowitz and P Krusell (2000). The role of investment-specific technological change in the business cycle. *European Economic Review*, 44, 91–115.

Inklaar, R (2007). Cyclical productivity in Europe and the United States: Evaluating the evidence on returns to scale and input utilization. *Economica*, 74, 822–841.

International Monetary Fund (IMF) (2007). *World Economic Outlook (April) — Spillovers and Cycles in the Global Economy*, Chapter 4 (Decoupling the train? Spillovers and cycles in the global economy), pp. 121–160.

International Monetary Fund (IMF) (2008). *World Economic Outlook (October) — Financial Stress, Downturns, and Recoveries*, Chapter 6 (Divergence of current account balances across emerging economies), pp. 197–240.

Kumamura, M (2006). Trade and business cycle co-movements in Asia-Pacific. *Journal of Asian Economics*, 17, 622–645.

Kwack, SY and LY Sun (2005). Economies of scale, technological progress, and the sources of economic growth: Case of Korea. *Journal of Policy Modeling*, 27, 265–283.

Ministry of Economy, Trade and Industry, Japan (METI) (2005). *White Paper on International Economy and Trade 2005*. Tokyo: METI.

Miyagawa, T and Y Imamura (2003). Keikijunkan no kokusaitekihakyuu [Empirical analysis on international business cycle spillovers in the Asia-Pacific region]. In *Keikijunkan to keikiyosoku [Business cycles and business forecast (sic)]*, K Asako and S Fukuda (eds.), pp. 337–370. Tokyo: University of Tokyo Press. (in Japanese)

Moneta, F and R Rüffer (2009). Business cycle synchronization in East Asia. *Journal of Asian Economics*, 20, 1–12.

Ng, ECY (2010). Production fragmentation and business-cycle comovement. *Journal of International Economics*, 82, 1–14.

Shin, K and Y Wang (2004). Trade integration and business co-movements: The case of Korea with other Asian countries. *Japan and the World Economy*, 16, 213–230.

Stock, JH and MW Watson (2005). Understanding changes in international business cycle dynamics. *Journal of the European Economic Association*, 3, 968–1006.

Takeuchi, F (2011a). Structural FAVAR ni yoru sekaikeizai no youinbunseki [A decomposition of global business cycles using Structural FAVAR]. *Economic Analysis* 184 (Economic and Social Research Institute, Cabinet Office, Government of Japan), pp. 75–98. (in Japanese)

Takeuchi, F (2011b). Yuroken no sangyoukouzou no henka to keikijunkan eno eikyou [The industrial structural change and its impact to business cycles in Euro zone]. In *Sekaidoujifukyo to Keikijunkanbunseki* [*Great Recession in the Global Economy and Business Cycle Analyses* (*sic*)], K Asako, N Iizuka and T Miyagawa (eds.), pp. 285–307. Tokyo: University of Tokyo Press. (in Japanese)

Takeuchi, F (2011c). The role of production fragmentation in international business cycle in East Asia. *Journal of Asian Economics*, 22, 441–459.

CHAPTER 3

FINANCIAL MARKET LINKAGE IN EAST ASIAN COUNTRIES*

Kyosuke Shiotani

Bank of Japan
2-1-1 Nihonbashi Hongokucho
Chuo-Ku, Tokyo 103-8660, Japan
kyousuke.shiotani@boj.or.jp

Yoichi Matsubayashi

Faculty of Economics, Kobe University
Rokkodai, Nada-Ku, Kobe 657-8501, Japan
myoichi@econ.kobe-u.ac.jp

1. Introduction

The rise in world economy's globalization has increased the degree of global linkage in economic fluctuations. New global linkages are taking shape, especially in Japan, the United States and in East Asian countries due to the various changes in economic structures.

Lehman Shock in 2008 triggered a rapid deterioration of real economies in the United States, Japan and European countries. On the other hand, the "decoupling hypothesis" predicted that the American financial crisis would have little impact on East Asian countries, and

---

*Views expressed in this chapter are those of the authors and do not necessarily reflect the official views of the Bank of Japan.

other emerging countries. However, due to the presence of various economic links, emerging countries were not exempted from the global recession.

There are few conceivable factors for links between economies of developed and emerging countries, but financial market linkage is a most vital factor in transmission of short-term economic shock. In particular, a stock market shock is transmitted instantly to a country, not just in the same country, but also in stock markets all over the world. For example, the American stock market crash in 1987 known as "Black Monday", the Mexican currency crisis in 1992, the Asian financial crisis between 1997 and 1998, the global financial crisis that triggered Lehman Brothers to file for bankruptcy in September 2008 and the European sovereign debt crisis in 2010 have all triggered a sharp fluctuation in stock prices around the world.

This document will explore the global linkage of stock prices throughout the United States, Japan and East Asian countries, as well as study the cause for that linkage by employing quantitative analysis using new statistical methods. Regarding global linkage of stock prices, there has been an abundance of empirical analysis in the past, but studies that have deeply explored economic factors behind those linkages are nearly nonexistent. The analysis in this document successfully employs a new statistical method that has gained popularity in recent years — the Bayesian Network analysis, to gain new insight previously unattained through traditional analysis on international linkage of stock prices. Specifically that the stock price shock which caused a ripple effect on East Asian countries, with the United States as the epicenter, changed overtime. Transmission of stock price fluctuations has been increasing throughout the East Asian region, especially against a backdrop of regional intra-trade network development in the early 2000s. Additionally, during this period a unique situation was observed where stock price fluctuations in the United States impacted South Korea and China first, and subsequently both of these country fluctuations were then transmitted to Japan.

This chapter is organized as follows. The next section surveys some of the empirical literatures about financial market linkage and transmission mechanism. In Sec. 3, we will discuss the Bayesian network approach, which is a statistical model that we will use in this chapter. In Sec. 4, a detailed empirical analysis is conducted. Some conclusions are summarized in Sec. 5.

2. Literature Review

The oldest studies on international transmissions of stock prices date back to the 1970s. Levy and Sarnat (1970), Agmon (1972), Ripley (1973), Panton *et al.* (1976) and Hilliard (1979) have used weekly and monthly data in an attempt to verify transmissions, with all reporting that the correlation among countries is generally weak. Considering that in the 1960s and 1970s, which were the focus of the analyses, capital transactions were strongly regulated by nations, and international financial markets were not sufficiently integrated, these findings can be considered reasonable.

Styles of analysis have diversified from the 1980s. Considering first the correlation of international stock markets, it is vital to observe transmissions from the perspective of return rate (first moment) or of variance of return rate (second moment). Errunza and Losq (1985), Taylor and Tonks (1989), Campbell and Hamao (1992), Eun and Shim (1989) and Longin and Solnik (1995) focused on international transmissions in price–earnings ratio, concluding that generally the correlation is strong. Conversely, many analyses have focused on the volatility of the return rate, including Hamao *et al.* (1990), Theodossiou and Lee (1993), Koutmos and Booth (1995), Liu and Pan (1997), In *et al.* (2001), Jang and Sul (2002), Leong and Felmingham (2003), Darrat and Benkato (2003), Cifarelli and Paladino (2004), Hoti (2005), Chuang *et al.* (2007), Chelley-Steely (2000), Karolyi (1995), Arshanapalli *et al.* (1997) and Steely (2006). Many of these analyses attempt to verify, by use of so-called ARCH-type time series analysis, whether the conditional variance in stock prices in relevant countries are affected by the variance in stock price return rate in other countries.

Target areas for analysis have typically centered on transmissions among developed countries such as the United States and Europe or the United States and Japan. However, from the 1990s, analysis has been active in stock price transmissions among emerging market countries, especially in Asia. Examples include Wong *et al.* (2004), Johnson and Soenen (2002), Masih and Masih (1999), Wongswan (2006), Ghosh *et al.* (1999), Kim and Rogers (1995), In *et al.* (2001) and Liu and Pan (1997). A general summary of these analyses follows.

Kim and Rogers (1995) examined correlations in stock price volatility using monthly data for Japan, the United States and South Korea from 1985 to 1992. The results showed that changes in volatility of the U.S. and Japanese market affected volatility in South Korea just after its stock market began trading and that increases in volatility in Japan had a greater effect on the Korean market than did increases in volatility in the United States.

In *et al.* (2001) using VAR-EGARCH, examined stock market volatility correlation in Hong Kong, South Korea and Thailand during the Asian crisis (1997–1998), showing two-way propagation of volatility between Hong Kong and South Korea, and propagation of volatility from South Korea to Thailand. They also indicated that Hong Kong played an important role in the propagation of volatility.

Ghosh *et al.* (1999) used the cointegration test to analyze stock price fluctuations in the United States, Japan, the Philippines, Indonesia, Thailand, Singapore, Malaysia, Taiwan, South Korea, India and Hong Kong for the period from March 1997 to December 1997. Based on these findings, Hong Kong, India, South Korea and Malaysia demonstrated a cointegration relationship with the United States, while Indonesia, the Philippines and Singapore demonstrated a cointegration relationship with Japan, showing that the latter countries and the Japanese economy were closely connected.

Masih and Masih (1999), using monthly data from February 1992 to June 1997, applied the cointegration test to stock price fluctuations in Japan, the United States, the United Kingdom, Germany, Hong Kong, Singapore, Thailand and Malaysia. From the findings, the United States and United Kingdom had a major impact on fluctuations in Asian countries, while Japan and Germany did not have as great an impact. Furthermore, stronger transmissions in financial policies and economies may underlie the stronger interdependence among stocks in Asian nations. Johnson and Soenen (2002) used Geweke Unidirectional Feedback Measures to examine stock price fluctuations in Japan, Australia, China, Hong Kong, Malaysia, New Zealand, Singapore, India, Indonesia, South Korea, the Philippines, Taiwan and Thailand from 1988 to 1998. The findings pointed to a strong transmission between Australia, Hong Kong, China, Malaysia, New Zealand and Singapore to the Japanese market of that time, especially from 1994. Moreover it was evident that a high correlation among macro variables tended to indicate a high correlation among stock prices.

Wong *et al.* (2004), using the cointegration test, analyzed stock price fluctuations in the United States, the United Kingdom, Japan, Malaysia, Thailand, South Korea, Taiwan, Singapore and Hong Kong from 1981 to 1986, from 1987 to 1996 and from 1997 to 2002. Hong Kong showed cointegration with the United States and the United Kingdom. From Taiwan's and Singapore's cointegration relationship with Japan, transmissions between developed countries and Asian countries were observed from 1987, further strengthening after the Asian currency crisis. Moreover it was seen that the portfolio variance effect through investment in newly developing nations has lessened. From these findings, the possibility is high that the strengthening of economic ties underlies the strengthening of transmissions between Asian stock markets and the stock market in Japan (the United States) in recent years. However, the analyses also contain inadequacies, as follows. First, the analyses fundamentally address only the relationship between two countries. Second, they look at the impact of developed countries with emerging countries, without conversely analyzing the impact of emerging markets on developed countries like Japan. Third, the relationships among the countries are not consistent in the analyses. Drawing upon the research discussed, the unique contributions made by this study can be summarized in the following two points. First, this study expressly examines the environment behind the international transmissions of the stock price, and the background against which those transmissions are strengthened. As noted earlier, there is considerable existing research on international transmissions of stock prices. Most analyses, however, seem to have limited awareness on the issue of whether international transmissions are growing or not; research like this study, with deeper interest in identifying the factors that increase the transmissions is almost nonexistent. Second, this study investigates the mechanisms by which the U.S. stock market shock propagated to the East Asian region. Towards that end, the following two points demand consideration.

The first point is the nature of the U.S. shock. The standard VAR estimates a vector autoregressive model, and from residual sequence information takes the approach of artificially applying shock in (for example) the form of one standard deviation of the residuals. In this situation, generating a real economic shock that varies over time is difficult, and analytical methods do not go beyond the realm of virtual test calculations (i.e., simulations). Further, VAR-based analysis deters sufficient investigation of changes in economic conditions that regulate the movements of variables.

The second point is that by using a new analytical technique, the Bayesian network, the characteristics of the first point can be scrutinized very effectively. The Bayesian network is a form of machine learning, like

NNJ; however, unlike the black box of neural networks that leave the relationship among variables unclear, the Bayesian network, by using the information in data to the fullest extent, highlights the causalities that exist among multiple variables as a probabilistic graphical model. These characteristics make this an ideal methodology to separate the transmission mechanisms in East Asian stock price volatility and to highlight the characteristics of the transmission patterns. In the second section, we lay out and introduce a framework for organising this Bayesian network.

3. Methodologies: Bayesian Network Model

In this section, we will discuss the Bayesian network approach, which is a statistical model that we will use to investigate the causality of stock price movement in the United States and East Asian countries. A Bayesian network is a probabilistic graphical model that represents a set of variables and their probabilistic independence. It can be used to examine causal relationships and can represent these relationships graphically, which can help us understand complex situations easily. In econometrics, the Bayesian network has been employed in a time series analysis. For example, Chen and Hsiao (2007) apply the technique to the identification of structural vector autoregression. However, econometricians have not yet investigated the use of the Bayesian network model as an effective instrument for time series analysis and econometrics. For some time, there has been very little application of the model in economic research.[1]

Despite having little application in economics, this approach does not differ greatly from other econometric techniques. There is a good deal of literature in economics for using probabilistic graphical models or machine learning techniques to analyze data and deriving complex functional relationships from it. Economists discuss causal relationships among variables with probabilistic graphical models in treatment effect literature [see Pearl (2000)]. The neural network is a common econometric tool to forecast time series data with complex nonlinearity, like currency

---

[1] Besides economics, there are a variety of applications for the Bayesian network in the fields of gene regulatory networks, protein structures, medicine, document classification, image processing and others. It is not only used for academic research but also for practical business purposes (vehicle navigational systems, blocking unwanted junk mail and so on). For more detail on its basic theories and applications, refer to textbooks like Bishop (2006) and Pourret *et al.* (2008).

exchange rates and other financial data [see Chapter 12 in Giles (2003)]. We can consider the Bayesian network as a technique that finds probabilistic graphical models depicting causal relationships among variables from a vast amount of data.[2]

4. Empirical Evidence

4.1. Data

The source for the stock price index is the Morgan Stanley Capital Index (abbreviated as MSCI), and a daily series is collected. We use a simple model that each node in the Bayesian network takes only two states, "up" if the stock index is up, and "down" if the stock index is down. As to the stock price analysis, "to what extent" the U.S. stock price affects the Asian stock markets daily, our simple model is not appropriate. However, our most important goal is accounting for the international linkage between the United States and East Asian countries. It is likely that our model is sufficient to examine the causal chain in these countries. In addition, we can avoid the problem that the distribution of stock price changes is complex, at least not a simple distribution like the Gaussian, and dedicate our efforts to finding the optimal Bayesian network model.

The countries analyzed are the United States, Japan, China, South Korea and Taiwan. As the core of the Asian NIES, South Korea and Taiwan have, along with Japan, built East Asian trade network. China, meanwhile, as the "world factory" since the 1990s, has been rapidly strengthening its economic power. By focusing on the five countries noted, detailed analysis of the stock price transmissions from the United States to East Asian countries, and of their underlying factors, should be possible.

4.2. Empirical study

First, we use the period of 1994 to 1995 as the sample for analysis. Per Fig. 1, U.S. stock price volatility at the time propagated directly to Japan and China, while neither direct propagation from the United States to South Korea and Taiwan, nor from Japan or China, is observed. In other

---

[2]The detailed explanations of Bayesian network model are summarized in the appendix.

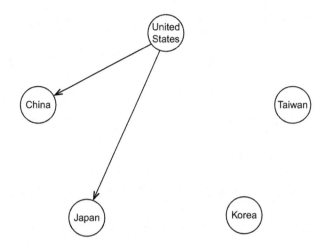

Fig. 1. Transmission mechanism, 1994–1995.

words, the propagation of the 1990s U.S. stock price shock into East Asia can be summed up as having been limited to direct spillover into Japan and China. The largest factor responsible for such a propagation route lies in the characteristics of trade structures.

Japan steadily increased exports of automobiles to the United States from the 1980s, reaching about one million autos per year in 1990. The number decreased slightly during that decade but maintained a level of about 800,000 autos. Such a stable trade structure with the United States necessarily affected Japanese exports, reflecting auto purchase trends in the United States. As an auto is produced from about 30,000 parts, a division of labor system pervaded associated factories. Therefore, as trends in car exports permeated widely through all of Japanese industry, the ripple effects influenced stock prices. Remarkable economic growth centered on East Asian NIES countries in the 1990s led to the expansion and deepening of trade networks in the region. However, as can be seen from Fig. 1, this strengthening of economic transmissions was not, in the mid-1990s, reflected in stock price transmissions.

China's route of reform and liberalization proceeded in earnest from the early 1990s, and trade with the United States grew sharply. According to Fukao *et al.* (1999), China's exports to the United States in 1990 were about $5.17 million in 1994 but have grown over four-fold to $21.47 million. Imports from the United States in 1990 were 6.57 million yuan, but had doubled to approximately 13.70 million yuan in 1994.[1] This rapid

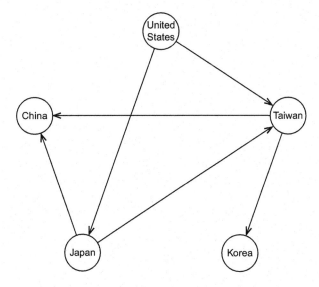

Fig. 2. Transmission mechanism, 1998–1999.

expansion of trade with the United States, as shown in Fig. 1, likely contributed to the direct spread of U.S. stock price volatility to China.

Next, we look at the spillover route from 1998 to 1999 based on Fig. 2. During this period, the Asian currency crisis erupted outward from Thailand, and financial markets in the Asian region were quite volatile. However, per Fig. 4, propagation into other Asian countries from South Korea, which experienced the currency crisis, was not observed.

On the other hand, unlike the early 1990s, propagation from Japan to other Asian countries was observed. This feature can essentially be seen as stemming from the expansion of trade with these countries. In 1998, however, the collapse of Yamaichi Securities and Hokkaido Takushoku Bank revealed a highly volatile domestic financial market in Japan. There is some possibility that this turmoil in the Japanese financial market affected the stock prices of neighboring Asian countries such as China and Taiwan. Furthermore, a spillover route from the United States to Japan can be clearly observed, in the same manner as Fig. 1.

How has the spillover mechanism changed in the 2000s? Figure 3 shows the situation from 2002 to 2003. Propagation in this period differs from that of the 1990s in the following three aspects.

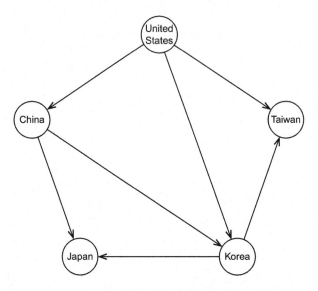

Fig. 3. Transmission mechanism, 2002–2003.

The first feature is that direct spillover from the United States to Japan is not observed. The second feature is that propagation from the United States to China, South Korea and Taiwan is evident. The third feature is that within the East Asian region, propagation to Japan and Taiwan via South Korea, and impact on Japan and South Korea via China, are observed.

To help understand the background that generates these mechanisms, Fig. 4 displays a comparison of Japanese, U.S. and East Asian trade flows between the 1990s and 2000s.

Figure 4 shows the changes in the trading volume from 2001 to 2005 if the average trading volume between 1991 to 1995 is normalized as 1. The figure shows that trading volume between Japan and the United States did not change much from the 1990s to 2000s. On the other hand, exports from the East Asian nations to Japan and the United States more than doubled in the 10-year period. The trading volume of the East Asian countries has shown such remarkable increase that both Japan and the States cannot disregard it. The extent of the transmission effect of the United States, Japan and East Asian nations' stock price has changed internationally through merchandize trading. Quantitative organization and verification on the changes in the trading flow amongst these three

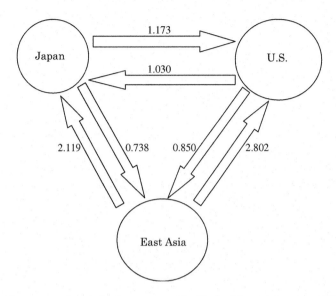

Fig. 4. Changes in the trade flow among the United States, Japan and East Asia.

regions have thus been done in advance. In addition, the term "East Asian nations" used here refers to the following eight countries: South Korea, China, Hong Kong, Singapore, Indonesia, Thailand, Malaysia and the Philippines. Figure 1 shows the changes in the trading volume from 2001 to 2005 if the average trading volume between 1991 to 1995 is normalized as 1.

Here, let us take a look at the other countries' relationships with China, which had the largest increase in trading volume amongst East Asian nations. As in Fig. 4, Table 1 shows the changes in the average volume from 2001 to 2005 if the average import and export volume of China from 1991 to 1995 was normalized to 1.

From this table, we can see that every country's export and import volume to and from China sharply increased during this period. From the above facts, we can verify that trade relations amongst these three regions have become extremely strong in the past ten years, and China's presence was particularly significant. Such a characteristic is bound to largely influence the international ripple effect of stock price volatility.

The most influential feature of the 2000s has been the economic rise of China and the deepening of East Asian trade networks. These two nascent movements are likely altering the nature of how U.S. stock price

Table 1. Trade volume with China.

	Export to China	Import from China
The United States	3.36	5.12
Japan	3.59	3.44
Korea	7.81	5.04
Hong Kong	2.29	2.01
Singapore	6.58	4.62
Indonesia	2.92	3.19
Thailand	7.61	5.04
Malaysia	5.23	6.86
Philippines	14.11	6.07

Source: IMF Direction of Trade.

shocks propagate to East Asia, by strengthening new economic transmissions as follows.

We assume that the demand for PCs in the United States is increasing. The expanded production accompanying this increased demand will take place not in the United States but in the "world factory", China. However, production in China is essentially assembly of the final goods — the PC units — and does not encompass production of semiconductors and other components that make up PCs. Those semi-finished goods are primarily manufactured in South Korea and Taiwan. In other words, expanded PC production in China boosts the production of intermediate goods in South Korea and Taiwan. Furthermore, the apparatus (general machinery) for manufacturing these semi-finished goods is mainly produced in Japan. In other words, the increase in demand for PCs from the United States spreads outward on a path that passes through China, South Korea and Japan. The mechanism by which the entire East Asian region functions as a type of production system has been established from the 2000s. The evolution and expansion of this mechanism has become apparent as a route of propagation, as shown in Fig. 4. Naturally, even in the 2000s, the U.S.–Japan trade structure, centered on the auto industry, is robust (auto exports to the United States since 1998 have expanded to over 1 million vehicles). However, a characteristic of the economic transmissions at the time, as outlined earlier, strengthened East Asian networks centered on China and South Korea constitute a relatively

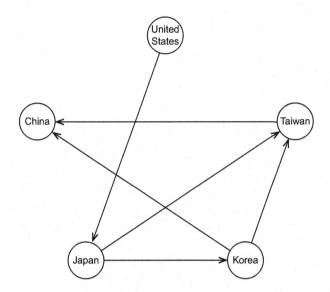

Fig. 5. Transmission mechanism, 2008–2009.

stronger factor, and as a result the stock price impact from the United States to Japan can be considered to have followed an indirect route.

Finally, we take a look at the international financial crisis that broke out from 2008 to 2009. As shown in Fig. 5, the propagation route in that period differs from those of both the 1990s and the early 2000s. In particular, we note that a direct route from the United States to Japan is revived and that propagation in the East Asian region is still present.

What factors underlie the U.S.–Japan stock price propagation route's renewed importance? The origin of the current international economic crisis is in the U.S. financial crisis. The Lehman Brothers bankruptcy in September 2008 raised concerns over similar risks of collapse of major U.S. financial institutions, causing funds to dry up in markets, especially the CP market. Against this backdrop of financial market confusion, various financial institutions quickly cut back on household loans. The household liquidity constraints rose suddenly, and excessive spending on the backs of loans quickly reversed itself into consumer restraint. Robust U.S. consumer spending was focused on durable goods demands, particularly cars, and included considerable imports from overseas. In short, the decline in U.S. domestic demand quickly reduced exports to the United States from Japan and other countries around the world. Growing credit risk in the

United States was also spreading rapidly to financial institutions around the world. Companies around the world found themselves struggling to raise funds, just as in the United States; coupled with decreased production due to shrinking exports, companies' financial condition began to deteriorate rapidly. The global recession grew via this process, and nations' imports and exports fell sharply through volume adjustment. In other words, the U.S.–Japan trade structure that had adapted steadily over time became evident in the financial crisis stemming from the United States, and this is likely to have highlighted anew the U.S.–Japan stock price transmissions. However, the East Asian production network's progress since the early 2000s remains robust, and no notable change is seen in those qualities during the late 2000s, and it seems that the propagation of stock price volatility within the East Asian region continues to exist as it was previously rooted in those characteristics.

5. Conclusion

In this chapter, the question of how stock price volatility originating in the United States propagates and spread to East Asian countries is quantitatively examined using a technique that has recently attracted attention, the Bayesian network. To summarize the analysis, the route by which U.S.-originating stock price shocks propagate can be observed to change over time, and cannot be explained only as a direct route from the United States to Japan. This study's contribution to the field can be summed up as the following two items: the environmental factors underlying international stock price transmissions, specifically during U.S.-originated shocks, and the mechanisms by which the economic transmissions propagated to the East Asian region. Since the late 1990s, along with the deepening of the East Asian intraregional economic network, the propagation of U.S.-originated stock price shocks to East Asian stock prices have become complex. In contrast, during the early 2000s, impacts on stock prices going from East Asia to Japan have been observed. However, the current global economy is experiencing negative shocks of very high magnitude from the U.S. financial crisis, throwing U.S.–Japan trade transmissions into relief once more.

By using the Bayesian network method for this analysis, we have obtained very compelling findings which indicate that the structure and strength of the interdependence of variables may vary with the type of source shock and with the economic environment that underlies the variables. These findings can be widely mapped to the macro economy in general, which simultaneously means broadening the applicability of Bayesian networks. The range of applications for the same technique for international transmissions of the price of financial assets other than stocks, for the mechanism by which monetary policy effects spread and so on is very promising. We hope that this study contributes to the foundation for such applications.

Appendix: Concept and Structure of Bayesian Network

A.1. *Basic concept*

A Bayesian network consists of nodes, a set of variables and links that represent probabilistic or causal relationships among nodes. For instance, we can show a causal model for the relationship among stress, smoking and lung cancer. To simplify the situation, let us assume that we have the events {yes, no} for stress, smoking and lung cancer. If smoking is the cause of lung cancer and stress is the cause of smoking, we can draw a flow-chart as shown in Fig. A.1. We call stress the parent node of smoking and smoking the parent node of lung cancer.

In a mathematical expression, consider the nodes as $X_1, X_2, ..., X_n$, we can write the joint distribution for a Bayesian network as

$$P(X_1, X_2, ..., X_n)\prod_{i=1}^{n} p(X_i \mid Pa(X_i)), \tag{1}$$

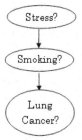

Fig. A.1. Causality between stress, smoking and lung cancer.

where $Pa(X_i)$ represents parents for X_i. As an example, for the network in Fig. A.1, the joint distribution can be calculated as follows.

$P(Stress, Smoking, Cancer) = P(Cancer \mid Strees, Smoking) \, P(Stress, Smoking)$
$= P(Cancer \mid Smoking) \, P(Smoking \mid Stress) \, P \, (Stress)$
$= P(Cancer \mid Smoking) \, P(Stress, Smoking).$ \hfill (2)

This causal model implies that stress relates to lung cancer. However, stress only encourages people to smoke and is not the direct cause of lung cancer. We can assume that if a person has stress, but does not smoke, his/her risk of lung cancer is low. On the other hand, if he/she has no stress but he/she smokes, his/her risk is high. In other words, stress and lung cancer would be dependent, but conditioning on smoking would be independent, and so long as smoking is held as a constant, yes or no, stress cannot affect lung cancer.

In the same way, we choose the other model in which both stress and smoking are the causes of lung cancer. The graphical expression is shown in Fig. A.2, and we can write the joint distribution as

$P(Stress, Smoking, Cancer) = P(Cancer \mid Strees, Smoking) \, P(Stress, Smoking)$
$= P(Cancer \mid Stress, Smoking) = P(Stress) \, P(Smoking).$ \hfill (3)

The last example is that smoking relates to lung cancer, but is not the cause of cancer. Stress is the cause of smoking and lung cancer as shown in Fig. A.3. Then the joint distribution would be

$P(Stress, Smoking, Cancer) = P(Smoking, Cancer \mid Stress) \, P(Stress)$
$= P(Smoking \mid Stress) \, P(Cancer \mid Stress) \, P(Stress)$
$= P(Smoking \mid Stress) \, P(Stress, Smoking).$ \hfill (4)

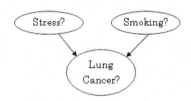

Fig. A.2. Causality between stress, smoking and lung cancer.

Fig. A.3. Causality between stress, smoking and lung cancer.

As in the above discussion, we can construct the joint distribution for a Bayesian network model given a probabilistic structure or a causal chain.[3]

A.2. Parameter estimation

Our goal is to find the best causal model for explaining the international stock price movement in the U.S. and in East Asian countries, based on real data. Before discussing how to search for the best model, we will consider the construction of a parametric model based on a given Bayesian network model, and estimate the parameters from the data.

Let θ_{ijk} be the parameter corresponding to the conditional probability for $x_i = k$, given $pa(X_i)$ is the j th pattern. In the case of Fig. A.2, an example is the parameter p of the Bernoulli distribution given {smoking = yes} and {Stress = yes}, $P(Cancer \mid Stress, Smoking)$. Let Θ be the parameter set,

$$\Theta = \{\theta_{ijk}\} \ \{i = 1, \ldots, n; j = 1, \ldots, q_i; k = 0, \ldots, r_i - 1\}. \tag{5}$$

Then, we can write the likelihood for parameter set Θ given that data X is expressed as

$$P(X \mid \Theta) = \prod_{i=1}^{n} \prod_{j \sim 1}^{q_i} \frac{\sum_{k=0}^{r_i-1} N_{ijk}!}{\prod_{k=0}^{r_i-1} N_{ijk}!} \prod_{k=0}^{r_i-1} \theta_{ijk}^{N_{ijk}} \propto \prod_{i=1}^{n} \prod_{j \sim 1}^{q_i} \prod_{k=0}^{r_i-1} \theta_{ijk}^{N_{ijk}}, \tag{6}$$

---

[3]Using the theory of Bayesian statistics, we can refine the Bayesian network with additional data and improve the accuracy of the analysis. We can understand its process easily with spam filter software. A spam filter software with a Bayesian network algorithm can learn the characteristics of emails classified as spam by the user, and increase the accuracy of classification. Everyone has probably experienced that spam filter software misclassifies a lot of emails in the first use after its installation, but gradually it can distinguish spam accurately.

where N_{ijk} is the number of data, the i th variable $= k$ and its parent node set takes the j th pattern. We can get the maximum likelihood estimator for this model by choosing θ_{ijk}, maximizing $p(X \mid \Theta)$. Other than this maximum likelihood estimator, the Bayesian estimator is commonly used.

A.3. Learning the Bayesian network

The most important part of our Bayesian network analysis is how to search for the best model by using the real data for statistical learning of causal relationships. We encounter difficulties in this procedure because there are many directions of links for each node. If we cannot guess the model and a certain number of nodes exist, it follows that there is a vast number of competitive networks. For this task, we need a powerful computer and an effective algorithm. The first question we have to ask is how to evaluate competitive networks to choose the optimal Bayesian networks. As in other model selection problems, information criteria such as the Akaike information criterion or Bayesian information criterion are employed in comparing the networks. In this chapter, we will use the Minimum Description Length (MDL) as the model selection criterion. The MDL for network B, MDL_B, is defined as follows:

$$MDL_B = -2l(\Theta_B, X) + k_B (\log N), \tag{7}$$

where $l(\Theta_B, X)$ denotes the maximum log likelihood of network B given data set X. Θ_B is the parameter set for network B, and k_B is the number of parameters. The second term represents the length of describing network B. Bouckaert (1994) and Suzuki (1993, 1999) show the effectiveness of network learning with MDL. Thus, our goal is to find the model that has the shortest description of the original data.

To find the optimal network structure which has the highest MDL, we will use the greedy search algorithm. The basic idea of this algorithm is to find the global optimal structure that makes the locally optimum choice at each stage. It follows the procedure below.

1. Start with a Bayesian network B_i and calculate the network score according to MDL.
2. Generate the local neighbor networks by either adding, removing or reversing an edge of the network and then calculating the scores for the local neighbor networks.

3. Choose the network with the highest score as B_{i+1}. If the score for B_{i+1} is larger than the one for B_i, update A and go back to step 1. If not, take the original B_i as the local solution.

References

Agmon, T (1972). The relations among equity markets: A study of share price co-movements in the United States, United Kingdom, Germany, and Japan. *Journal of Finance*, 27, 839–855.

Arshanapalli, B, J Doukas and LHP Lang (1997). Common volatility in the industrial structure of global capital markets. *Journal of International Money and Finance*, 16, 189–209.

Bishop, C (2006). *Pattern Recognition and Machine Learning*. Berlin: Springer-Verlag.

Bouckaert, RR (1994). Probabilistic network construction using the minimum description length principle. Technical Report UU-CS-94-27, Utrecht University.

Campbell, JY and Y Hamao (1992). Predictable stock returns in the United States and Japan: A study of long term capital market integration. *Journal of Finance*, 47, 43–70.

Chelley-Steely, PL (2000). Interdependence of international equity market volatility. *Applied Economic Letters*, 7, 341–345.

Chen, P and C Hsiao (2007). Learning causal relations in multivarate time series data. *Economics eJournal, Discussion Paper* 2007–15.

Chuang, I-Y, JR Lu and K Tswei (2007). Interdependence of international equity variances: Evidence from east asian markets. *Emerging Market Review*, 8, 311–327.

Cifarelli, G and G Paladino (2004). The impact of the Argentine default on volatility co-movements in emerging bond markets. *Emerging Markets Review*, 5, 427–446.

Darrat, AF and OM Benkato (2003). Interdependence and volatility spillovers under market liberalization: The case of Istanbul stock exchange. *Journal of Business Finance and Accounting*, 30, 1089–1114.

Errunza, V and E Losq (1985). The behavior of stock prices on LDC markets. *Journal of Banking and Finance*, 9, 561–575.

Eun, CS and S Shim (1989). International transmission of stock market movements. *Journal of Financial and Quantitative Analysis*, 24, 241–256.

Fukao, K, K Kiyota and S Yonekawa (1999). COE Chinese Trade Data: Calculation method in 1988–1994. *Discussion Paper Series*, No.99-DOJ-95, Research Institute of International Trade and Industry, Ministry of International Trade and Industry, Japan.

Ghosh, A, R Saidi and KH Johnson (1999). Who moves the Asian-pacific stock markets — U.S. or Japan? Empirical evidence based on the theory of cointegration. *Financial Review*, 34, 159–170.

Giles, D (2003). *Computer-Aided Econometrics (Statistics: A Series of Textbooks and Monographs)*. New York: Marcel Dekker.

Hamao, Y, RW Masulis and V Ng (1990). Correlations in price changes and volatility across international stock markets. *Review of Financial Studies*, 3, 281–308.

Hilliard, JE (1979). The relationship between equity indices on world exchanges. *Journal of Finance*, 34, 103–114.

Hoti, S (2005). Modelling country spillover effects in country risk ratings. *Emerging Markets Review*, 6, 324–345.

In, F, S Kim, JH Yoon and C Viney (2001). Dynamic interdependence and volatility transmission of Asian stock markets: Evidence from the Asian crisis. *International Review of Financial Analysis*, 10, 87–96.

Jang, H and W Sul (2002). The Asian financial crisis and the co-movement of Asian stock markets. *Journal of Asian Economics*, 13, 94–104.

Johnson, R and L Soenen (2002). Asian economic integration and stock market comovement. *Journal of Financial Research*, 25, 141–157.

Karolyi, GA (1995). A multivariate GARCH model of international transmissions of stock returns and volatility: The case of the United States and Canada. *Journal of Business and Economic Statistics*, 13, 11–25.

Kim, SW and JH Rogers (1995). International stock price spillovers and market liberalization: Evidence from Korea, Japan, and the United States. *Journal of Empirical Finance*, 2, 117–133.

Koutmos, G and GG Booth (1995). Asymmetric volatility transmission in international stock markets. *Journal of International Money and Finance*, 14, 747–762.

Leong, SC and B Felmingham (2003). The interdependence of share markets in the developed economies of East Asia. *Pacific-Basin Finance Journal*, 11, 219–237.

Levy, H and M Sarnat (1970). International diversification of investment portfolios. *American Economic Review*, 60, 668–675.

Liu, YA and M Pan (1997). Mean and volatility spillover effects in the U.S. and Pacific-Basin stock markets. *Multinational Finance Journal*, 1, 47–62.

Longin, F and B Solnik (1995). Is the correlation in international equity returns constant: 1960–1990? *Journal of International Money and Finance*, 14, 3–26.

Masih, AMM and R Masih (1999). Are Asian stock market fluctuations due mainly to intra-regional contagion effects? Evidence based on Asian emerging stock markets. *Pacific-Basin Finance Journal*, 7, 251–282.

Panton, DB, VP Lessiq and OM Joy (1976). Comovement of international equity markets: A taxonomic approach. *Journal of Financial and Quantitative Analysis*, 11, 415–432.

Pearl, J (2000). *Causality: Models, Reasoning, and Inference*. UK: Cambridge University Press.

Pourret, O, P Naim and B Marcot (eds.) (2008). *Bayesian Networks: Practical Guide to Applications*. New York: John Wiley & Sons.

Ripley, DM (1973). Systematic elements in the linkage of national stock market indices. *Review of Economics and Statistics*, 55, 356–361.

Steely, JM (2006). Volatility transmission between stock and bond markets. *Journal of International Finance markets, Institutions and Money*, 16(1), 71–86.

Suzuki, J (1993). A construction of Bayesian networks from databases on an MDL principle. *Proc. of Ninth Conf. on Uncertainty in Artificial Intelligence*, pp. 263–273.

Suzuki, J (1999). Learning Bayesian belief networks based on the MDL principle: An efficient algorithm using Branch and Bound technique. *IEICE Transactions on Fundamentals*, E82-D(2), 356–369.

Taylor, M and I Tonks (1989). The internationalisation of stock markets and the abolition of exchange controls. *Review of Economics and Statistics*, 26, 265–272.

Theodossiou, P and U Lee (1993). Mean and volatility spillovers across major national stock market: Further empirical evidence. *Journal of Financial Research*, 16, 337–350.

Wong, WK, J Penm, RD Terrell and KY Ching (2004). The relationship between stock markets of major developed countries and Asian emerging markets. *Journal of Applied Mathematics and Decision Sciences*, 8, 201–218.

Wongswan, J (2006). Transmission of information across international equity markets. *Review of Financial Studies*, 19, 1157–1189.

CHAPTER 4

THE IMPACT OF EAST ASIAN FTAS ON THE STRUCTURE OF DEMAND

Hikari Ban

Faculty of Economics, Kobe Gakuin University
1-1-3 Minatojima, Chuo-ku, Kobe, 650–8586, Japan
ban@eb.kobegakuin.ac.jp

1. Introduction

The global recession triggered by the Lehman Shock accompanied a significant and rapid reduction in global trade. In evidence, in 2009, the real growth rate of world GDP was just −2.3% and the real growth rate of world trade was only −10.6% (World Bank, 2011). As far as Japan is concerned, exports began to contract after the fourth quarter of 2008 and the recession appeared to become more serious. Using quarterly data to measure the percentage changes compared to the corresponding periods in the previous year, the real growth rates of Japanese exports were 4.1% (2008:Q3), −13.5% (2008:Q4), −36.9% (2009:Q1), −29.6% (2009:Q2) and −23.1% (2009:Q3). At the same time, the corresponding real GDP growth rates were −0.6%, −4.7%, −9.3%, −6.6% and −5.6%, respectively. The percentage contributions of private consumption, private non-residential investment and net exports to changes in real GDP (2009:Q1) were −2.2%, −2.7% and −3.6%, respectively (National Accounts of Japan, 2012).

These experiences suggest that the diversification of foreign demand is important for the stabilization of East Asian economies. Therefore, in this chapter our objective is to examine the impact of East Asian free trade agreements (FTAs) on the demand structure using computable general equilibrium (CGE) analysis and input–output (I–O) analysis. A number of studies have already employed CGE analysis to study the effects of FTAs in East Asia, including Kawasaki (2003), Urata and Kiyota (2003) and Ando (2009). In terms of model specifics, we employ the multiregion and multisector Global Trade Analysis Project (GTAP) CGE model.

To better understand international interdependence, I–O analysis with an international I–O table provides useful information, with relevant work on international labor division and global production networks including studies by Hummels *et al.* (2001), Fujikawa *et al.* (2005), Wang and Wei (2009) and Koopman *et al.* (2010). In the most relevant study, Bems *et al.* (2010, 2011) examine the collapse of trade during the global recession of 2008–2009. We employ international I–O tables constructed using the GTAP database following Bems *et al.* (2010, 2011), but instead consider the degree of dependence on foreign final demand.

2. Framework and Data

2.1. CGE and I–O analysis

We begin by explaining the role of the CGE and I–O analyses in this study. The construction of a basic CGE model typically includes assumptions on the equilibrium conditions for the factor and goods markets and zero-profit conditions. It also usually assumes a constant return-to-scale production function. Given utility maximization and cost-minimizing behavior, demand is then endogenously determined. The quantities supplied are then determined to match the quantities demanded. From the perspective of the substitution of inputs and adjustments in the factor market, we may thus interpret the CGE model as being somewhere between the long and short run (a "middle-run" model).

In contrast, the construction of a basic I–O model includes only goods market conditions such that it does not guarantee factor market equilibrium. Given final demand, the equilibrium outputs are determined under fixed input coefficients and constant prices. Therefore, we can more properly interpret an I–O model as a short-run model in which final demand is exogenous.

In this chapter, we analyze the impact of East Asian FTAs using two steps. In the first step, we investigate the middle-run effects of FTAs using a static CGE model. In the second step, we analyze the changes in demand structure caused by FTAs by applying I–O analysis to pre- and post-simulation international I–O tables.

2.2. The GTAP model

To investigate the impacts of East Asian FTAs, we use the GTAP model and database maintained at Purdue University since 1992.[1] This section briefly describes the essentials of the GTAP model. To start with, the GTAP model incorporates market equilibrium conditions for factors and goods and zero-profit conditions in a similar manner to a basic CGE model. The model also includes several kinds of taxes and subsidies so that users can also evaluate the effects of policy change.

One particular feature of the GTAP model is the assumption of two global sectors. The first is a global banking sector that assembles savings from each region and distributes investment to each region in such a way that the rate of change in the expected rate of return on capital equalizes across regions. The second is a global transportation sector that purchases international transport services from regions and supplies international transport services. This assumption solves the problem of a lack of information about which particular regional transport services are associated with particular imports.

Figure 1 depicts the production structure in the GTAP model. This has a Leontief structure with zero elasticity of substitution at the top level and a constant elasticity of substitution (CES) structure at the lower level. The model employs the Armington approach in that firms first determine the source of their imports and then compare the prices of domestic goods and the optimal mix of imports.

In the GTAP model, a regional household plays the role of both a private household and a government. The regional household receives endowment income and net tax revenue and expends regional income on private and public commodities and saving. Figure 2 illustrates the utility function of the regional household in the GTAP model. As shown, this employs a constant difference of elasticity (CDE) structure at the first level of private household demand.

---

[1] See Hertel (1997) and the GTAP Web page (http://www.gtap.agecon.purdue. edu/, accessed April 17, 2012) for details.

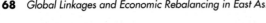

Fig. 1. Production structure in the GTAP model.

Source: Based on Hertel (1997).

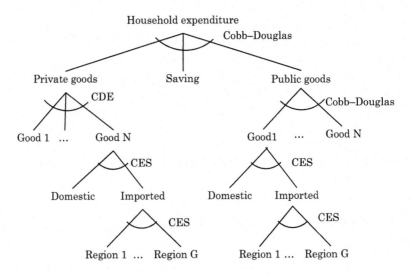

Fig. 2. Regional household expenditure in the GTAP model.

Source: Based on Hertel (1997).

2.3. The I–O model

Under a constant returns-to-scale production function, we represent inter-mediate demand as the product of the output and input coefficients.

Therefore, the market equilibrium condition for goods in the case of N goods (N industries) and G countries is as follows:

$$x_i^s = \sum_{r=1}^{G} \sum_{j=1}^{N} u_{ij}^{sr} x_j^r + \sum_{r=1}^{G} f_i^{sr}, \quad i=1\ldots N, \quad s=1\ldots G \qquad (1)$$

where $x_{i'}^s$ a_{ij}^{sr} and f_i^{sr} are the gross output of industry i in country s, the input coefficient indicating the amount of intermediate good i produced in country s required to produce a unit of good j in country r and final demand for good i produced in country s from country r, respectively.

Equation (1) can be represented in matrix form by:

$$
\begin{pmatrix} \mathbf{x}^1 \\ \mathbf{x}^2 \\ \vdots \\ \mathbf{x}^G \end{pmatrix} =
\begin{pmatrix} \mathbf{A}^{11} & \mathbf{A}^{12} & \cdots & \mathbf{A}^{1G} \\ \mathbf{A}^{21} & \mathbf{A}^{22} & \cdots & \mathbf{A}^{2G} \\ \vdots & \vdots & \ddots & \vdots \\ \mathbf{A}^{G1} & \mathbf{A}^{G2} & \cdots & \mathbf{A}^{GG} \end{pmatrix}
\begin{pmatrix} \mathbf{x}^1 \\ \mathbf{x}^2 \\ \vdots \\ \mathbf{x}^G \end{pmatrix} +
\begin{pmatrix} \mathbf{f}^1 \\ \mathbf{f}^2 \\ \vdots \\ \mathbf{f}^G \end{pmatrix}, \qquad (2)
$$

where $\mathbf{x}^s$ is the $N \times 1$ vector of gross output in country s, $\mathbf{A}^{sr}$ is the $N \times N$ input coefficient matrix giving the intermediate use in country r of goods produced in country s and $\mathbf{f}^s$ is a $N \times 1$ vector of the final demand for goods produced in country s from all countries.

$$
\mathbf{x}^s = \begin{pmatrix} \mathbf{x}_1^s \\ \mathbf{x}_2^s \\ \vdots \\ \mathbf{x}_N^s \end{pmatrix}, \mathbf{A}^{sr} =
\begin{pmatrix} a_{11}^{sr} & a_{12}^{sr} & \cdots & a_{1N}^{sr} \\ a_{21}^{sr} & a_{22}^{sr} & \cdots & a_{2N}^{sr} \\ \vdots & \vdots & \ddots & \vdots \\ a_{N1}^{sr} & a_{N2}^{sr} & \cdots & a_{NN}^{sr} \end{pmatrix}, \mathbf{f}^s =
\begin{pmatrix} f_1^{s1} + f_1^{s2} + \cdots f_1^{sG} \\ f_2^{s1} + f_2^{s2} + \cdots f_2^{sG} \\ \vdots \\ f_N^{s1} + f_N^{s2} + \cdots f_N^{sG} \end{pmatrix}.
$$

Let $\mathbf{I}$ and $\mathbf{B}^{sr}$ be the $N \times N$ identity matrix and the $N \times N$ Leontief inverse matrix, respectively. We can then express (2) in block matrix notation as[2]:

$$
\begin{pmatrix} \mathbf{x}^1 \\ \mathbf{x}^2 \\ \vdots \\ \mathbf{x}^G \end{pmatrix} =
\begin{pmatrix} \mathbf{I} - \mathbf{A}^{11} & -\mathbf{A}^{12} & \cdots & -\mathbf{A}^{1G} \\ -\mathbf{A}^{21} & \mathbf{I} - \mathbf{A}^{22} & \cdots & -\mathbf{A}^{2G} \\ \vdots & \vdots & \ddots & \vdots \\ -\mathbf{A}^{G1} & -\mathbf{A}^{G2} & \cdots & \mathbf{I} - \mathbf{A}^{GG} \end{pmatrix}^{-1}
\begin{pmatrix} \mathbf{f}^1 \\ \mathbf{f}^2 \\ \vdots \\ \mathbf{f}^G \end{pmatrix}
$$

$$
= \begin{pmatrix} \mathbf{B}^{11} & \mathbf{B}^{12} & \cdots & \mathbf{B}^{1G} \\ \mathbf{B}^{21} & \mathbf{B}^{22} & \cdots & \mathbf{B}^{2G} \\ \vdots & \vdots & \ddots & \vdots \\ \mathbf{B}^{G1} & \mathbf{B}^{G2} & \cdots & \mathbf{B}^{GG} \end{pmatrix}
\begin{pmatrix} \mathbf{f}^1 \\ \mathbf{f}^2 \\ \vdots \\ \mathbf{f}^G \end{pmatrix}. \qquad (3)
$$

---

[2] See Wang *et al.* (2009) and Miller and Blair (2009, pp. 76–82).

If we know the values of the input coefficients, we can introduce the Leontief inverse matrix $\mathbf{B}^{sr}$, which is the total requirements matrix. This consists of elements that imply the amount of total output in country s directly and indirectly required for one unit of final demand in country r. Therefore, given final demand, we can calculate equilibrium gross output. We can use (3) to find the amount of gross output of good i in country s, which is derived from the final demand in country r and any ripple effects from the change in final demand in country r. For example, given a final demand vector $(f_1^{1r} f_2^{1r} \dots f_N^{Gr})'$, we can calculate the amount of gross output in each country required for final demand in country r. In addition, given a vector of the change in final demand in country r $(\Delta f_1^{1r} \Delta f_2^{1r} \dots \Delta f_N^{Gr})'$, we can assess the impact on gross output in all countries.

2.4. Database

For the CGE analysis, we use the GTAP 7 Database, which corresponds to the global economy in 2004 with 113 countries/regions and 57 industries. We aggregate this data into eight regions and ten industries as shown in Tables 1 and 2.[3] The production factors are land, natural resources, unskilled labor, skilled labor and capital.

The I–O analysis detailed in the preceding section requires an input coefficients matrix. We calculate this as follows:

$$a_{ij}^{sr} = \frac{VM_{ij}^{sr}}{VX_j^r}, \tag{4}$$

where VM_{ij}^{sr} is total purchases by industry j in country r from industry i in country s and VX_j^r is the value of gross output of industry j in country r. Unfortunately, the GTAP database does not contain data on VM_{ij}^{sr} ($s \neq r$), that is, purchases of imported intermediate goods by industry j in country r from industry i in country s. In addition, as the GTAP database does not contain data for VF_i^{sr}, that is, the value of final demand for goods i produced in country s from country r, we follow basically the procedure in Bems *et al.* (2010, 2011). Let VEX_{i*}^{sr} be the total value of exports from industry i in country s to country r, VIM_{ij}^{*r} be the total purchases of imported

---

[3] See Tables A.1 and A.2 in the Appendix for additional details on the respective aggregation by country/region and industry.

Table 1. Country/region aggregation.

	Code	Definition
1	CHN	China
2	JPN	Japan
3	KOR	South Korea
4	TWN	Taiwan
5	ASEAN	Nine of the ten members of the Association of Southeast Asian Nations (ASEAN) (excepting Brunei)
6	U.S.	United States
7	EU	Twenty-five of the 27 members of the European Union (EU) (excepting Bulgaria and Romania)
8	RoW	Rest of the world

Table 2. Industry aggregation.

	Code	Definition
1	Primary	Agriculture, forestry, fishing, mining
2	Food	Food processing
3	Textiles	Textiles and wearing apparel
4	Chemical	Chemicals
5	MotorTrans	Motor vehicles and transport equipment
6	Electro	Electronic equipment
7	Machine	Machinery and equipment
8	Light	Light manufacturing
9	Heavy	Heavy manufacturing
10	Services	Services

intermediate good i by industry j in country r and VIF_i^{*r} be the total value of final demand for imported good i from country r, which the GTAP database contains. We assume:

$$VM_{ij}^{sr} = VEX_{i*}^{sr} \left(\frac{VIM_{ij}^{*r}}{\sum_j VIM_{ij}^{*r} + VIF_i^{*r}} \right), \ s \neq r. \tag{5}$$

$$VF_i^{sr} = VEX_{i*}^{sr} \left(\frac{VIF_i^{*r}}{\sum_j VIM_{ij}^{*r} + VIF_i^{*r}} \right), \ s \neq r. \tag{6}$$

These assumptions mean that the share of imported goods i from country s in total imported goods i is the same across both industries and in final demand. Although these assumptions are rather strong, this method is helpful when investigating the international trade of intermediate goods in this first analytical approach.

3. CGE Analysis

3.1. *Simulation scenario*

The simulation in this chapter is designed to evaluate the impact of the East Asian FTAs on the economy. As such, the simulation involves the complete removal of any *ad valorem* import tariffs between any East Asian countries. Existing export subsidies and taxes are unaltered.

Table 3 provides details on bilateral tariff rates in East Asia. The first four columns represent the tariff rates of products exported from Japan to each destination and the last column represents the tariff

Table 3. Bilateral tariff rates by source and destination (%).

Source	JPN				CHN
Destination	CHN	KOR	TWN	ASEAN	JPN
Primary	4.0	12.6	7.8	4.9	4.6
Food	16.1	38.3	23.1	25.8	19.2
Textiles	14.1	9.4	7.6	18.2	8.8
Chemical	8.6	6.6	3.1	7.7	0.2
MotorTrans	22.4	7.2	20.9	23.4	0.0
Electro	3.4	1.5	0.5	1.1	0.0
Machine	6.9	6.4	2.5	4.4	0.0
Light	8.8	6.2	3.5	10.9	3.7
Heavy	5.7	3.3	3.8	7.3	0.7
Services	0.0	0.0	0.0	0.0	0.0

Source: GTAP 7 Database.

rates on products exported from China to Japan. Even if the tariff rates on disaggregated imported products are the same across countries, the tariff rates on aggregated imported products are not, because the composition of disaggregated imported products in aggregated imported products differs across countries. However, Table 3 is useful for obtaining a rough indication of East Asian tariff rates. In general, we can see that the tariff rates on products exported to Japan are generally lower than those on products exported from Japan, and the tariff rates on electronic products are lower than those on other products.

3.2. Simulation results

Table 4 indicates the effects of FTAs on real GDP, the volume of exports, the terms of trade and the equivalence valence (EV) for each region. The third column provides the rate of change of the volume of exports from each region. As shown, the exports of East Asian regions under FTAs increase more than 3%, whereas the exports of other regions do not change as much. These results suggest that international trade inside East Asia appears to increase with the presence of FTAs. However, the effects of FTAs on GDP in East Asia do not appear to be large, even though South Korea, Taiwan and ASEAN exhibit a relatively higher rate of increase in GDP. Turning to EV, not only non-FTA member regions but also China exhibit negative effects on EV, caused mainly by deterioration

Table 4. Effects of East Asian FTAs on the macroeconomy.

	GDP %	Volume of exports %	Terms of trade %	Change in EV in $ millions
CHN	0.01	7.41	−0.33	−1,237
JPN	0.02	3.18	1.45	9,129
KOR	0.31	4.24	1.06	4,545
TWN	0.20	3.28	1.14	3,124
ASEAN	0.32	3.03	0.29	5,031
U.S.	0.00	−0.04	−0.32	−5,063
EU	−0.02	0.05	−0.10	−6,155
RoW	−0.02	0.02	−0.30	−8,385

Source: GTAP simulation.

in their terms of trade. We define the terms of trade as the ratio of the export and import price indexes. As shown later, some industries in China can lower their export prices through a decrease in imported intermediate goods prices. That is one reason for the observed deterioration in the terms of trade.

Table 5 details the changes in output for each industry in East Asia. It is interesting that the effects on output by industry are relatively large compared with the effects on GDP. Although the expanding industries differ across countries, an increase in net exports accompanies most, with some exceptions. This suggests that exports drive the increases in output. Of particular note, outputs from the textiles and wearing apparel industries in South Korea and Taiwan, the chemical and machine industries in Taiwan and the food industry in ASEAN all increase at a higher rate, with GDP in these regions also growing at a higher rate.

It is also notable that the outputs and net exports of the electronic equipment industries in Japan, South Korea, Taiwan and ASEAN decrease, whereas those for China and in non-FTA members increase (Outputs: U.S. 1.4%, EU 1.4%, RoW 2.0%). This appears to be related to three main factors: the initial tariff rate, the share of imports in total intermediate goods and the change in factor prices. As shown in Table 3, compared with other

Table 5. Impact of East Asian FTAs on output (%).

	CHN	JPN	KOR	TWN	ASEAN
Primary	1.1	−1.3	−1.6*	−1.3	−0.4
Food	3.7	−1.4	−1.6	−2.5	6.2
Textiles	2.6	−0.4	7.7	16.5	−1.3
Chemical	−3.8	1.1	1.3	7.6	1.5
MotorTrans	−3.9	2.4	0.9	2.7*	−9.2
Electro	3.4	−2.0	−1.8	−10.8	−1.1
Machine	−2.6	1.1	−3.0	7.8	3.7*
Light	−0.5	−0.3	−0.9	2.0	−2.0
Heavy	−1.9	1.1	3.2	3.5	−1.5
Services	−0.1	0.0	0.1*	−0.3	0.1*

Note: An asterisk (*) indicates that the signs of the change in the rate of output and net exports are not the same.
Source: GTAP simulation.

Table 6. Share of exports shipped to East Asia (%).

	CHN	JPN	KOR	TWN	ASEAN
In intermediate goods exports					
Pre	31.4	50.9	54.8	62.7	42.5
Post	37.9	57.8	61.4	68.2	47.0
In final goods exports					
Pre	21.4	23.0	22.5	38.1	20.5
Post	26.1	29.4	27.6	44.0	24.2
In total exports					
Pre	27.1	39.0	41.3	54.3	33.9
Post	32.9	46.0	47.9	60.2	38.2

Source: GTAP simulation.

products, the tariff rates on electronic equipment are low. However, the tariff rates for electronic equipment imported from China and exported to China are generally higher than in other countries/regions. Imported goods also have a large share of intermediate input costs in the electronic equipment industry (China 42.4%, Japan 10.8%, South Korea 49.1%, Taiwan 50.4%, ASEAN 52.7%). Therefore, China benefits from sales prices in terms of both destination and production cost. By way of contrast, FTAs increase wage and capital rental rates in FTA member regions, but lowers them in non-FTA member regions. This change in factor prices increases the output and net exports of electronic equipment in non-FTA member regions.

Because of East Asian FTAs, international trade inside the FTA member regions increases. Table 6 details the share of exports destined for East Asia in terms of intermediate goods, final goods and total exports, where "Pre" and "Post" indicate the shares calculated using pre- (benchmark) and post-simulation data, respectively.[4] We can see that East Asia's share of exports of intermediate goods is higher than its share of final goods exports. In particular, the East Asian share of intermediate goods exports exceeds 50% in Japan, South Korea and Taiwan.

---

[4]To calculate the East Asian shares we used international I–O tables constructed using the GTAP database and assumptions (5) and (6).

Table 7. Change in cost structure with East Asian FTAs (%).

	CHN	JPN	KOR	TWN	ASEAN
Share of imported goods in total intermediate inputs					
Pre	15.8	7.8	22.6	32.7	30.6
Post	17.3	8.0	23.8	33.4	32.2
Share of imported goods from East Asia in imported intermediate inputs					
Pre	52.5	33.8	42.3	52.0	42.0
Post	59.5	35.9	52.7	55.2	49.0
Share of imported goods from East Asia in total intermediate inputs					
Pre	8.3	2.6	9.6	17.0	12.8
Post	10.3	2.9	12.5	18.4	15.8

Source: GTAP simulation.

In addition, Table 6 indicates that as the result of FTAs, the shares of exports shipped to East Asia increase for both intermediate and final goods exports. Examining the share of intermediate goods exports by industry, we can see that the East Asian share increases across all industries with the exception of services. We also observe relatively higher increases in the primary, food and textiles and wearing apparel industries.[5] Automobiles and transport equipment in Japan and South Korea and light manufactures in Japan and Taiwan also exhibit increases of more than 10% points.

As far as production cost structure is concerned, we can readily recognize a deepening of East Asian production networks. Table 7 provides information on the average shares of imports in total intermediate inputs, imports from East Asia in imported intermediate inputs and imports from East Asia in total intermediate inputs by region. Here, we measure the values of the intermediate inputs at producer prices. We should note that Japan has a relatively low share of imported intermediates, while Taiwan has a relatively high share. As shown in Table 7, FTAs clearly increase the share of imported intermediate goods from East Asia.

---

[5] For example, the East Asian share of intermediate goods exports by industry went from 59.8% to 82.2% in primary industry in China, from 54.6% to 74.1% in the food industry in Japan and from 57.5% to 70.9% for the textile and wearing apparel industry in South Korea.

Further, by investigating the shares of intermediate goods by industry and region, we can see that because of FTAs, the share of East Asian intermediate goods increases across all industries in FTA member regions. These increases are relatively higher (in % points) in the food (6.3%), textiles and wearing apparel (6.5%) and heavy manufacturing (8.2%) industries in South Korea, the automobile and transport equipment industry (9.2%) in Taiwan and the textiles and wearing apparel (9.3%) and automobile and transport equipment (10.7%) industries in ASEAN.

This static CGE analysis suggests that although East Asian FTAs do not have a large macroeconomic impact, they may bring about relatively large changes in the demand structure in some industries. East Asian FTAs thus appear to increase international trade and extend production networks within East Asia.

4. Input–Output Analysis

This section reports the results of the simple I–O analysis discussed in Sec 2. First, we construct two international I–O tables based on the pre-simulation (benchmark) and post-simulation GTAP database following Bems *et al.* (2010, 2011). Second, we calculate the input coefficients and the Leontief inverse matrix using Eq. (4). We then examine the degree of dependence on foreign final demand and the ripple effects using system equations (3).

4.1. *Dependence on foreign final demand*

Table 8 presents the share of output induced directly and indirectly from final demand in the U.S. and the EU to gross output. For example, final demand from the U.S. and the EU directly and indirectly induces 10.5% of the gross output of primary industry in China when using the pre-simulation database. Roughly speaking, the degree of dependence on the U.S. and the EU is relatively low in Japan, moderate in China and South Korea and high in Taiwan and ASEAN. By industry, the degree of dependence on the U.S. and the EU is relatively lower in the primary, food and services industries and higher for electronic equipment, except Japan, and for the textiles and wearing apparel industries for ASEAN. In addition, the share of output induced directly and indirectly from final demand in the U.S. and the EU is relatively high for the automobile and

Table 8. Foreign final demand dependence on the U.S. and the EU (%).

	CHN		JPN		KOR		TWN		ASEAN	
	Pre	Post	Pre	Post	Pre	Post	Pre	Post	Pre	Post
Primary	10.5	10.1	2.2	2.1	4.1	4.3	5.8	5.6	15.9	14.7
Food	7.4	6.8	1.0	0.9	2.8	2.7	3.6	3.7	11.8	10.5
Textiles	25.6	24.8	7.9	9.0	27.3	26.8	34.3	31.8	44.5	46.5
Chemi	25.1	25.1	18.3	17.4	23.2	22.2	30.8	28.7	32.4	31.2
MotorTrans	16.5	17.0	32.2	29.3	34.2	30.9	29.0	29.5	15.8	17.2
Electro	46.1	45.9	23.6	22.2	43.9	42.6	45.0	43.8	48.4	47.5
Machine	24.6	24.6	22.9	21.0	24.9	22.8	28.1	24.8	30.5	29.0
Light	32.6	31.8	8.5	8.0	17.6	16.5	35.5	32.5	31.8	31.0
Heavy	19.1	18.8	13.9	13.2	16.8	16.1	24.9	23.3	19.6	18.9
Services	8.4	8.2	3.3	3.1	5.8	5.3	11.0	10.2	14.1	13.3

Source: Author calculations using pre- and post-simulation international I–O table.

transport equipment industries across Japan, South Korea and Taiwan. As for the impact of FTAs, we can see that the degree of dependence on the U.S. and the EU falls in most industries.

Table 9 represents the share of output directly and indirectly induced from final demand in each region to total gross output. The region in the column heading indicates the region where final demand arises. For example, as shown in the first row, 67.5% of total gross output in China originates from final demand in China, 4.1% from Japan, 0.9% from South Korea, 0.4% from Taiwan, 1.5% from ASEAN, 9.2% from the U.S. and 8.5% from the EU.

As shown in Table 9, we can see that although the gross output of all five regions depends most on domestic final demand, the share of domestic final demand in total final demand ranges from 46.0% (Taiwan) to 83.9% (Japan). The domestic final demand shares in the U.S., the EU and the RoW (not shown) are 90.7%, 86.5% and 77.4%, respectively, using the pre-simulation data. All other things being equal, larger economies tend to exhibit larger shares of domestic final demand in total final demand.

As for the impact of FTAs, we find that the shares of output induced from final demand in East Asia increase, while the shares arising from the U.S., the EU, and the home country decline. Moreover, we can readily observe these trends across most industries. However, there are a few

Table 9. Domestic and foreign final demand dependence by region (%).

	CHN	JPN	KOR	TWN	ASEAN	U.S.	EU
CHN							
Pre	67.5	4.1	0.9	0.4	1.5	9.2	8.5
Post	66.3	4.9	1.4	0.5	1.9	9.1	8.3
JPN							
Pre	1.8	83.9	0.7	0.6	1.1	4.4	3.5
Post	2.3	83.6	0.8	0.6	1.5	4.1	3.3
KOR							
Pre	5.4	3.2	63.0	0.5	1.7	8.2	6.9
Post	6.5	3.4	62.5	0.6	2.4	7.7	6.5
TWN							
Pre	11.5	4.9	1.3	46.0	3.4	12.3	10.6
Post	13.7	5.0	1.4	45.1	4.2	11.4	9.8
ASEAN							
Pre	4.3	5.7	1.3	0.7	52.5	10.4	12.6
Post	5.1	6.4	1.7	0.9	51.9	10.1	12.0

Source: Author calculations using pre- and post-simulation international I–O tables.

exceptions. For example, the share of final demand from the home country and from East Asia increases for electronic equipment in Japan, South Korea, Taiwan and ASEAN because of the decrease in the net exports of electronic equipment discussed earlier.

We can see that the degree of dependence on China increases relatively more in Japan, South Korea, Taiwan and ASEAN, while the degree of dependence on Japan increases in China. Although the influence of the U.S. and the EU declines across all of the East Asian regions, the extent of the decrease appears relatively small such that their overall importance in terms of final demand remains relatively high.

4.2. Ripple effects

The second I–O analysis examines how the ripple effects of final demand in a specific region change with the presence of East Asian

Table 10. Ripple effects from a 1% increase in U.S. final demand (%).

	CHN		JPN		KOR		TWN		ASEAN	
	Pre	Post	Pre	Post	Pre	Post	Pre	Post	Pre	Post
Primary	0.05	0.05	0.01	0.01	0.02	0.02	0.03	0.03	0.07	0.07
Food	0.04	0.03	0.01	0.01	0.02	0.02	0.02	0.03	0.06	0.05
Textiles	0.12	0.11	0.04	0.05	0.16	0.15	0.21	0.19	0.26	0.28
Chemical	0.13	0.14	0.10	0.09	0.12	0.12	0.17	0.16	0.14	0.14
MotorTans	0.09	0.09	0.21	0.19	0.19	0.17	0.16	0.16	0.06	0.06
Electro	0.24	0.24	0.12	0.11	0.23	0.22	0.22	0.22	0.25	0.25
Machine	0.13	0.13	0.13	0.12	0.12	0.11	0.16	0.14	0.15	0.14
Light	0.20	0.19	0.05	0.05	0.10	0.09	0.21	0.19	0.14	0.14
Heavy	0.10	0.10	0.08	0.07	0.09	0.09	0.14	0.13	0.09	0.09
Services	0.04	0.04	0.02	0.02	0.03	0.03	0.06	0.05	0.05	0.05

Source: Author calculations using pre- and post-simulation international I–O tables.

FTAs. Table 10 details the ripple effects calculated using the pre- and post-simulation database when final demand in the U.S. increases by 1%. Table 10 indicates that as a result, primary industry output in China increases by 0.05%. Naturally, industries that have a relatively large share of output induced from final demand in the U.S. exhibit relatively large impacts.

Comparison of the ripple effects using the pre- and post-simulation data indicates that the impact of the latter is smaller in almost all industries than when using the pre-simulation database. However, the degree of the decrease is very small. For example, the ripple effects decrease final demand by at most 0.02% points in the automobile and transport equipment industries in Japan and South Korea, and in the textiles and wearing apparel, machine and light manufacturing industries in Taiwan.

The ripple effects on the East Asian regions caused by a change in final demand from the EU are almost the same as for the U.S. Further, Table 11 details the ripple effects when final demand in Japan increases by 1%. Although East Asian FTAs increase the ripple effects of Japan on other East Asian countries and regions, they are still lower than the ripple effects from the U.S. or the EU in most industries. The exceptions are the food and textiles and wearing apparel industries in China and the primary and food industries in South Korea, Taiwan and ASEAN.

Table 11. Ripple effects from a 1% increase in Japan final demand (%).

	CHN		JPN		KOR		TWN		ASEAN	
	Pre	Post	Pre	Post	Pre	Post	Pre	Post	Pre	Post
Primary	0.03	0.04	0.95	0.94	0.03	0.05	0.05	0.06	0.08	0.09
Food	0.05	0.08	0.97	0.97	0.03	0.05	0.06	0.06	0.05	0.09
Textiles	0.13	0.16	0.81	0.74	0.05	0.06	0.06	0.07	0.05	0.05
Chemical	0.05	0.06	0.63	0.62	0.06	0.06	0.07	0.07	0.08	0.08
MotorTans	0.03	0.03	0.45	0.44	0.01	0.01	0.03	0.03	0.04	0.04
Electro	0.08	0.08	0.58	0.59	0.07	0.08	0.11	0.11	0.11	0.12
Machine	0.05	0.06	0.48	0.47	0.05	0.04	0.05	0.05	0.11	0.11
Light	0.05	0.06	0.83	0.82	0.04	0.05	0.06	0.06	0.08	0.09
Heavy	0.04	0.05	0.67	0.66	0.05	0.06	0.05	0.06	0.06	0.07
Services	0.02	0.02	0.93	0.93	0.02	0.02	0.02	0.02	0.02	0.03

Source: Author calculations using pre- and post-simulation international I–O tables.

5. Conclusion

In this chapter, we analyzed the impacts of East Asian FTAs mainly on the structure of demand by combining static CGE and I–O analysis. Our findings suggest that East Asian FTAs appear to have little effect on the macroeconomy as a whole, but much greater effects on industry. In brief, FTAs will increase international trade and deepen production networks inside East Asia. Although the share of production induced from final demand in the U.S. and the EU declines with the presence of FTAs, the magnitude of this decline is relatively small and the degree of dependence on the U.S. and the EU remains relatively high. This particular result appears to relate to the size of the U.S. and EU economies and to the fact that the decrease in the share of production is largely induced from domestic final demand.

As a final requirement, we discuss some of the limitations of the present analysis. First, in the CGE analysis, the assumption of full employment brings about an increase in the wage rate for FTA members and a decrease in the wage rate for non-members. Therefore, the results of the simulation may underestimate the shifting of the source of imports from FTA non-members to members. Second, in terms of data, we require more information about international input–output flows. Finally, to obtain a better grasp of global production networks, we should employ newer conceptual frameworks, such as in Koopman *et al.* (2010).

Appendix

Table A.1. Country/region aggregation.

Code	GTAP region
CHN	China
JPN	Japan
KOR	South Korea
TWN	Taiwan
ASEAN	Cambodia, Indonesia, Lao People's Democratic Republic, Myanmar, Malaysia, Philippines, Singapore, Thailand, Vietnam
U.S.	United States
EU	Austria, Belgium, Cyprus, Czech Republic, Denmark, Estonia, Finland, France, Germany, Greece, Hungary, Ireland, Italy, Latvia, Lithuania, Luxembourg, Malta, Netherlands, Poland, Portugal, Slovakia, Slovenia, Spain, Sweden, United Kingdom
RoW	Australia, New Zealand, Rest of Oceania, Hong Kong, Rest of East Asia, Rest of Southeast Asia, Bangladesh, India, Pakistan, Sri Lanka, Rest of South Asia, Canada, Mexico, Rest of North America, Argentina, Bolivia, Brazil, Chile, Colombia, Ecuador, Paraguay, Peru, Uruguay, Venezuela, Rest of South America, Costa Rica, Guatemala, Nicaragua, Panama, Rest of Central America, Caribbean, Switzerland, Norway, Rest of European Free Trade Association (EFTA), Albania, Bulgaria, Belarus, Croatia, Romania, Russian Federation, Ukraine, Rest of Eastern Europe, Rest of Europe, Kazakhstan, Kyrgyzstan, Rest of Former Soviet Union, Armenia, Azerbaijan, Georgia, Islamic Republic of Iran, Turkey, Rest of Western Asia, Egypt, Morocco, Tunisia, Rest of North Africa, Nigeria, Senegal, Rest of Western Africa, Central Africa, South Central Africa, Ethiopia, Madagascar, Malawi, Mauritius, Mozambique, Tanzania, Uganda, Zambia, Zimbabwe, Rest of Eastern Africa, Botswana, South Africa, Rest of South African Customs Union.

Source: Author.

Table A.2. Industry aggregation.

Code	GTAP industry
Primary	Paddy rice, Wheat, Cereal grains nec, Vegetables, fruit, nuts, Oil seeds, Sugar cane, sugar beet, Plant-based fibers, Crops nec, Cattle, sheep, goats, horses, Animal products nec, Raw milk, Wool, silkworm cocoons, Forestry, Fishing, Coal, Oil, Gas, Minerals nec
Food	Meat: cattle, sheep, goats, horse, Meat products nec, Vegetable oils and fats, Dairy products, Processed rice, Sugar, Food products nec, Beverages and tobacco products
Textiles	Textiles, Wearing apparel
Chemical	Chemical, rubber, plastic products
MotorTrans	Motor vehicles and parts, Transport equipment nec
Electro	Electronic equipment
Machine	Machinery and equipment nec
Light	Leather products, Wood products, Paper products, publishing, Metal products, Manufactures nec
Heavy	Petroleum, coal products, Mineral products nec, Ferrous metals, Metals nec
Services	Electricity, Gas manufacture, distribution, Water, Construction, Trade, Transport nec, Sea transport, Air transport, Communication, Financial services nec, Insurance, Business services nec; Recreation and other services, Public administration, defense, health, education.

Source: Author.

References

Ando, M (2009). Impacts of FTAs in East Asia: CGE simulation analysis. *RIETI Discussion Paper Series* 09-E0–37, The Research Institute of Economy, Trade and Industry, Tokyo.

Bems, R, RC Johnson and K-M Yi (2010). Demand spillovers and the collapse of trade in the global recession. *IMF Economic Review*, 58, 295–326.

Bems, R, RC Johnson and K-M Yi (2011). Vertical linkages and the collapse of global trade. *American Economic Review*, 101, 308–312.

Fujikawa, K, M Shimoda and T Watanabe (2005). The structure of international division of labor in the Asia-Pacific region — An empirical study using IDE international IO tables. *Konan Economic Papers*, 46, 1–34.

Hertel, TW (ed.) (1997). *Global Trade Analysis — Modeling and Applications.* Cambridge: Cambridge University Press.

Hummels, D, J Ishii and K-M Yi (2001). The nature and growth of vertical specialization in world trade. *Journal of International Economics*, 54, 75–96.

Kawasaki, K (2003). The impact of free trade agreements in Asia. *RIETI Discussion Paper Series* 03-E-018, The Research Institute of Economy, Trade and Industry, Tokyo.

Koopman, R, W Powers, Z Wang and S-J Wei (2010). Give credit where credit is due: Tracing value added in global production chains. *NBER Working Papers* w16426, The National Bureau of Economic Research, Cambridge.

Miller, RE, PD Blair (2009). *Input-Output Analysis Foundations and Extensions.* Cambridge: Cambridge University Press.

National Accounts of Japan (2012). Quarterly estimates of GDP: October–December 2011 (The Second Preliminary). Available at http://www.esri.cao. go.jp/jp/sna/data/data_list/sokuhou/files/2011/qe114_2/pdf/jikei_1.pdf [accessed on 17 April 2012].

Urata, S, K Kiyota (2003). The impacts of an East Asia FTA on foreign trade in East Asia. *NBER Working Papers* w10173, The National Bureau of Economic Research, Cambridge.

Wang, Z, W Powers and S-J Wei (2009). Value chains in East Asian production networks — An international input–output model based analysis. *Office of Economics Working Paper* 2009–10-C, U.S. International Trade Commission, Washington DC.

World Bank (2011). The global Outlook in Summary, 2009–2013. Available at http://siteresources.worldbank.org/EXTGBLPROSPECTS/Resources/ GEP2012aTable1.xlsx [accessed on 10 September 2012].

CHAPTER 5

INFLATION TARGETING IN SOUTH KOREA, INDONESIA, THE PHILIPPINES AND THAILAND: THE IMPACT ON BUSINESS CYCLE SYNCHRONIZATION BETWEEN EACH COUNTRY AND THE WORLD*

Takeshi Inoue

Institute of Developing Economies
3-2-2 Wakaba Mihama-Ku, Chiba 261-8545, Japan
takeshi_inoue@ide.go.jp

Yuki Toyoshima

Graduate School of Economics, Kobe University
2-1, Rokkodai, Nada-Ku, Kobe 657-8501, Japan
makenaizard@yahoo.co.jp

Shigeyuki Hamori

Faculty of Economics, Kobe University
2-1, Rokkodai, Nada-Ku, Kobe 657-8501, Japan
hamori@econ.kobe-u.ac.jp

*An earlier version of this article was presented as IDE Discussion Paper 328.

1. Introduction

For the last two decades, a growing number of countries have introduced what is known as "inflation targeting". Inflation targeting (IT) is generally defined as a monetary policy framework wherein the central bank would adjust the policy interest rate to keep the conditional inflation forecast close to the inflation target, and to achieve price stability and low inflation as the primary objectives of monetary policy. In the initial phase, IT was adopted mainly in developed countries. Due to successful experience especially in terms of price stabilization, the introduction of IT has spread not only to other developed countries but also to emerging and developing countries, currently amounting to approximately 30 countries.

With the number of IT countries increasing, recent literature has placed much more emphasis on this policy framework, examining it from a variety of viewpoints. Among other things, most studies empirically indicate the positive impacts of IT on domestic macroeconomic variables. For instance, Neumann and von Hagen (2002) state that the introduction of this framework has permitted IT countries to reduce inflation to low levels and to curb the volatility of inflation and interest rates. In addition, Levin *et al.* (2004) suggests that IT plays a role in anchoring inflation expectations and in reducing inflation persistence. Furthermore, Mishkin and Schmidt-Hebbel (2007) show that IT actually helps countries achieve lower inflation in the long term. Earlier empirical literature tended to explore IT largely in industrial countries, as there was limited evidence of IT in less developed countries partly because of the lack of data as well as the credibility problem of central banks. As data and experience have gradually accumulated, however, growing numbers of empirical studies have analyzed the impact and/or the effectiveness of the IT framework in emerging and developing countries. In line with this recent trend, this chapter focuses on the last decade of experience in IT for selected Asian countries, such as South Korea, Indonesia, the Philippines and Thailand.

Specifically, in this chapter, we attempt to analyze the extent to which the adoption of IT in these Asian countries has affected their business cycle synchronization with the rest of the world. To this end, we apply the dynamic conditional correlation (DCC) model developed by Engle (2002). This is a relatively novel approach, since the surveyed literature indicates that empirical studies tend to characterize IT by estimating the monetary reaction function for each country. Our empirical evidence states that the adoption of IT in Asia has little impact on business cycle synchronization with the rest of the world and that the effect is positive in some of the countries, if any. This is basically consistent with Flood and Rose (2010), in spite of the different methodologies applied. Apart from this, in the second part of this chapter, we also summarize the history of monetary policy in each of these countries.

This chapter is organized as follows. The next section briefly sets out the historical background and specific features of IT in South Korea, Indonesia, the Philippines and Thailand. In Sec. 2, we survey the recent empirical literature on IT focusing on these Asian countries. Based on the Engle (2002) procedure, the third section empirically analyzes whether and to what extent the adoption of IT in Asia has affected business cycle synchronization with the rest of the world. The final section offers concluding observations regarding this chapter.

2. Background and Features of IT in the Four Asian Countries

IT is typically defined as a monetary policy framework in which the central bank explicitly sets the inflation target, controls the policy rate to close the gap between the announced target and the expected inflation, and aims to achieve price stabilization and low inflation. In this section, we briefly review IT in South Korea, Indonesia, the Philippines and Thailand in terms of the circumstances under which IT was introduced, the practical characteristics, and the inflation developments before and after adoption.

2.1. *South Korea*

For a few decades before IT, South Korea had conducted its monetary policy under monetary targeting. The Bank of Korea (BOK) set the M1 growth rate as the intermediate target in 1976 and changed the target to the M2 growth rate in 1979. Largely because of the stability of M2 demand, the bank had been able to keep it closer to the target value until the middle of the 1990s (Kim and Park, 2006, pp. 141–142). However, since changes in the trust account system in 1996 made the demand for M2 unstable, the BOK added a broader monetary aggregate called MCT to the list of intermediate targets (*ibid.*, pp. 141–142).[1] Subsequently, the

---

[1] MCT is the sum of M2, the certificate of deposits, and the money in trust.

usefulness of M2 and MCT substantially declined with the diversification of financial products as well as due to the change in the required reserve system in 1997.

Under this circumstance, the financial crisis that began in Thailand in July 1997 spread to South Korea at the end of the year. To cope with the crisis, under the IMF program, the government set about broad-based structural reform, a part of which it began monetary policy reform and amended the BOK Act. This revised central bank act that came into effect in April 1998 ensures the political and institutional independence of the BOK, clearly sets out price stability as the primary objective of the BOK, and announces the shift of its policy framework to IT. Since then, the bank has decided on the inflation target in consultation with the government and has conducted monetary management by controlling short-term interest rates. Later, South Korea switched to pure inflation targeting in 2001, up until which time the central bank made public the inflation target, setting M3 growth as the operational target (*ibid.*, p. 142).[2]

Since the adoption, South Korea has modified IT in several respects. One of them is the changes in the benchmark indicator. In the early years, the inflation target was based on the CPI inflation rate. In 2000, it was changed to the core CPI inflation rate, which strips out the prices of petroleum products and non-grain agricultural products from the CPI. However, since 2007, the CPI inflation rate has been again used as the benchmark indicator. In addition, after introducing IT in 1998, the BOK came to establish an annual inflation target every year, but from 2004 onward, a medium-term inflation targeting system has been put in place in line with the entry into the effect of the revision of the central bank act in 2004.[3] Another major change regards the policy rate. Following the introduction of IT, the Monetary Policy Committee, the policy-making body of the BOK, defined the uncollateralized overnight call rate as the policy rate, and set the target level of the call rate every month. In March 2008, the policy rate was switched from the call rate to the Bank of Korea Base Rate (Base Rate), while the BOK continues to use the call rate as an

---

[2] In 2001, the BOK decided to set the M3 growth not as the intermediate target but as the monitoring range. Since 2003, the bank has carefully monitored the movement of M3 as an information variable for the conduct of monetary policy.

[3] From 2000 to 2003, the BOK announced the medium-term inflation target as well as the annual inflation target based on the average core inflation. The medium-term target was set at 2.5% from 2000 to 2002 and at 2.5%–3.5% for 2003.

(%)

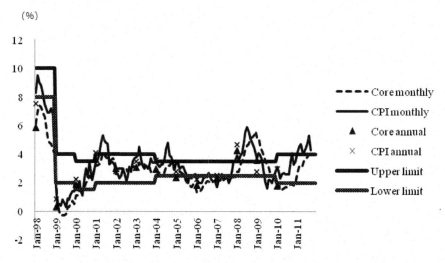

Fig. 1. Actual inflation and the inflation target in South Korea.

Source: Compiled by the authors from the BOK (various issues) and the BOK web page (http://ecos.bok.or.kr/EIndex_en.jsp) [accessed on 14 October 2011].

operational target and seeks to ensure that it does not deviate too widely from the Base Rate by using its policy instruments such as open market operations.[4]

Figure 1 and Table 1 depict both the developments of the inflation target and the actual inflation rate after the adoption of IT in South Korea. From Fig. 1, on a monthly basis, it seems that the inflation rate has sometimes deviated from the target range. However, given that average annual inflation determines whether the inflation target is achieved or not, they show that actual inflation has been often times within the target range, that is, in six years out of nine years.

2.2. Indonesia

For many years, as Indonesia's central bank, Bank Indonesia (BI) had conducted monetary policy by using mainly base money as the operational instrument to control other monetary aggregates and thus inflation

---

[4]The BOK Base Rate is the standard rate applied to transactions between the central bank and the counterpart financial institutions.

Table 1. Actual inflation and the inflation target in South Korea.

Time horizon	Target indicator	Target range %	Performance evaluation	Actual rate %
1998	CPI Inflation	9.0±1.0	Annually	7.5
1999		3.0±1.0		0.8
2000	Core CPI	2.5±1.0		1.9
2001	Inflation	3.0±1.0		3.6
2002				3.0
2003				3.1
2004–2006		2.5–3.5	Average	2.3
2007–2009	CPI Inflation	3.0±0.5	during the Term	3.3
2010–2012		3.0±1.0	Annually	2.9

Source: The same sources as those from Fig. 1.
Note: The actual rate for 2010–2012 represents the inflation rate for 2010.

(Alamsyah *et al.*, 2001, p. 311). In addition, the BI had used the nominal exchange rate with a pre-announced crawling band as the main anchor of monetary policy and implemented the steady depreciation of the rupiah in order to maintain international competitiveness rather than control inflation itself (McLeod, 1997, p. 22). Although the use of base money as the operational instrument seemed to have been effective in the 1980s and early 1990s, this approach using quantity targets was challenged thereafter, as the relationship between money aggregates and nominal income became tenuous in the mid-to-late 1990s due to the instability in the income velocity of money resulting from global financial innovations and deregulation (Alamsyah *et al.*, 2001, p. 311; Mariano and Villanueva, 2006, p. 218).[5] Thus, the BI attempted to gradually shift its policy from quantity targeting to price (interest rate) targeting, and has widened the exchange rate tolerance

---

[5]So far, there have been several empirical studies to examine the stability of money demand functions in Indonesia with different techniques and specifications. Some studies using sample data from before 2000, such as Bahmani-Oskooee and Rehman (2005) and James (2005), state that the money demand function is stable, whereas more recent studies using data from even after 2000, such as Narayan (2007) and Kubo (2009), indicate the instability of money demand functions for Indonesia.

band to ease the conflict with monetary policy (Alamsyah *et al.,* 2001, p. 312).

Nevertheless, this attempt to move to the price targeting approach was postponed due to the turbulence caused by the Asian financial crisis, and targeting of the monetary base continued to be used after the crisis as a temporary measure (*ibid.,* pp. 312, 314). Affected by the crisis, the crawling band exchange rate regime was abandoned in August 1997, and the rupiah was allowed to float. As a result, the rupiah depreciated significantly, and soon after this, the BI sharply increased the short-term interest rate, which proved fatal to the banking and real estate sectors (Mariano and Villanueva, 2006, p. 218). Reacting to these developments, the BI injected large-scale liquidity into the banking system, but the excessive monetary creation exerted further pressure on the exchange rate, doing the same to prices (*ibid.,* p. 219). Accordingly, the bank re-absorbed the excess liquidity from the banking system by targeting the monetary base (Alamsyah *et al.,* 2001, p. 314).

Under these circumstances, a new central bank act was enacted in May 1999. This legislation clearly prescribed that the primary objective of monetary policy is to achieve and maintain the stability of the rupiah's value. It also provided the BI with the legal independence as well as the authority to formulate and implement monetary policy considering the inflation target that the bank set. Subsequently, the central bank act was amended in 2004, which empowered the government to set the inflation target (Mariano and Villanueva, 2006, p. 220).

Although the BI has explicitly announced the inflation target since 2000 following the enactment of the new central bank act in 1999, it was in July 2005 that Indonesia formally adopted IT and replaced the previous policy framework using base money as the policy instrument. Under the IT framework, the Board of Governors of the BI set "the BI rate" as the policy instrument to reflect the monetary policy stance.[6] For 2000 and 2001, the inflation target was set for the core CPI, which excludes the impacts of government-administered prices and income policy on the CPI. However, in 2002 it was changed to be based on the headline CPI (*ibid.,* p. 219). Figure 2 shows the developments of actual inflation and the

---

[6] In addition, the BI rate is used as a reference rate in monetary control operations to ensure that the weighted average of one-month Bank Indonesia Certificates (SBI) rate derived in open market operation auctions remains at around the level of the BI rate (Siregar and Goo, 2010, p. 116).

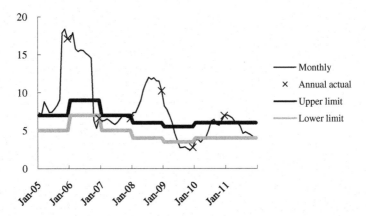

Fig. 2. Actual inflation and the inflation target in Indonesia.

Source: Compiled by the authors from the web pages of the BI (http://www.bi.go.id/web/ en) and BPS-Statistics Indonesia (http://dds.bps.go.id/eng/) [accessed on 16 December 2011].

inflation targets in Indonesia after the introduction of IT in 2005. From this figure, we find that it was only two times during the seven years from 2005 to 2011 that actual inflation was within the inflation target range.

2.3. The Philippines

Pursuant to the 1987 Philippine Constitution and the new central bank act of 1993, the Bangko Sentral ng Pilipinas (BSP) was established in July 1993 as the central bank of the Philippines, which took over from the Central Bank of Philippines (CBP), established in 1949. Unlike the previous legislation, the new central bank act that took effect in July 1993 explicitly stated the maintenance of price stability conducive to balanced and sustainable growth as the primary objective of the BSP, and also gives the central bank fiscal and administrative autonomy which the CBP did not have.

Since the establishment, the BSP followed the monetary aggregate targeting approach to monetary policy. Beginning in the latter half of 1995, this approach was modified to put greater emphasis on price stability instead of rigidly observing the targets set for monetary aggregates. The reason was that the relationship between quantitative monetary targets and inflation had weakened due to structural breaks in the income velocity of money and due to volatilities and instabilities in the money multiplier caused by financial liberalization (Lim, 2008, p. 276). Under this modified framework, as far as inflation was below or at the target level, the BSP tolerated money supply in excess of the programmed level (Mariano and Villanueva, 2006, p. 211). However, this semi-IT framework was based on current inflation, rather than forecast inflation (*ibid.*, p. 211).

Following this transitional phase, in January 2000, the BSP's policy-making body, the Monetary Board, approved in principle the shift from monetary targeting to inflation targeting, and two years later, the BSP formally adopted IT as a framework for conducting monetary policy. The inflation target is defined in terms of the average year-on-year change in the CPI over the calendar year and is set by the government through an inter-agency economic planning body — the Development Budget and Coordination Committee. Initially, the inflation target was set in terms of a range. In 2006, the government re-specified the inflation target from a range target to a point target with a tolerance interval of ±1.0% points starting in the target for 2008. In addition to this modification, in July 2010, the BSP also announced the shift from a variable annual inflation target to a fixed inflation target for the medium-term, and set the inflation target of 4.0±1.0% for the period of 2012–2014. In order to achieve the inflation target, the BSP has so far used the overnight repurchase rate and reverse repurchase rate as the primary policy instruments.

Figure 3 illustrates the developments of the actual inflation rate and the inflation target in the Philippines since the adoption of IT in 2002. This figure shows that after the failure to meet the target from 2002 to 2008, headline inflation has been within the pre-announced target range for 2009 and 2010. In cases where the BSP fails to achieve the inflation target, the BSP governor issues an "Open Letter to the President". This outlines the reasons why actual inflation did not fall within the target, along with the steps that will be taken to bring inflation towards the target. So far, the BSP has issued this letter to the President six times in total for the inflation target from 2003 to 2008.

2.4. Thailand

For a long time after the Second World War, Thailand adopted a fixed exchange rate regime. Since 1984, the value of the baht had been pegged to a basket of currencies, although the financial crisis that occurred in July 1997 posed challenges to Thailand's monetary policy. Following both the

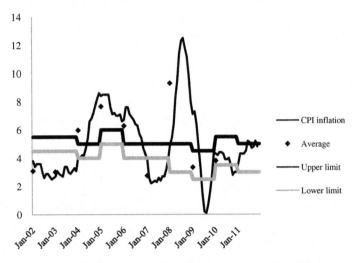

Fig. 3. Actual inflation and the inflation target in the Philippines.

Source: Compiled by the authors from the BSP (various issues) and the web pages of the BSP (http://www.bsp.gov.ph/downloads/Publications/FAQs/targeting.pdf) and the National Statistical Office (http://www.census.gov.ph/) [accessed on 13 December 2011].

Note: The base year for CPI inflation is 1994 for the period from January 2002 to December 2003, 2000 for January 2004 to May 2011, and 2007 for June 2011 onward.

adoption of the floating exchange rate system and the IMF program, a monetary targeting regime was adopted (Phuvanatnaranubala, 2005, p. 272). Under this regime, the Bank of Thailand (BOT) set the daily and quarterly monetary base targets and put upward pressure on interest rates if base money was running ahead of the medium-term targets, and put downward pressure on interest rates if base money was below such targets (Fane, 2005, p. 176). However, as the relationship between the money supply and output growth became less stable over time, the targeting of the money supply was deemed inappropriate. Moreover, with the exit from the IMF program, it became necessary for the authorities to identify a new appropriate policy anchor. Accordingly, in April 2000, the BOT appointed the Monetary Policy Board (MPB) as the policy-making body and officially announced the adoption of IT with the main objective of maintaining price stability by the following month.

The MPB defined the quarterly average of core inflation as the policy target and set the core inflation target at between 0.0%–3.5% per year. Core inflation is expressed in terms of the year-on-year percentage change of the CPI, which excludes fresh food and energy prices. In addition, the

MPB decided to use the 14-day repurchase rate as the key policy rate to signal the monetary policy stance. In July 2001, a new Monetary Policy Committee (MPC) was formed and took over the MPB's function and responsibility as the policy-making body.

In March 2008, the Bank of Thailand Act was amended for the first time in over 60 years. Before then, although the BOT had been granted *de facto* independence in the conduct of monetary policy, the amended act clearly states the BOT's objectives and responsibilities as the nation's central bank in maintaining monetary stability, the stability of the financial system, and the stability of the payment system. The new act requires that the MPC set out the inflation target in conjunction with the Minister of Finance each December for the following year, with formal approval from the Cabinet (Grenville and Ito, 2010, p. 82). At this juncture, the MPC and the Minister of Finance have carefully considered the appropriateness of the inflation target, and in order to reduce the probability of deflation, the MPC adjusted the target range from 0.0%–3.5% to 0.5%–3.0% per annum in 2009 (BOT, 2009, p. 8). In addition, the MPC changed the policy rate from the 14-day repurchase rate to the one-day repurchase rate from January 2007 onward.

Figure 4 illustrates the developments of the inflation rate and the inflation target in Thailand. From April 2000 to July 2011, actual inflation

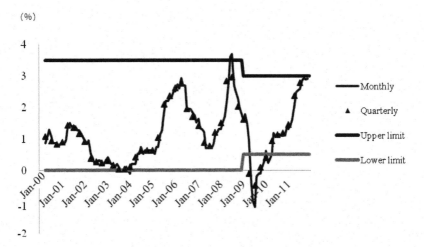

Fig. 4. Actual inflation and the inflation target in Thailand.

Source: Compiled by the authors from the BOT web page (http://www.price.moc.go.th/price/cpi/index_new_e.asp) [accessed on 5 December 2011].

was within the target range for 42 quarters, that is, more than 90% of the total time. The inflation rate remained below the lower bounds of the target from 2009 Q2 until 2010 Q1, which was mainly caused by the effects from the government's cost-of-living reduction measures and the 15-year free-of-charge education program (BOT, 2010, p. 9).

2.5. Effectiveness of IT in the four Asian countries

After the Asian financial crisis in 1997, the four Asian countries excluding the Philippines adopted monetary targeting, accompanying the shift to the flexible exchange rate regime. Only the Philippines introduced monetary targeting before the crisis. Due to financial innovation and deregulation, however, the relationship between the money supply and output growth became less stable over time. Accordingly, the effectiveness of monetary targeting appeared to have been eroded, which encouraged these countries to switch to the alternative IT framework in Asia. Since the introduction of IT, the achievement of the inflation target has varied across the countries. In Thailand and South Korea, actual inflation has relatively fallen well within the target range, while Indonesia and the Philippines have quite often failed to meet the target.

Typically, the main objectives of the IT framework are to achieve stable price levels and low inflation. In order to briefly assess to what extent the four Asian countries achieved these objectives, in Table 2, we

Table 2. Inflation performance in the Asian IT countries.

	Before inflation targeting				After inflation targeting			
	Average	SD	Max	Min	Average	SD	Max	Min
South Korea	5.6	2.0	9.3	2.8	2.9	1.0	4.7	0.8
	(5.4)	(1.7)	(8.4)	(3.0)	(2.6)	(1.1)	(4.2)	(0.3)
Indonesia	8.7	3.0	12.6	5.1	6.8	2.9	11.1	2.8
The Philippines	6.8	1.7	9.3	4.0	5.3	2.4	9.3	2.8
Thailand	5.0	1.4	6.2	1.8	1.1	0.8	2.3	0.1

Source: Calculated by the authors from IMF (2011) and the same sources as those from Figs. 1, 2, 3 and 4, as well as Table 1.

Note 1: All values are calculated for the same period before and after the adoption of IT. We exclude the first year of the IT regime's implementation.

Note 2: The numbers in parenthesis are based on core inflation.

report on basic statistics for the inflation rate in each country, comparing the sample mean, standard deviation, and the maximum and minimum before and after IT. From this table, it is found that each number except the standard deviation in the Philippines has been smaller than those prior to the IT period, suggesting that the inflation rate has been lower and less volatile since the introduction of IT. Therefore, although the achievement of the inflation target actually varies across the countries, the IT frameworks in these Asian countries generally seem to have achieved some positive results, at least in terms of low and stable inflation.

3. Literature Review

In recent years, a growing body of empirical studies has analyzed IT in emerging and developing countries. In the previous section of this chapter, we simply observed the basic statistics, while in this section we review the recent empirical literature on the performance of IT focusing on the emerging countries in Asia.

First, concerning South Korea, Kim and Park (2006) analyze the monetary reaction function of the BOK to infer the way in which the bank conducted monetary policy during the IT period. Following Clarida *et al.* (1998, 2000), they estimate the reaction function for the period 1999 to August 2005 and find that the coefficients of both the deviation of inflation from the target and the output gap from the potential level are positive and significantly different from zero, though the estimates of the output gap are relatively small. Therefore, Kim and Park (2006) point out that the BOK adjusts interest rates in response to changes in inflationary pressure, and that the BOK also includes stabilizing the output gap as policy objectives. Next, Sánchez (2010) calculates the BOK's parameters in the policy objective function to characterize the monetary policy in South Korea during the IT period. Empirical results show that the central bank appears to have pursued an optimal policy geared towards achieving price stability, while displaying a significant degree of interest rate smoothing. He also states that the BOK's loss function is estimated to include negligible weights on output and exchange rate variability.[7]

---

[7] Besides, Hoffmaister (2001) and Eichengreen (2004) also examine monetary policy management in South Korea.

Concerning the Philippines, Salas (2006) explores the BSP's monetary policy behavior during the entire sample from January 1992 to September 2003 and the three sub-periods. By employing the forward-looking model by Clarida *et al.* (1998, 2000), he points out that the shift to IT in the Philippines was accompanied by string responses to inflationary pressures and an apparent disregard of the output deviations from trend. In addition, Angeles and Tan (2007) examine whether the inclusion of the output gap in the central bank's estimated reaction function would improve the conduct of IT in the Philippines. They conduct counterfactual simulations by replacing the interest rate equation from the VAR model with the Taylor rule, and unlike Salas (2006), find that the adoption of a Taylor-type rule involving the use of the output gap minimizes the deviations of inflation from the target.

Regarding Thailand, McCauley (2006) estimates the monetary policy reaction function for the BOT, augmenting the Taylor rule with the change in the effective exchange rate. Taking the results with different variables and sample periods together, he states that the BOT's policy in the IT period can be most plausibly modeled using the bank's next-year forecast of inflation and that no specification finds a response of the policy rate to the exchange rate. In addition, Payne (2009) examines the impact of IT on inflation volatility in Thailand using monthly data during the period of 1965 to 2007. The estimation results obtained from the ARIMA–GARCH model indicates that the inflation targeting adopted marginally reduced the degree of volatility persistence in response to inflationary shocks. Moreover, Siregar and Goo (2010) employ the Markov-switching VAR framework to test for the shift in the monetary policy rules of the central banks in Thailand and Indonesia. The result shows that the IT policy in these countries has largely been flexible during the stable period, whereas a greater policy focus has been placed on anchoring inflationary expectation during the turbulent period.

Finally, Prasertnukul *et al.* (2010) analyze how the adoption of IT has influenced exchange rate pass-through and its volatility in South Korea, Indonesia, the Philippines and Thailand during the sample period from January 1990 to June 2007. The empirical results indicate that adopting IT caused a decline in exchange rate volatility in all four countries, while it helped reduce exchange rate pass-through only in South Korea and Thailand. Besides, Taniguchi and Kato (2011) assess the monetary policy rule under IT by estimating the monetary policy reaction functions in the

IT countries in Asia and Malaysia. The results indicate that there seems to be a linkage between the adoption of IT and the monetary policy rule emphasizing the stabilization of inflation excluding such in the Philippines. They also state that South Korea seems to have adopted a forward-looking policy rule under IT, while Indonesia and Thailand seems to have adopted a backward-looking rule.

As mentioned above, the literature survey on IT in the Asian countries generally suggests that under the IT regime, the central bank in each country pays much more attention to inflation developments when conducting monetary policy. In this chapter, we investigate the impact of IT on the economy from a different viewpoint than the literature surveyed. More specifically, in the following section, we attempt to evaluate whether and to what extent the adoption of IT in the Asian countries has affected their business cycle synchronization with the rest of the world.

4. Impact of IT Adoption on Business Cycle Synchronization with the Rest of the World

4.1. *Empirical techniques*

This section examines the dynamic conditional correlation between the world's business cycle and that of the four countries in this study that adopt inflation targeting; and this chapter adopts the following two-step approach. In the first step, we estimate the conditional correlations using the dynamic conditional correlation (DCC) model developed by Engle (2002).[8]

In the second step, AR (1) models are applied to model the conditional correlations derived from the first step. Specifically, the dummy variables signifying the period that adopt each countries' inflation targeting and financial crisis period are included to test whether the inflation targeting and the financial crisis significantly altered the dynamics of the estimated conditional correlations between the global business cycle and that of the four countries; that is:

$$D\hat{C}C_t = \delta_0 + \delta_1 D\hat{C}C_{t-1} + \gamma_0 Dummy_t^i + \gamma_1 Crisis_t + \nu_t, \qquad (1)$$

---

[8]See Appendix for details.

where $D\hat{C}C_t$ is the conditional correlation estimated from the first step and v_t is the white noise. Estimating Eq. (1), the dummy variable $Dummy_t^i$ ($i = 1, \cdots, 4$) and $Crisis_t$ is determined by the financial crisis; that is:

$$Dummy_t^1 = \begin{cases} 0 & (t = 03/1996,\ldots,03/1998) \\ 1 & (t = 04/1998,\ldots,06/2011) \end{cases}$$

$$Dummy_t^2 = \begin{cases} 0 & (t = 03/1996,\ldots,06/2005) \\ 1 & (t = 07/2005,\ldots,06/2011) \end{cases}$$

$$Dummy_t^3 = \begin{cases} 0 & (t = 03/1996,\ldots,12/2001), \\ 1 & (t = 01/2002,\ldots,06/2011) \end{cases} \tag{2}$$

$$Dummy_t^4 = \begin{cases} 0 & (t = 03/1996,\ldots,04/2000) \\ 1 & (t = 05/2000,\ldots,06/2011) \end{cases}$$

$$Crisis_t = \begin{cases} 0 & (t = 03/1996,\ldots,08/2008) \\ 1 & (t = 09/2008,\ldots,06/2011), \end{cases}$$

where the dummy variable $Dummy_t^1$ shows the South Korea dummy, $Dummy_t^2$ shows the Indonesia dummy, $Dummy_t^3$ shows the Philippines dummy, and $Dummy_t^4$ shows the Thailand dummy.

4.2. Data

We employ monthly data on the JCER (Japan Center for Economic Research) World Business Climate Index from March 1996 to June 2011. This sample period is chosen on the basis of the availability of data from the Japan Center for Economic Research. We use the global index and the index of the four countries adopting inflation targeting: South Korea, Indonesia, the Philippines and Thailand. In addition, we estimate the following two main cases and four sub-cases considering the time trend of the data and the pairs of countries.

Case 1: In case of including the time trend of data

    1-1: World versus South Korea
    1-2: World versus Indonesia
    1-3: World versus the Philippines
    1-4: World versus Thailand

Case 2: In case of excluding the time trend of data

2-1: World versus South Korea
2-2: World versus Indonesia
2-3: World versus the Philippines
2-4: World versus Thailand

In Case 2, we removed the time trend using the Hodrick–Prescott (HP) filter.

4.3. Empirical results

First, we estimated the DCC models for each pairs of the business climate index. Next, we apply AR (1) models with a dummy variable representing each countries' inflation targeting and financial crisis period to the evolution of the estimated dynamic conditional correlations.

Tables 3 and 4 show the estimate results of the AR (1) models. As for Case 1, the constant terms (δ_0) are all positive and significant at the 5% significance level. The coefficients of AR terms (δ_1) are also significant for all cases excluding Case 1-1, with values of less than unity. The inflation

Table 3. Regression of the correlation evolution for the world and the four countries in Case 1.

	Coefficient	Std. error	t-Statistic	Prob.
Case 1-1: World versus South Korea				
δ_0	0.262	0.036	7.312	0.000
δ_1	0.106	0.077	1.381	0.169
γ_0	0.004	0.029	0.141	0.888
γ_1	0.038	0.020	1.859	0.065
Adjusted R-squared	0.020			
Case 1-2: World versus Indonesia				
δ_0	0.031	0.008	3.746	0.000
δ_1	0.822	0.046	18.050	0.000
γ_0	−0.001	0.004	−0.196	0.845
γ_1	0.011	0.007	1.723	0.087
Adjusted R-squared	0.766			

(*Continued*)

Table 3. (*Continued*)

	Coefficient	Std. error	*t*-Statistic	Prob.
Case 1-3: World versus the Philippines				
δ_0	0.019	0.007	2.573	0.011
δ_1	0.893	0.035	25.805	0.000
γ_0	0.009	0.007	1.305	0.194
γ_1	0.013	0.008	1.652	0.100
Adjusted *R*-squared	0.893			
Case 1-4: World versus Thailand				
δ_0	0.057	0.016	3.605	0.000
δ_1	0.836	0.039	21.215	0.000
γ_0	0.023	0.008	2.708	0.008
γ_1	0.024	0.009	2.675	0.008
Adjusted *R*-squared	0.876			

Table 4. Regression of the correlation evolution for the world and the four countries in Case 2.

	Coefficient	Std. error	*t*-Statistic	Prob.
Case 2-1: World versus South Korea				
δ_0	0.005	0.012	0.425	0.671
δ_1	0.953	0.024	40.126	0.000
γ_0	0.009	0.010	0.877	0.382
γ_1	0.011	0.008	1.498	0.136
Adjusted *R*-squared	0.936			
Case 2-2: World versus Indonesia				
δ_0	0.026	0.009	3.034	0.003
δ_1	0.879	0.039	22.611	0.000
γ_0	0.002	0.003	0.745	0.458
γ_1	0.002	0.004	0.614	0.540
Adjusted *R*-squared	0.813			

(*Continued*)

Table 4. (*Continued*)

	Coefficient	Std. error	*t*-Statistic	Prob.
Case 2-3: World versus the Philippines				
δ_0	0.028	0.008	3.308	0.001
δ_1	0.869	0.037	23.316	0.000
γ_0	0.010	0.005	2.066	0.040
γ_1	0.015	0.006	2.602	0.010
Adjusted *R*-squared	0.921			
Case 2-4: World versus Thailand				
δ_0	0.051	0.016	3.181	0.002
δ_1	0.856	0.038	22.522	0.000
γ_0	0.028	0.010	2.711	0.007
γ_1	0.021	0.011	2.032	0.044
Adjusted *R*-squared	0.896			

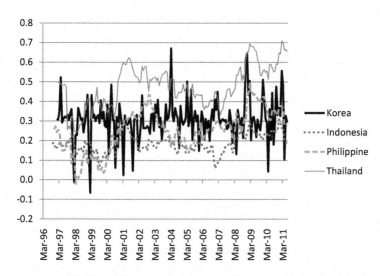

Fig. 5. DCCs of the world versus the four countries in Case 1.

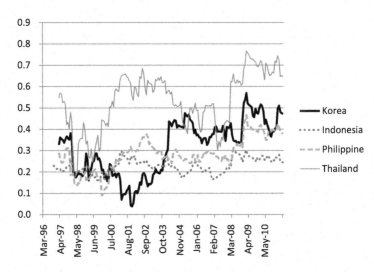

Fig. 6. DCCs of the world versus the four countries in Case 2.

targeting dummy (γ_0) and financial crisis dummy (γ_1) are positively significant at the 1% significance level in Case 1-4. As for Case 2, the constant terms (δ_0) are positively significant at the 5% significance level in all cases excluding Case 2-1. The coefficients of AR terms (δ_1) are significant for all cases with values of less than unity. The inflation targeting dummy (γ_0) and financial crisis dummy (γ_1) are positively significant at the 5% significance level in Cases 2-3 and 2-4. As for Case 2, the adjusted R-squared is higher than Case 1 in all sub-cases.

5. Conclusion

Before inflation targeting (IT), the four Asian countries, that is, South Korea, Indonesia, the Philippines and Thailand, commonly adopted monetary targeting. Due to financial innovation and deregulation, however, the relationship between money supply and output growth became less stable over time, which encouraged these countries to switch their policy framework from monetary targeting to IT.

Looking at the achievement of inflation targets, these countries show different outcomes. In Thailand and South Korea, actual inflation has relatively fallen well within the target range, while Indonesia and the Philippines have quite often failed to meet the target. Therefore, the achievement of the inflation target varied across these countries, although the basic statistics such as the mean and standard deviation indicate that the numbers were generally smaller than those prior to the IT period, suggesting that the IT framework in Asia seems to have succeeded in attaining the objectives of low and stable inflation.

In recent years, a growing body of empirical studies has been conducted to analyze IT in the Asian emerging countries. These empirical studies tend to characterize IT by estimating the monetary reaction function for each country and generally confirm that the central banks under the IT regime have paid substantial attention to inflation developments when conducting monetary policy. In this chapter, we investigate the impact of IT on the economy from a different viewpoint than the surveyed literature. Specifically, we analyze whether and to what extent the adoption of IT in these countries has affected international business synchronization by employing the dynamic conditional correlation (DCC) model developed by Engle (2002). From this analysis, we find that IT in Asia has little effect on business cycle synchronization with the rest of the world and that the effect is positive in some of the countries, if any.

In relevant literature, Flood and Rose (2010) examine whether the advent of IT in developed and developing countries including the Asian countries can be linked to the rising international synchronization of the business cycle by applying different methods, and they point out that countries that target inflation seem to have cycles that move slightly more closely with foreign cycles. Therefore, our findings basically seem to be consistent with the evidence from Flood and Rose.

Appendix

The first step of the DCC model is to estimate the following equations:

$$r_t \setminus I_{t-1} \sim N(0, D_t R_t D_t)$$
$$D_t^2 = diag\{\omega_i\} + diag\{\kappa_i\} \circ r_{t-1} r_{t-1}' + diag\{\lambda_i\} \circ D_{t-1}^2$$
$$\varepsilon_t = D_t^{-1} r_t$$
$$Q_1 = \bar{Q} \circ (\iota\iota' - A - B) + A \circ \varepsilon_{t-1} \varepsilon_{t-1}' + B \circ Q_{t-1}$$
$$R_t = diag\{Q_t\}^{-1} Q_t diag\{Q_t\}^{-1}$$

where r_t is the CPI inflation rate, D_t is the conditional volatility, R_t is the conditional correlation, ε_t is the standardized residual, Q_t is the covariance matrix, $\bar{Q}$ is the unconditional covariance matrix, ι is a vector of ones and where $\circ$ is the Hadamard product of two identically seized matrices, which is computed simply by element-by-element multiplication. The second equation expresses a univariate generalized autoregressive conditional heteroskedasticity (GARCH) process. ω_i, κ_i, and λ_i are the parameters of the GARCH process. The third equation expresses the standardized residual, the fourth one expresses the conditional covariance matrices, and the fifth one expresses the conditional correlations. If A, B, and $(\iota\iota' - A-B)$ are positive semidefinites, then Q will be positive semidefinite.

References

Alamsyah, H, C Joseph, J Agung and D Zulverdy (2001). Towards implementation of inflation targeting in Indonesia. *Bulletin of Indonesian Economic Studies*, 37, 309–324.

Angeles, R and MA Tan (2007). The contribution of the output gap to the conduct of inflation targeting in the Philippines. *Philippine Review of Economics*, 44, 99–123.

Bahmani-Oskooee, M and H Rehman (2005). Stability of the money demand function in Asian developing countries. *Applied Economics*, 37, 773–792.

Ball, L and N Sheridan (2005). Does inflation targeting matter? In *The Inflation Targeting Debate*, BS Bernanke and M Woodford (eds.), pp. 249–276. Chicago: University of Chicago Press.

Bangko Sentral ng Pilipinas (BSP) (2005). Annual Report 2004. BSP, Manila.

Bangko Sentral ng Pilipinas (2006). Annual Report 2005. BSP, Manila.

Bangko Sentral ng Pilipinas (2007). Annual Report 2006. BSP, Manila.

Bangko Sentral ng Pilipinas (2008). Annual Report 2007. BSP, Manila.

Bangko Sentral ng Pilipinas (2009). Annual Report 2008. BSP, Manila.

Bangko Sentral ng Pilipinas (2010). Annual Report 2009. BSP, Manila.

Bangko Sentral ng Pilipinas (2011). Annual Report 2010. BSP, Manila.

Bank of Korea (BOK) (1999). Annual Report 1998. BOK, Seoul.

Bank of Korea (2000). Annual Report 1999. BOK, Seoul.

Bank of Korea (2001). Annual Report 2000. BOK, Seoul.

Bank of Korea (2002). Annual Report 2001. BOK, Seoul.

Bank of Korea (2003). Annual Report 2002. BOK, Seoul.

Bank of Korea (2004). Annual Report 2003. BOK, Seoul.

Bank of Korea (2007). Annual Report 2006. BOK, Seoul.

Bank of Korea (2010). Annual Report 2009. BOK, Seoul.

Bank of Korea (2011). Annual Report 2010. BOK, Seoul.

Bank of Thailand (BOT) (2009). Inflation Report January 2009. BOT, Bangkok.

Bank of Thailand (2010). Inflation Report April 2010. BOT, Bangkok.

Clarida, RH, J Gali and M Gertler (1998). Monetary policy rules in practice: Some international evidence. *European Economic Review*, 42, 1033–1067.

Clarida, RH, J Gali and M Gertler (2000). Monetary policy rules and macroeconomic stability: Evidence and some theory. *Quarterly Journal of Economics*, 115, 147–180.

Eichengreen, B (2004). Monetary and exchange rate policy in Korea: Assessments and policy issues. *CEPR Discussion Paper*, 4676, October.

Engle, RF (2002). Dynamic conditional correlation: A simple class of multivariate generalized autoregressive conditional heteroskedasticity models. *Journal of Business and Economic Statistics*, 20, 339–350.

Fane, G (2005). Post-crisis monetary and exchange rate policies in Indonesia, Malaysia and Thailand. *Bulletin of Indonesian Economic Studies*, 41, 175–195.

Flood, RP and AK Rose (2010). Inflation targeting and business cycle synchronization. *Journal of International Money and Finance*, 29, 704–727.

Grenville, S and T Ito (2010). An Independent Evaluation of the Bank of Thailand's Monetary Policy under the Inflation Targeting Framework, 2000–2010. The website of the Bank of Thailand. Available at http://www.bot.or.th/Thai/MonetaryPolicy/Documents/GrenvilleItoV10(Oct22).pdf.

Hoffmaister, AW (2001). Inflation targeting in Korea: An empirical exploration. IMF Staff Papers, 48.

International Monetary Fund (IMF) (2011). International Financial Statistics. November, IMF, Washington D.C.

Ito, T and T Hayashi (2004). Inflation targeting in Asia. *HKIMR Occasional Paper*, 1, March.

James, GA (2005). Money demand and financial liberalization in Indonesia. *Journal of Asian Economics*, 16, 817–829.

Kim, S and YC Park (2006). Inflation targeting in Korea: A model of success? *BIS Papers*, 31, pp. 140–164.

Kubo, A (2009). Monetary targeting and inflation: Evidence from Indonesia's post-crisis experience. *Economics Bulletin*, 29, 1805–1813.

Levin, AT, FM Natalucci and JM Piger (2004). The macroeconomic effects of inflation targeting. *Federal Reserve Bank of St. Louis Review*, 86, 51–81.

Lim, J (2008). Central banking in the Philippines: From inflation targeting to financing development. *International Review of Applied Economics*, 22, 271–285.

Mariano, RS and DP Villanueva (2006). Monetary policy approaches and implementation in Asia: The Philippines and Indonesia. *BIS Papers*, 31, pp. 207–226.

McCauley, RN (2006). Understanding monetary policy in Malaysia and Thailand: Objectives, instruments and independence. *BIS Papers*, 31, pp. 172–198.

McLeod, RH (1997). Survey of recent developments. *Bulletin of Indonesian Economic Studies*, 33, 3–43.

Mishkin, FS and K Schmidt-Hebbel (2007). Does inflation targeting make a difference? *NBER Working Paper Series*, 12876.

Mohanty, MS and M Klau (2004). Monetary policy rules in emerging market economies: Issues and evidence. *BIS Working Paper*, 149.

Narayan, PK (2007). Is monetary targeting an option for Bank Indonesia? *Journal of Asian Economics*, 18, 726–738.

Neumann, MJM and J von Hagen (2002). Does inflation targeting matter? *Federal Reserve Bank of St. Louis Review*, 127–148.

Payne, JE (2009). Inflation targeting and the inflation-inflation uncertainty relationship: Evidence from Thailand. *Applied Economics Letters*, 16, 233–238.

Pétursson, TG (2004). The effect of inflation targeting on macroeconomic performance. *Working Paper*, 23, Central Bank of Iceland, Reykjavik.

Phuvanatnaranubala, T (2005). Globalisation, financial markets and the operation of monetary policy: The case of Thailand. *BIS Papers*, 23, pp. 269–274.

Prasertnukul, W, D Kim and M Kakinata (2010). Exchange rates, price levels, and inflation targeting: Evidence from Asian countries. *Japan and the World Economy*, 22, 173–182.

Salas, JMIS (2006). The BSP's monetary policy reaction function from 1992 to 2003. *Philippine Review of Economics*, 43, 23–48.

Sánchez, M (2010). What does South Korean inflation targeting target? *Journal of Asian Economics*, 21, 526–539.

Santiprabhob, V (2001). Bank of Thailand's inflation targeting: Recent performance and future challenges. BOT Symposium 2001, SP/06/2001.

Siregar, RY and S Goo (2010). Effectiveness and commitment to inflation targeting policy: Evidence from Indonesia and Thailand. *Journal of Asian Economics*, 21, 113–128.

Taniguchi, H and C Kato (2011). Assessing the performance of inflation targeting in East Asian economies. *Asian-Pacific Economic Literature*, 25, 93–102.

CHAPTER 6

GLOBALIZATION AND ECONOMIC GROWTH IN EAST ASIA

Fengbao Yin

Graduate School of Economics, Kobe University
2-1, Rokkodai, Nada-Ku, Kobe 657-8501, Japan
hemuxiao@hotmail.com

Shigeyuki Hamori

Faculty of Economics, Kobe University
2-1, Rokkodai, Nada-Ku, Kobe 657-8501, Japan
hamori@econ.kobe-u.ac.jp

1. Introduction

The simultaneous progress of globalization and regionalization marks a characteristic feature of the global economy in recent years. The systemic framework supporting globalization has changed from the General Agreement on Tariffs and Trade (GATT) to the World Trade Organization (WTO). However, the excessive expansion of the WTO (157 countries) has stymied its ability to form a consensus and left the organization at an impasse. Promoting the liberalization of foreign trade and investment is not easy amid efforts to coordinate the intricate intertwinement of member countries' national interests by multilateral negotiations. Disappointment and disgust with WTO negotiations has been tipping the scale strongly in favor of Free Trade Areas or Free Trade Agreements (FTA) established bilaterally between countries. Amid progressing globalization, the trend today is towards regionalism, of which East Asia can be regarded as a typical example.[1]

Beginning in the 1950s, economic growth in East Asian countries started with the establishment of nation states accompanied by the building of national economies. From the 1980s, liberalization was promoted both for trading in merchandise and for financial transactions with a view to further accelerating economic growth. In other words, countries actively took steps to open themselves to capitalism by going global. Multinational corporations, such as those in Japan, introduced mass production competition in East Asia, beginning in the mid-1980s. This competition resulted in organic linkages between production bases that were previously scattered across East Asia. The resulting strengthening of mutual interdependence brought about independent development mechanisms in the region that were not prone to the influence of trends in countries outside the region. In particular, after the Asian currency and financial crisis at the end of the 1990s, East Asian countries hit by the crisis found they were not getting the help they had anticipated from countries outside the region. They realized that intra-regional cooperation, such as FTAs, was necessary if a recurrence of the crisis was to be prevented. This realization was the event that brought East Asia's regionalization to light.

The strongest criticism leveled at regionalism is that it supports inward-turned, closed-off regional blocks, and so threatens to obstruct global liberalization. However, East Asia's regionalism has been propelled by the creation of stabilization measures in the face of economic uncertainty brought about by globalization, which differs from the exclusive economic blocks of the 1930s.

Ultimately, the emergence of regionalism is a stopgap measure to fill a void in the absence of prospects for quick global liberalization through the WTO. Indeed, one could say that the global economy today is running on the two wheels of multilateralism's international trade liberalization negotiations centered on the WTO and economic cooperation based on the regionalism between multiple countries.

---

[1] In this chapter, East Asia means the region comprised of Northeast Asia, consisting mainly of China, Japan and South Korea, and Southeast Asia, which is also referred to as ASEAN (Association of Southeast Asian Nations) region. For the purposes of the analysis, however, the scope of subject countries may be changed as necessary for the analysis.

This chapter, which concerns itself with the effects of globalization on East Asia, attempts empirical research mainly of internationalisation intertwining with globalization and regionalization in East Asia. The chapter starts with a review of East Asia's economic integration over time, before explaining the performance of globalization in East Asia using globalization indicators. Finally, the chapter concludes with an empirical analysis of the effects of globalization on East Asia, both before and after the Asian currency crisis. The objective of this chapter is to establish the true shape of the unique frameworks created in East Asia, which has benefited tremendously from the wave of globalization.

2. The Formation of the East Asian Economic Sphere

This section argues that, while East Asian countries are diverse, the region's remarkable economic growth has been associated with increasingly close trade relationships between countries, a strengthening of mutual dependence. With reference to statistical data related to the "*de facto* integration*" among East Asian countries, the following explanation focuses on the economic development behind this expansion of foreign trade and the factors promoting economic integration.

2.1. Diversity in East Asia

East Asia consists of numerous countries and regions, diverse in terms of ethnicities, languages and religions. Mutual differences also exist between the region's countries with respect to social and political systems, with wide disparities in land areas, population sizes and levels of economic development. Table 1 shows key economic indicators for 15 countries and regions. The data is from 2010, the most recent available.

The East Asia region comprises a mixture of economies at various stages of development. A comparison of GDP, for example, shows extreme economic disparities, on the basis of volume, between China and Laos, and on a per-capita basis between Japan and Myanmar. However, it is because of these economic disparities and economic complementary relations between the member countries that the region's foreign trade and international investment are flourishing. The two columns on the right side of Table 1 show the real economic growth rates before and after the Asian currency crisis. As can be seen from the table, East Asian countries and regions after the crisis display high economic growth rates in instances

Table 1. Key economic indicators for countries and regions in East Asia (2010).

	Land area (1,000 sq. km)	Population (million)	GDP (U.S. $, billion)	GDP per capita (U.S. $)	Total trade (U.S. $, billion)	Economic growth rate (real, annual %)	
						1985–1996	1997–2008
Japan	364.60	127.45	5458.84	42831.05	1598.67	3.05	0.94
South Korea	98.73	48.86	1014.48	20756.69	1034.71	8.56	4.12
China	9572.90	1338.30	5926.61	4428.46	3246.01	10.04	9.90
(Hong Kong)	1.04	7.07	224.46	31757.81	988.31	6.26	3.65
(Taiwan)	36.19	23.14	430.84	18618.64	525.84	7.81	4.11
Indonesia	1811.57	294.56	706.56	2945.58	336.25	7.51	2.95
Malaysia	328.55	28.40	237.80	8372.83	420.42	8.32	4.33
Philippines	298.17	93.26	199.59	2140.12	142.55	3.66	4.16
Thailand	510.89	69.12	318.52	4608.10	430.45	9.13	3.24
Singapore	0.70	5.08	208.77	41122.19	822.68	8.51	5.05
Brunei	5.27	0.40	14.39*	37414.31*	15.24*	1.71	1.65
Vietnam	310.07	86.94	106.42	1224.19	175.96	6.74	7.07
Lao PDR	230.80	6.20	7.30	1176.66	56.34	5.39	6.53
Cambodia	176.52	14.14	11.24	795.17	12.77	—	9.08
Myanmar	667.58	61.19	45.43	742.44	16.00	2.14	12.22

Note: The data for China's land area is from the Encyclopedia Britannica; * denotes data of 2008.
Source: WDI (2011); Taiwan data from ADB (2011); Myanmar data IMF (2011).

where economic expansion has started comparatively late, such as Vietnam. Comprised as it is of a diversity of countries and regions, East Asia provides various location advantages, a unique characteristic in the context of the region's rapid economic development.

2.2. De facto economic integration

Despite the diversity in the relations among East Asian countries in terms of economic disparity, depth of historical interaction, and differences in social and political systems, regional integration is progressing in East Asia in step with the strengthening global trend towards regional economic integration. To date, through foreign trade and investment, East Asia has been building relations of intra-regional mutual dependency. Basic statistics are provided by foreign trade matrices that track the changes in the flow of foreign trade between countries over time. These statistics can be used to measure the strengthening of mutual dependencies in foreign trade among East Asian countries.

East Asian countries' strong growth is reflected in their foreign trade statistics. Table 2 provides a comprehensive foreign trade matrix for regions and countries in East Asia. This matrix includes statistics for the three central economies in East Asia (China, Japan and ASEAN[2]) as well as the United States, as the country with the strongest influence in the Asia Pacific region. This data casts into relief East Asia's characteristic features in global foreign trade over the last 25 years.

Table 2 also shows period-to-period growth rates in foreign trade between pairs of referenced economic entities. The values for 1985 were selected for this data set because 1985 marks the year of the Plaza Accord, which had a massive impact on the structure of global trade. The Asian currency crisis occurred in 1997, so the figures are split into two periods around this point. The purpose of this demarcation is to demonstrate regions' and countries' foreign trade performance before and after the Asian currency crisis.

Table 3 compares the size of East Asia's foreign trade (total value of foreign trade and intra-regional foreign trade ratios) with that of two big groups, namely NAFTA and the EU.

---

[2] As a result of large economic disparities, the combination of Indonesia, Malaysia, Philippines, Singapore and Thailand is generally called ASEAN-5, while ASEAN overall is referred to as ASEAN-10.

Table 2. Matrix of East-Asia centered regional foreign trade and its growth rates (Units: U.S. $, million; percent).

Exporting from		China	Japan	Export to ASEAN-5	East Asia	The United States	World
China	1985	7,148	6,091	2,804	16,043	2,336	27,329
	96/85	4.99	5.07	3.15	5.17	**11.44**	5.53
	1996	35,658	30,888	8,830	82,903	26,731	151,165
	10/96	6.95	3.89	**15.66**	6.97	**10.61**	**10.45**
	2010	247,994	120,262	138,236*	577,866	283,679	1,580,400
Japan	1985	12,590		11,261	42,551	66,684	177,189
	96/85	1.73		6.38	4.07	1.70	2.32
	1996	21,827		71,898	173,201	113,174	411,302
	10/96	6.86		1.57	2.39	1.06	1.88
	2010	149,626		112,868*	413,970	120,483	771,720
ASEAN-5	1985	930	16,351	12,937	36,030	13,900	68,553
	96/85	10.25	2.85	5.87	4.83	4.40	4.81
	1996	9,531	46,677	75,992	174,191	61,100	329,499
	10/96	14.56	2.19	3.54	3.75	1.74	3.32
(ASEAN-10)	2010	138,791*	102,364*	268,852*	653,459*	106,177*	1,094,542*

(*Continued*)

Table 2. (*Continued*)

Exporting from		China	Japan	ASEAN-5	East Asia	The United States	World
							Export to
East Asia	1985	21,377	31,722	32,287	122,385	117,757	364,210
	96/85	4.93	3.75	6.23	5.22	2.45	3.64
	1996	105,338	118,820	201,090	638,695	288,164	1,325,848
	10/96	6.57	2.37	3.17	3.61	2.18	3.44
	2010	692,300	282,113	636,540*	2,308,524	629,518	4,560,641
United States	1985	3,856	22,631	8,039	47,511		213,146
	96/85	3.11	2.98	5.29	3.80		2.92
	1996	11,978	67,536	42,508	180,535		622,949
	10/96	7.67	1.08	1.66	1.72		2.05
	2010	91,878	72,645	70,434*	311,139		1,277,630
World	1985	38,189	110,199	58,797	276,070	327,543	1,874,100
	96/85	4.09	2.85	5.72	4.34	2.43	2.83
	1996	156,201	313,533	336,386	1,196,774	794,753	5,300,740
	10/96	8.17	1.97	2.81	3.28	2.24	2.83
	2010	1,275,590	617,694	944,196*	3,928,334	1,779,810	14,994,300

Notes: (1) The value of China's foreign trade with China refers to trade by mainland China with Taiwan and Hong Kong; exports by countries and regions to Taiwan reflect the values of Taiwanese import statistics (CIF base) converted to an FOB base by multiplying by 0.9; an asterisk designates ASEAN-10 values. (2) East Asia comprises China, Japan, South Korea, Hong Kong, Taiwan and ASEAN-5 (values for 2010 are for ASEAN-10, comprising ASEAN-5, Brunei, Vietnam, Lao PDR, Cambodia and Myanmar).
Source: Compiled from IMF Direction of Trade Statistics Yearbooks and Taiwan Trade Statistics.

Table 3. Comparison of the foreign trade volumes of East Asia, NAFTA and EU.

		Northeast Asia	ASEAN	East Asia	NAFTA	EU
Total trade	1985	513	127	640	740	1,444
(billion U.S. $)	1996	1,857	666	2,523	1,959	4,222
	2010	6,450	2,039	8,489	4,381	10,210
Intra-regional	1985	26.13	20.32	38.23	38.70	59.84
trade ratio	1996	36.56	22.82	50.64	44.71	67.01
(%)	2008	37.75	27.06	52.51	49.47	65.93
	2010	40.29	26.37	54.39	42.84	65.64

Notes: (1) ASEAN data reflect ASEAN-10 for 2008 and 2010, and ASEAN-5 for other years; EU data reflect EU27 for 2008 and 2010, and EU25 for other years.

(2) Northeast Asia is comprised of China, Japan, South Korea, Taiwan and Hong Kong. NAFTA is comprised of the United States, Canada and Mexico.

(3) Countries' exports to Taiwan have been converted to FOB by multiplying the values of the Taiwanese import statistics (CIF base) by 0.9.

Source: Compiled from IMF Direction of Trade Statistics Yearbooks and statistics by Department of Statistics, Ministry of Finance, Taiwan.

In terms of trade volume, in 1985, East Asia and NAFTA were not that different, both being around U.S. $0.7 trillion, while the gap between East Asia and the EU was roughly twice as large, at around U.S. $1.444 trillion. Thanks to the rapid growth in intra-regional foreign trade, by 1996, the difference between East Asia and North America had already inverted, and subsequently continued to widen. By 2010, the gap was 1.94 times that between East Asia and NAFTA and 0.83 times the gap between East Asia and the EU.

With regards to the intra-regional foreign trade ratio in East Asia, the following points are worth noting. The East Asian intra-regional foreign trade ratio rose from 38.2% in 1985 to 54.4% in 2010. This number is less than the 65.6% intra-regional foreign trade ratio for the EU, but far higher than NAFTA's ratio of 42.8%. Moreover, Table 3 shows the characteristic trend of strengthening intra-regional mutual relations in East Asia. First, if East Asia is divided into sub-regions of Northeast Asia and ASEAN, each of the sub-regional internal trade ratios falls short of East Asia as a whole. This observation applies at all points in time. What this point demonstrates

Table 4. Bilateral export intensity in East Asia by country and region.

Export destination	Import destination	Japan		China		Japan, China, and South Korea		ASEAN-10	
		1996	2010	1996	2010	1996	2010	1996	2010
Japan				1.79	2.34	1.09	1.82	2.64	2.32
China		3.42	1.84			2.23	0.79	1.01	1.39
South Korea		2.05	1.45	2.96	3.00	1.85	2.04	2.29	1.79
ASEAN-5		2.37	2.30	0.97	1.32	1.81	1.63	3.63	4.08
	Indonesia	4.32	3.95	1.39	1.20	3.21	2.27	2.28	3.35
	Malaysia	2.25	2.51	0.81	1.52	1.66	1.77	4.22	4.03
	Philippines	2.99	3.66	0.54	1.33	1.87	2.02	1.94	3.37
	Singapore	1.37	1.12	0.91	1.25	1.29	1.26	3.06	4.78
	Thailand	2.82	2.53	1.13	1.33	1.93	1.54	3.63	3.60

Source: Calculated based on IMF Direction of Trade Statistics 1997, 2011.

is that the geographic region of East Asia, as the combination of ASEAN, Japan, China, South Korea, Hong Kong and Taiwan, is able to form a territory that provides a single, large expanse for economic activity. This is highly meaningful for today's foreign trade with its emphasis on economies of scale. Second, after two crises (the Asian currency and economic crisis of 1997 and the global financial crisis of 2008), only East Asia displays stable increases in its intra-regional foreign trade ratio. The NAFTA intra-regional foreign trade ratio declined after 2008, and that of the EU fell on both occasions.

Both the EU and NAFTA are subject to regional governance with binding legal effects, while East Asia has no regulations for regional integration other than the loose ASEAN framework. In this sense, the high economic mutual dependence among East Asian countries has been referred to as "*de facto* integration" (Hiratsuka, 2006).

Lastly, this section concludes with an analysis of the degree of foreign trade linkage for East Asia overall using the Trade Intensity Index. The bilateral export intensity is an indicator of bias in the foreign trade relations between two countries. Indicator readings of 1 or higher point to a close foreign trade relationship between two countries.[3]

Table 4 reveals that, overall, the values for the bilateral export intensity between two countries or regions in East Asia are often 1 or higher. These values show that the region's growing foreign trade is raising intraregional mutual interdependence and points to an ongoing formation of close, independent economic networks. In particular, the markets of China and ASEAN-10 are becoming more important to East Asian countries and regions. Moreover, each country shows strong ties with ASEAN-10. Of these, Singapore is most integrated with ASEAN-10 (4.78) and has established a central position in the ASEAN region.

2.3. Formation factors

There are various factors promoting economic integration in East Asia. The following sections discuss the most significant of these, in particular, the Plaza Accord, the Asian currency crisis, the two organizations of ASEAN and APEC, and the emergence of China.

2.3.1. The Plaza Accord

In the context of the regionalization of East Asia, the 1985 Plaza Accord was a formative event.[4]

The Plaza Accord provided the strongest momentum for the strategy of export-oriented industrialization (EOI) that was widely adopted across the East Asia region. In the mid 1980s, the group of countries at the time referred to as newly industrialized countries (NICs)[5] was in the so-called

---

[3] The bilateral export intensity is calculated according to the following formula: Bilateral export intensity = (Value of exports from Country i to Country j/Total value of exports of Country i)/(Value of global exports to Country j/Value of global exports). (Hirakawa *et al.*, 2007, p. 227)

[4] On September 22, 1985, the Group of Five (G5: U.S., Japan, Germany, U.K. and France) finance ministers and central bank governors held a meeting at the Plaza Hotel in New York and agreed to depreciate the U.S. dollar in a concerted action of the five countries.

[5] In this chapter, both NICs and NIEs (Newly Industrializing Economies) refer to the same four Asian countries and regions (South Korea, Singapore, Taiwan and Hong Kong).

"easy stage" after promoting industrialization. However, they were suffering under an economic recession due to the narrowness of their domestic markets. To exit from the recession, the NICs shifted from their previous strategies of foreign capital control and import substitution industrialization (ISI) to an EOI strategy.

Acting in concert with East Asia's shift to an EOI strategy, Japanese industry also shifted its focus to EOI investment. The impetus for this development was provided by the Plaza Accord of September 1985. Spurred into action by the rapid yen appreciation caused by the Plaza Accord, combined with a serious labor shortage, Japanese industry shifted domestic production bases to locations in the NICs and ASEAN-5, associated with a rapid proliferation of overseas business initiatives.

Prompted by the same motives, multinational corporations of the NICs also started to invest in ASEAN-5. These, in turn, achieved rapid industrialization due in large part to the investments made by multinational corporations. Moreover, after the Asian currency crisis, this circle widened to include China. Under its policy of "Reform and Opening" in the 1980s, China advanced towards a market economy regime, as well as being late starters among the ASEAN countries. The result was an unparalleled series of economic successes across a wide region. This industrial transition process is also referred to as the "Flying-Geese Pattern of Development".[6]

In this way, the broad-based and sustained move to East Asia made after th Plaza Accord by Japanese multinational corporations significantly contributed to rendering the region a part of the tripartite global economy alongside the EU and NAFTA.

2.3.2. The Asian currency crisis

The 1997 Asian currency crisis came as a serious blow to the growing East Asian economy. Under the impact, most countries in East Asia in 1998 posted negative real GDP growth rates. For example, Indonesia and Thailand show a decline of 13.1% and 10.5%, respectively. Various lessons can be drawn from the Asian currency crisis.

---

[6]The Flying Geese Theory refers to an empirical law discovered by Kaname Akamatsu through statistical research that describes the catch-up industrialization pattern that is typical of late industrializing countries.

Weak economies were obviously a factor in the crisis, and indiscriminate financial liberalization threatening the supply of short-term funds was driving Asian economies to the brink. However, in the context of globalization, international institutions such as the IMF and GATT, created as structural elements of the Pax Americana, had especially promoted the process of financial liberalization. Consequently, much criticism has been leveled at the United States and international institutions, particularly the IMF. For example, according to J. E. Stiglitz, the 2001 Nobel Prize laureate for economics, the prime factor causing the currency crisis in East Asia was the coerced economic reform by the IMF and the U.S. Department of the Treasury, enforced as aggressive unilateralism against East Asia to advance U.S. interests. Stiglitz points out that already from the end of the 1980s until the start of the 1990s, the countries of East Asia were under pressure to fully liberalize capital (Stiglitz, 2002).

Occasioned by the Asian currency crisis, drastic changes occurred in the region. Here, the United States presented itself as uncooperative in providing funds to Asia and hostile to the creation of an Asian Monetary Fund (AMF). The IMF's faulty remedies as the crisis broke and the stance of the United States engendered distrust, connected to the realization that East Asia needed intra-regional economic cooperation. From this insight sprang the move for a regionalism straddling country-specific frameworks. Initially, in the field of economics, the commercial relations between East Asian countries broadened. As a conspicuous development, trade and investment increased between the East Asian economies (Japan, South Korea and ASEAN) and China. Symbolic of this development is China's ascent in 2004 to the position of Japan's biggest partner in foreign trade. Beginning in the mid 1990s, conferences started to be held involving ASEAN, China, Japan and South Korea, with a diversity of cooperative efforts getting under way. The intention of these conferences, referred to as ASEAN+3 (ASEAN plus Japan, China and South Korea), is generally understood to be the promotion of cooperation in the East Asia region, given that member countries are East Asian. Another very notable development in East Asia after the Asian economic crisis is regionalism's remarkable rise to prominence, typically in the form of FTAs.

2.3.3. APEC and ASEAN

Currently, a number of layering frameworks exist for the Asia Pacific region. Among them, APEC and ASEAN form two important organizations for the economic integration of East Asia.

Until the inception of APEC in 1989, ASEAN was the only organization that had signed treaties with nations in the Asia Pacific region.[7,8] APEC was not originally welcomed by ASEAN amid open concerns that ASEAN's position and role might be diminished by being imbedded into APEC. Although key members of ASEAN belong also to APEC, the antagonism between ASEAN and APEC began from the inception of APEC as members engaged in efforts to maximize their national interest.

Beginning with the 5th APEC Ministerial Meeting in Seattle, a powerful U.S. initiative has rapidly been gathering information for an economic cooperative organization for the Asia Pacific region, to the extent that at the 6th APEC Ministerial Meeting in 1994, the Bogor Declaration provided for the fully industrialized countries to liberalize their foreign trade and investment by 2010, with industrializing countries to follow suit by 2020. The formation of the ASEAN Free Trade Area (AFTA), by ASEAN in a bid to accelerate intra-regional economic cooperation, must be seen as an expression of opposition to APEC and a reflection of fear of its possible merger into APEC.

Moreover, additional players among the many economic frameworks existing in the Asia Pacific region and concepts under research or under negotiation are the ASEAN Free Trade Area (AFTA), East Asia Free Trade Area (EAFTA), and the Comprehensive Economic Partnership in East Asia (CEPEA), centered around ASEAN,[9] and the North American

---

[7] ASEAN was incepted on August 8, 1967, in Bangkok, Thailand. The original five member countries were Thailand, Malaysia, Singapore, Indonesia and the Philippines (ASEAN-5). These were subsequently joined by Brunei (January 8, 1984), Vietnam (July 28, 1995), Lao PDR and Myanmar (July 23, 1997), and Cambodia (April 30, 1994) to form ASEAN-10, marking the formation of a regional body that covered all of Southeast Asia.

[8] APEC is short for Asia-Pacific Economic Cooperation. Proposed by Australia's then-Prime Minister, Bob Hawke, APEC's first Ministerial Meeting took place in November 1989 in Canberra. Although it was established after ASEAN, APEC is significantly larger, currently with 21 members. APEC has two main purposes: the liberalization of foreign trade and investment, and economic cooperation.

[9] The idea of a greater East Asian economic sphere is being contemplated in dual track with EAFTA, guided by China and South Korea, and CEPEA, proposed by Japan, but ASEAN holds the key to whether these two concepts will be referred to official inter-governmental negotiations. The former consists of ASEAN+3 and the latter of ASEAN+6.

Free Trade Agreement (NAFTA) and the Trans-Pacific Partnership (TPP) centered around the United States.

By its nature, APEC is not so much a regional as a trans-regional body whose charge is limited to reflecting the voice of East Asia (Ravenhill, 2000). ASEAN, by contrast, bringing to bear its special geo-political nature, even though it is an association of countries much smaller than Japan and China, stresses compliance with ASEAN's leadership position in promoting cooperation in East Asia. ASEAN, hit hard by the Asian currency crisis, resurged on the merits of building the ASEAN+10 country-to-country network and rose again to a central position in the network of Asian (Pacific) nations. (See the next section).

2.3.4. China's ascent to prominence

Along with progressing globalization, China's economy grew dramatically. Based on 2010 data, China accounts for 9.4% of global GDP, 9.3% of global exports (global No. 1), and 8.2% of global imports (global No. 2). China's foreign currency reserves at the end of March 2006 totaled U.S. $853.7 billion, overtaking Japan and marking the global top rank, and as of end-March 2011, for the first time exceeded U.S. $3 trillion.

China, an exception to the Kuznets proposition, is a country with a high degree of external exposure.[10] Since the establishment in 1992 of China's strategy of an export-driven economy, China's export industry has been propelling the country's strong growth. In 2009, China outpaced Germany in exports and rose to the top of the global rankings. China's exports have attracted and enlarged imports, especially from East Asian countries. However, although China is able to sustain a one-country production structure based on low-tech products, it needs intermediate materials and technologies from East Asian countries for products that are based on mid-range and advanced technologies. The expansion of foreign trade between East Asia and neighboring China

---

[10] An empirical law of the Kuznets proposition postulates that, between two countries, a lower degree of external economic dependency attaches to the one with the larger economy and population. In global economic history, only China does not conform to this law. Since the start of the 1990s, China's degree of foreign trade dependency has for the most part been fluctuating in the 30–40% band. In 2000 and 2001, it exceeded 40% and in 2003, China's degree of foreign trade dependency reached 60%.

reinforced the ripple effects on intra-regional foreign trade in East Asia. In other words, China's proliferating shipments of products to the world have spurred the globalization of the East Asian economy, while the growth in imports of intermediate materials and components from intra-regional suppliers necessary for China's manufacturing has promoted regionalization, thus involving forces that operate in two different directions. In this sense, China works like a magnet for East Asian intra-regional foreign trade.

Moreover, along with its economic development, China has been taking pains to meet its responsibilities as a major economic force. This was particularly true during the two economic crises, when China's performance was conspicuous. In 1998, China's government kept the USD/CNY exchange rate steady to mitigate the ill effects of the Asian currency crisis. In the interim, China-bound exports from ASEAN-5 countries were rising in volume, while China's exports suffered. Subsequently, in stark contrast to the theory of a threatening China, in truth, China's production and foreign trade expansion have contributed much to broadening East Asia's international division of labor. Moreover, after the global financial crisis, real global economic growth in 2009 turned negative at a rate of 2.0%, with a particularly steep fall of 4.3% in the emerging economies. Meanwhile, East Asia has been seen to post robust growth at a pace of 9.2%, driven by the Chinese economy. In the short term, China may be regarded as the engine of growth not only of East Asia but also of the global economy.

3. The Globalization of East Asia

The previous section demonstrated that East Asia forms a single economic entity marked by *de facto* economic integration. The following section will consider the process of the region's globalization.

3.1. The KOF index of globalization

Properly defining globalization is not without its problems. Measuring globalization is prone to entail yet more problems. A quantification of the degree of globalization by country was prepared by Dreher at the KOF Swiss Economic Institute. He based his quantification on 23 items in the three main dimensions of globalization, as defined by Keohane and Nye, namely the economic, social and political dimensions (Dreher, 2006, p. 1092).[11] The economic sub-index is measured using actual economic flows, such as foreign trade and foreign direct investment, with added economic restrictions put on metrics, such as imports and capital balance. The social sub-index is built from trilateral data related to personal contacts, information flows and culture proximity. The political sub-index is computed using data such as the number of international organization memberships as proxy variables. Sub-indices are constructed in a way such that the items associated with each dimension are converted based on a scale from zero to ten according to the method used by Gwartney and Lawson (2002), whereupon the respective weights are aggregated. Then the indices of economic, social and political globalization are combined into a single index of overall globalization, providing the respective weight for each dimension. The single index is named after the KOF index of Globalization. The KOF index takes values between 0 and 100, with higher values representing stronger globalization.

3.2. The globalization of East Asia based on the KOF index

This section starts with a look at the evolvement of East Asia's globalization gleaned directly from the data charts. Figure 1 shows the development of globalization as measured by KOF indices for the period from 1970 until 2008 for global regions and for the global average. From the data, it is apparent that, as compared to other regions, Europe is leading by far in the development of globalization. Specifically, globalization has continued to deepen after the transformation from EC to EU provided under the Maastricht Treaty (ratified in 1991 and put into effect in 1993).

In Asia, by comparison, the globalization of East Asia has been progressing steadily since 1970. After outpacing North America in the 1980s, beginning in the mid-1990s, the globalization of East Asia rapidly approached that of Europe. However, this vigor later weakened and globalization fell below that of Europe. These developments respectively reflect the impact of the 1985 Plaza Accord and the 1997 Asian currency and financial crisis mentioned in the previous section. Although both

---

[11] We use the 2011 version of this index as documented in Dreher et al. (2008) which is available at http://globalization.kof.ethz.ch/.

events had positive effects on the regional integration of East Asia, the crisis of 1997 was clearly a hindrance to globalization in East Asia.

Table 5 shows the results for the 2008 indices as well as the overall index for 1970 and the changes between 1970 and 2008. In 2008, of 186 countries, the top three positions were held by EU members. Belgium scores highest at 92.60 points. In contrast, the United States retreated to the 27th rank from the top position it held in 2000. ASEAN member Myanmar marked the bottom at just 22.72 points. Moreover, ASEAN member Singapore scored highest in Asia with the 18th rank on the global scale. This result reflects Singapore's high score for economic integration, which is leading other countries. Notably, despite their 2nd and 3rd ranks in global economic volume, Japan and China ranked 44th and 73rd, respectively, in the summary ratings because of their backwardness in opening their economies. China displays the fastest rise for the 1970–2008 period, with an increase of 42.42 points from 18.57 points in 1970 to 60.99 points in 2008.

3.3. *Advance of globalization by country and region*

The following section discusses the development of globalization (especially economic globalization) in East Asia by individual country and region, divided into Japan, China, South Korea and ASEAN.

3.3.1. *Japan*

Since joining GATT in 1955, Japan's government has given little attention to bilateral negotiations and not participated in regional free trade treaties (FTAs and customs unions). Instead they have favored multilateralism centered on maintaining and strengthening the multilateral foreign trade systems provided by GATT and its successor organization, WTO.

Into the 1970s, Japan initiated full-scale direct foreign investment (DFI) activities. However, DFI into East Asia was meant to secure natural resources. Beginning in the mid-1980s, intra-regional transactions in East Asia began to proliferate as Japanese corporations set up overseas bases in the region. This development needs some explaining. The background was provided by severe trade friction with the United States. Subsequently, the 1985 Plaza Accord occasioned a period of explosive growth in direct foreign investment by Japanese corporations.

Table 5. Ratings of globalization (2008).

	Economic integration		Social integration		Political integration		Summary rating		
	2008		2008		2008		1970	2008	1970–2008
1. Belgium	90.95	(5)	90.43	(3)	98.13	(3)	70.71	92.60	21.86
2. Austria	87.58	(12)	91.74	(2)	97.37	(4)	55.89	91.67	35.78
3. Netherlands	90.72	(6)	88.91	(5)	95.11	(7)	67.30	91.17	23.87
18. Singapore	96.80	(1)	78.81	(22)	75.05	(77)	59.67	84.39	24.72
27. United states	71.64	(50)	78.36	(25)	93.60	(15)	61.60	79.84	18.24
37. Malaysia	73.80	(43)	65.05	(58)	85.91	(45)	40.87	73.22	32.35
44. Japan	57.71	(92)	66.90	(48)	88.60	(34)	36.92	69.14	32.22
54. South Korea	61.59	(79)	53.38	(86)	89.17	(32)	27.06	65.57	38.51
60. Thailand	67.05	(60)	49.06	(104)	81.58	(59)	26.64	63.97	37.33
73. China	50.88	(103)	53.28	(89)	86.65	(41)	18.57	60.99	42.42
84. Indonesia	61.73	(77)	32.61	(145)	87.11	(39)	23.12	57.23	34.11
85. Philippines	53.49	(98)	41.55	(129)	85.56	(50)	27.76	57.22	29.46
184. Kiribati			30.43	(153)	21.67	(188)	35.91	26.89	–9.02
185. Solomon Islands			24.29	(177)	27.91	(181)	24.14	25.75	1.61
186. Myanmar			14.02	(197)	35.53	(169)	4.07	22.72	18.65

Note: The countries are ranked according to their overall index scores in 2008. Numbers in parentheses signify global rankings.
Source: Compiled by the author using 2011 KOF Index of Globalization data.

In 1998–1999, Japan's stance on trade changed to a multilateral trade strategy that sought to promote FTAs in addition to the previous multilateralism, which was driving foreign trade liberalization through multilateral negotiations at GATT and the WTO.[12] The first FTA negotiation counterpart was Singapore.[13] In December 1999, following Singapore's proposals at a meeting of government leaders in Singapore, it was agreed to set up a joint study group. In September 2000, the study group issued a report that led to the commencement of negotiations in January 2001 and to an actual agreement in October 2001. In January 2002, an Economic Partnership Agreement (EPA) was concluded with Singapore, which took effect in November 2002. After the conclusion of the Japan–Singapore Economic Partnership Agreement, amid widening activities to engage in economic cooperation centered on ASEAN, Japan too began to take active steps towards establishing economic cooperative agreements, including FTAs, with countries in East Asia. In addition to a general global trend towards FTAs, the background to this development was provided by the fact that Japan was unilaterally raising its dependence on East Asia.

To date, however, the predominant view is that Japan's agricultural sector is a major obstacle to Japan's FTA strategy. Given Japan's difficult bargaining position surrounding agricultural products, trade-offs that Japan finds acceptable will have to be re-defined and strategies re-formulated. At the end of 2011, Japan's Prime Minister Noda announced plans to participate in negotiations to allow Japan to participate in the Trans-Pacific Partnership. With sweeping tariff reductions on agricultural products now unavoidable, Japan is under acute pressure to reform its agricultural sector.

3.3.2. South Korea

South Korea's economic development strategies have been fashioned after their Japanese counterparts. As a result, in the period from 1963 until 1996, South Korea experienced economic success with annual economic growth rates as high as 8.8%, often referred to as South Korea's "Han river

---

[12] Japan's government uses the term economic partnership agreement (EPA) instead of FTA. EPA connotes greater comprehensiveness than FTA.

[13] The earlier conclusion of the Japan–Singapore Economic Partnership Agreement is owing to easier negotiations facilitated by the fact that foreign trade in agricultural products is essentially not included.

economic miracle". The consensus is that, during this period of economic success, South Korea maintained a state-directed economy. Since the 1960s, amid efforts by the South Korean government to promote full-scale export-oriented industries, exports (and later foreign direct investment) of South Korean corporations have been rising. Along with economic development, calls started to be made to open domestic markets and to revaluate the won. Under pressure from its economic partner countries, South Korea submitted to an economic liberalization program designed to establish a market economy. In 1993, South Korea's administration, under Kim Young-sam, initiated financial market liberalization and globalization and accelerated the implementation of liberalization measures to meet the membership requirements in order to acquire OECD membership in 1996.

In the wake of the 1997 financial crisis, South Korea experienced difficulties that it overcame not by closing domestic markets to the outside, but by accelerating its efforts at globalization. South Korea's administration under Kim Dae-jung, which emerged at the end of 1997 amid a worsening currency crisis, implemented four sweeping reform programs (finance, industry, labor and public sector) coerced by the IMF's pressure of conditionality. Under the strong leadership of President Kim Dae-jung, financially weak conglomerates were dismantled, non-performing loans were written off, the financial system was refloated, and solicitation was stepped up to attract foreign capital. As a result, South Korean economic policy shifted from government directives and national interventionalism on a grand scale to a market economy regime.

Moreover, like Japan, South Korea had maintained a government stance that emphasized multilateral foreign trade systems supported by GATT and the WTO. Until the start of the 2000s, South Korea was trailing Japan in its efforts at establishing FTAs, but it stepped up its activities at the beginning of 2003. By 2006, South Korea's negotiations had resulted in agreements with Chile, Singapore and the European Free Trade Association (EFTA), followed by ASEAN, India and the United States.

3.3.3. China

At the Third Plenary Session of the 11th CPC Central Committee in 1978, out of misgivings about the previous system of a centralized planned economy, China embarked on its policy of "Reform and Opening". Subsequently, along with developing a commodity-type market economy, China strengthened its links to international markets.

After the initial stage from the 1980s, Deng Xiaoping, in his "Southern Tour" in 1992, affirmed China's shift to a market economy as well as large-scale foreign investment, marking the full opening of the country to the outside. With 1992 as the watershed, the balance of foreign direct investment (FDI) into ASEAN and China inverted, with the gap continuing to widen thereafter. Using export-oriented foreign capital as leverage, China was able to maintain high economic growth rates over the long term and to further strengthen its position in global foreign trade. Since the start of the 1990s, China has been forming layers of frameworks to open increasingly wider areas to the outside, advancing from special economic zones to the coastal regions and still further to inland regions.

Moreover, with the country's WTO membership in 2001, the gates to China's economy were fully opened to the world. Achieving WTO membership was an epoch-making event. On the one hand, in its foreign trade, investment and service transactions, the step encouraged China's entry to international systems and the acceptance of their rules. On the other hand, it spurred the removal and mitigation of various barriers in China's economic relations, with the possibility of accelerating intra-regional investment and foreign trade. In particular, WTO membership placed China in the same policy environment as ASEAN countries, resulting in the confluence of China's and ASEAN countries' previously distinct production networks to form a large integrated production base covering the whole of East Asia.

Like others, China had been shy of multilateralism, but with the acquisition of ARF membership in 1994, changed its stance to actively pursuing multilateral arrangements. China had previously taken a cautious stance against FTAs, which it perceived as an "anti-regional block", but then changed to a more flexible approach in the face of an accelerating trend among other countries to enter into FTAs. Hence, it was China and not Japan who took the initiative in the creation of East Asia's regionalism. At the ASEAN–China Leaders Summit in 2000, China proposed to establish a working group to explore the possibility of an FTA between ASEAN and China. In 2001, China formally proposed an FTA to ASEAN. And at the ASEAN–China Leaders Summit held in Phnom Penh in November 2002, the China–ASEAN Free Trade Area (CAFTA) was inaugurated as government leaders were calling for the promotion of market integration in foreign trade and investment between ASEAN and China. The FTA between China and ASEAN marked an important step on the way to the integration of East Asian economies, which will likely serve as the foundation for a wider East Asian free trade area in the future.

3.3.4. ASEAN

The intra-regional cooperation among ASEAN countries, which has a history of over 40 years since its launch in the form of the Bangkok Declaration, is frequently cited as a success story of regional economic integration among developing nations. Internally, however, forces have been active within the ASEAN region that is working in two entirely different directions. One is a drive aimed at the independence of the ASEAN region. The other seeks economic integration with regional outsiders, with the ASEAN countries at the center.

In the first nine years after its formation in 1967, ASEAN's intra-regional cooperation underwent certain developments. The first ASEAN Summit in February 1976 marked the effective launch of ASEAN as a regional cooperative institution. The period from the 1970s until the 1980s saw the formation of the Preferential Trading Arrangements (ASEAN PTA, 1977), the ASEAN Industrial Projects (AIP, 1976) and the ASEAN Industrial Complementation (AIC). Coordinating national interests proved difficult, however, and the hoped-for results failed to materialize. Into the 1990s, marking a more auspicious period for economic integration, AFTA, along with the ASEAN Industrial Cooperation (AICO) scheme and the ASEAN Investment (AIA) became a reality.

In particular, the AFTA agreement took ASEAN intra-regional economic cooperation to a new stage. Launched in 1993, AFTA aimed to remove tariffs and non-tariff barriers between member countries and to achieve complete liberalization of intra-regional foreign trade by 2015 with the creation of a free trade zone.[14] The main objective of AFTA is not to raise the intra-regional foreign trade ratio of ASEAN members, but to increase the competitive strength of ASEAN products in global markets. In other words, the main objective of AFTA is to attract FDI from outside

---

[14] In 1992, ASEAN launched AFTA, established the Common Effective Preferential Tariff (CEPT), and for applicable items (Include List, IL) set a zero-tariff goal to be reached by 2015. Subsequently, concurrent with an accelerated tariff reduction, the original members (ASEAN-5 plus Brunei), with some exceptions, lowered intra-regional tariffs to the 0%–5% range by 2002, so that reaching a zero-tariff by 2010 appeared possible. New members were required to lower intra-regional tariffs on CEPT items to 5% or less, with deadlines of 2006 for Vietnam, 2008 for Lao PDR and Myanmar, and 2010 for Cambodia, with a subsequent tariff cut to zero by 2015 (Ishikawa *et al.*, 2010).

the region to boost the competitive strength of products manufactured in ASEAN countries. Imada (1993) assesses AFTA as strongly proactive: "Considering the slow progress made by ASEAN in intra-regional economic cooperation over the last 25 years, AFTA can be credited as a quantum leap on the way to achieving it".

ASEAN has used FTAs as its foreign trade strategy, which it regards as a tool for attracting investment, and since 1993, has pursued a policy of FTA creation centered on East Asia. In 1997, the Hanoi Action Plan was agreed on as a roadmap to "Vision 2020", the future shape of ASEAN, which had ASEAN launch proactive campaigns for FTAs with extra-regional partners such as China and Japan. In addition, the action plan resulted in arrangements by the ASEAN Regional Forum and ASEAN+3, not only in the economic realm, but also in relation to political and national security issues. ASEAN initiatives also reached beyond regional boundaries to establish interaction with Europe. A result was the Asia Europe Meeting (ASEM), which probes for possible new cooperative relations based on an equal partnership between Asia and Europe.

Already before the formation of ASEAN+3, ASEAN had created channels for individual talks with extra-regional countries such as the United States, Australia, Canada, Japan, China and South Korea. In addition, after the creation of ASEAN+3, ASEAN maintained cooperative "ASEAN+1" cooperative frameworks between itself and Japan, China and South Korea. Today, ideas exist, with ASEAN at the core, for the East Asia FTA (EAFTA), comprised of ASEAN plus Japan, China and South Korea, and for the Comprehensive Economic Partnership in East Asia (CEPEA), consisting of ASEAN+3+3, that is, ASEAN plus Japan, China and South Korea, plus India, Australia and New Zealand. These multiple layers of cooperative relationships in East Asia exist because of the pre-existing system of ASEAN regimes and organizations. At present, the channels for talks provided by ASEAN+3 and ASEAN+1 serve as the propellants for promoting cooperation in the East Asia region.

4. The Effects of Globalization on East Asia

The previous section considered the globalization of Asia using the KOF indices. In the global economic terms, the economy of the East Asia region has enjoyed spectacularly high growth rates since the beginning of the 1970s. This section seeks to answer questions as to the magnitude of the benefits reaped from globalization and how the performance of globalization changed before and after the 1997 currency crisis and of the havoc it brought upon the East Asian economy (with the exception of China). The analysis is based on panel data. The data used for the analysis relate to individual East Asian countries for the years from 1985 until 2008.[15] The variables used for the analysis are the KOF overall indices and sub-indices, as well as variables frequently used for growth regression (general government final consumption expenditure; gross capital formation), variables for measuring human capital (school enrollment rate; life expectancy), and proxy variables for economic stability (inflation rate), among others. Table 6 shows the definitions for each variable.

4.1. Empirical analysis before the Asian currency crisis

The analysis starts with an examination of the relation between globalization and per-capita GDP in East Asia using data before the currency crisis for the period from 1985 until 1996. Table 7 shows the empirical results.

Table 7 shows high readings for all coefficients of determination adjusted for degrees-of-freedom, demonstrating a good fit with the model. Moreover, variables' coefficients are without exception significant at a significance level of 1%. In Cases 1 through 3, the overall globalization index coefficients are in all instances positive and statistically significant. Case 4 shows that the coefficients for three sub-indices are positive and statistically significant. The coefficient values suggest that economic integration and social integration contributed strongly to growth, while the contribution from political integration was low.

For government consumption variables and capital formation variables, the results are consistent with those of Dreher (2006). In other words, "Higher domestic investment as a share of GDP should lead to higher growth" and "Higher government consumption over GDP leads to lower growth". However, the inflation rate coefficient is positive and significant, contradicting the findings of Dreher (2006). Lastly, the two human capital proxy variables show a positive impact on economic growth. The demographic bonus is a major factor in enabling high savings and investment sustained over the

---

[15] Since data for the sample period were available only for China, Japan, South Korea and ASEAN-5, the empirical analysis was conducted using the data for these eight countries.

Table 6. Variable definitions.

Variable	Definition
Dependent Variable:	
Log (GDP per capita)	GDP per capita is gross domestic product divided by midyear population.
Independent Variable:	
KOF Index	Overall index of globalization; Index of economic integration; Index of social integration; Index of political integration.
General government final consumption expenditure (in percentage of GDP)	General government final consumption expenditure includes all government current expenditures for purchases of goods and services (including compensation of employees).
Gross capital formation (in percentage of GDP)	Gross capital formation consists of outlays on additions to the fixed assets of the economy plus net changes in the level of inventories.
Log (life expectancy)	Life expectancy at birth indicates the number of years a newborn infant would live if prevailing patterns of mortality at the time of its birth were to stay the same throughout its life.
School enrollment, secondary (gross)	Gross enrollment ratio is the ratio of total enrollment, regardless of age, to the population of the age group that officially corresponds to the level of education shown. Secondary education completes the provision of basic education that began at the primary level, and aims at laying the foundations for lifelong learning and human development, by offering more subject- or skill-oriented instruction using more specialized teachers.
Inflation rate (annual)	Measured by the consumer price index. The Laspeyres formula is generally used.

Source: World Bank (2011), except for KOF indices.

Table 7. Per capita GDP and globalization (1985–1996).

	Case 1	Case 2	Case 3	Case 4
Overall index of globalization	3.127	2.001	3.062	
	(19.81*)	(6.29*)	(19.67*)	
Index of economic integration				1.937
				(5.80*)
Index of social integration				1.934
				(9.33*)
Index of political integration				0.244
				(2.63*)
General government final	−4.303	−3.867	−3.909	−4.773
consumption expenditure	(−6.65*)	(−4.82*)	(−6.30*)	(−8.86*)
(in percentage of GDP)				
Gross capital formation	0.727	0.745	0.652	0.521
(in percentage of GDP)	(3.62*)	(3.18*)	(3.35*)	(3.04*)
Log (life expectancy)		3.120		
		(2.98*)		
School enrollment rate,		0.685		
secondary (gross)		(3.09*)		
Inflation rate			0.650	
			(3.09*)	
Number of observations	96	81	94	96
Adjusted *R*-square	0.893	0.998	0.897	0.999
Hausman test (Prob > *F*)	0.509	0.004	0.162	0.000

Notes: Robust (White) *t*-statistics are shown in parentheses.
*Significant at the 1% level, **significant at the 5% level, ***significant at the 10% level.

long term. Moreover, the World Bank in its 1993 report identifies an emphasis on education as a factor contributing to the high economic growth rates attained in Asian countries.[16]

---

[16] A report entitled "EAST ASIA MIRACLE: Economic Growth and Public Policy", published in 1993 by the World Bank, mentions "benign fundamental economic conditions" as a factor contributing to countries' strong growth. By implication, this refers to a savings rate of over 30% in preparation for the future and a labor force with a comparatively high education, which are considered fundamental conditions for self-sustained development.

4.2. Empirical analysis after the Asian currency crisis

To examine the change in the performance of globalization after the 1997 currency crisis, the sample period was changed to the years from 1997 to 2008. The empirical analysis was carried out using the same formularization as in Table 7. Table 8 shows the analysis results.

Table 8 shows that overall globalization index coefficients for Cases 1 through 3 are in all instance positive and statistically significant. However, a comparison with Table 7 reveals a tendency to contraction. This finding suggests that the influence of globalization on economic growth weakened after the crisis. As mentioned already in the discussion of Fig. 1, East Asia's globalization lost vigor after the crisis. In this context, the changes in the readings of the sub-index coefficients in Case 3 are worth noting. The economic integration and social integration coefficients have contracted. Specifically, the social integration index has declined from 1.934 in Table 7 to 0.523 in Table 8. In contrast, the political integration coefficient has climbed from 0.244 to 1.031. The coefficients for the capital formation variable in Tables 8 and 7 are almost unchanged. In Table 8, the government consumption and inflation coefficients are in many instances not statistically significant. As an intriguing point, life expectancy coefficients have risen strongly.

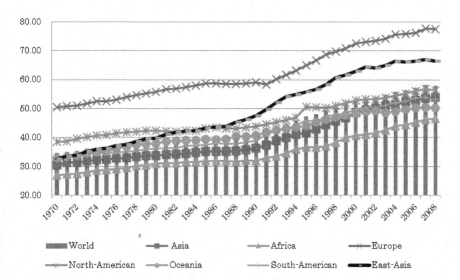

Fig. 1. East-Asia trends of globalization according to KOF indexes (1970–2008).

Note: East Asia comprises China, Japan, South Korea and ASEAN-5.

Source: Author's calculation using data from the KOF Index of Globalization.

Table 8. Per capita GDP and globalization (1997–2008).

	Case 1	Case 2	Case 3	Case 4
Overall index of globalization	3.034	0.936	3.042	
	(7.62*)	(2.10**)	(7.61*)	
Index of economic integration				1.591
				(3.95*)
Index of social integration				0.523
				(1.90***)
Index of political integration				1.031
				(3.47*)
General government final	−1.304	−2.583	−1.064	−0.971
consumption expenditure	(−1.04)	(−2.72*)	(−0.82)	(−0.74)
(in percentage of GDP)				
Gross capital formation	0.629	1.547	0.678	0.671
(in percentage of GDP)	(2.08**)	(4.29*)	(2.18**)	(2.28**)
Log (life expectancy)		7.368		
		(6.89*)		
School enrolment rate,		0.651		
secondary (gross)		(2.49**)		
Inflation rate			0.183	
			(0.74)	
Number of observations	96	74	96	96
Adjusted R-square	0.993	0.997	0.993	0.993
Hausman test (Prob > F)	0.006	0.000	0.005	0.016

Notes: Robust (White) t-statistics are shown in parentheses.
*Significant at the 1% level, **significant at the 5% level, ***significant at the 10% level.

Despite projections that the period of East Asia's demographic bonus is rapidly approaching its end owing to falling birth rates and demographic aging, the positive effects on economic growth are still strong.

5. Conclusion

This chapter analyzed the relation between globalization and economic growth in the East Asia region. An examination was conducted proving the *de facto* integration of East Asia, which, under the impact of globalization, has been forming close mutual linkages based on using foreign trade matrices, intra-regional foreign trade ratios, and bilateral export intensity (Tables 2, 3 and 4). Furthermore, an empirical analysis was conducted of the effects to check globalization on the economic growth of East Asia, both before and after the Asian currency economic crisis. The analysis results suggest a mild decline in globalization's influence on economic growth after the crisis.

However, East Asia has been the scene of a complex intertwinement of regionalism and globalization engendered by the region's original diversity and non-systemic integration. Currently, East Asia maintains a high intra-regional foreign trade ratio, and is gradually reducing its dependency on fully industrialized economies, including the United States. This suggests that extra-regional shocks, such as the one triggered by the U.S. sub-prime mortgage problem, might prove to have only a small recessionary impact on the region. Even so, private sector final consumption expenditure today is U.S. $10 trillion in the United States, U.S. $9 trillion in the EU, U.S. $3 trillion in Japan, and just U.S. $1.5 trillion in China. Compared to the United States and EU, intra-regional final demand in East Asia is still small, and maintaining growth on intra-regional demand alone might prove difficult.

East Asia's economy today is facing a new turning point. If intra-regional integration is to advance further, the integration achieved thus far in a *de facto* manner will need support from a more system-based approach to deeper integration. ASEAN and individual countries in East Asia, specifically Japan, China and South Korea, are on the one hand pining for the restructuring of domestic political systems to be better able to deal with the pressures from globalization. On the other hand, along with the formation of layering multilateral frameworks, seeking to give regionalization a concrete shape, concepts of the East Asian Community are being rolled out. With globalization through the WTO at an impasse, the question of how to proceed with the *de jure* integration will soon pose itself to East Asia.

References

Akamatsu, K (1943). *The Industrial Development of Newly Industrialized Countries, Ueda Teijiro Collection of Commemorative Essays, Kagaku Shugi Kougyousha.* (in Japanese)

ADB (2011). Key Indicators for Asia and the Pacific.

Dreher, A (2006). Does globalization affect growth? Evidence from a new index of globalization. *Applied Economics*, 38(10), 1091–1110.

Dreher, A, G Noel and M Pim (2008). *Measuring Globalisation — Gauging its Consequences*. New York: Springer.

Gwartney, J and R Lawson (2002). Economic freedom of the world: Annual report, http://www.freetheworld.org/

Hirakawa, H, K Ishikawa, N Kobayashi and A Ohara (eds.) (2007). *Globalization and Regional Integration of East Asia, Minerva Shobou*. (in Japanese)

Hiratsuka, D (ed.) (2006). *Strategies of East Asia — Economic Integration, Structural Reform, Framework Creation — Asia Economic Research Institute*. (in Japanese)

Imada, P (1993). Production and trade effect of an ASEAN free trade area. *The Developing Economies*, 31(1), 8.

IMF (2011). World Economic Outlook 2011 (WEO) — (1986, 1997, 2011) Direction of Trade.

Ishikawa, K *et al.* (2010). *Globalization and Regionalization of Southeast Asia, Asia Research Institute*, Asia Research Series No. 73, Asia University, Asia Research Institute. (in Japanese)

Kuroyanagi, Y (ed.) (2005). *Asian Regional Order and Strategies of ASEAN, Aiming at East Asian Partnership, Akashi Shoten*. (in Japanese)

Ohnishi, Y (ed.) (2006). *New Developments in Economic Relations between China and ASEAN — The Coming Age of Reciprocal Investment and FTA, Asia Economic Research Institute*, pp. 5–74. (in Japanese)

Ravenhill, J (2000). APEC Adrift: Implications for Economic Regionalism in Asia and the Pacific. *The Pacific Review*, 13(2), 319–333.

Stiglitz, J (2002). *Globalization and its Discontents*. New York: W.W. Norton & Company, Inc.

Watanabe, T (2004). *The Age of East Asian Economic Cooperation*, pp. 3–38. Japan: Toyo Keizai, Inc. (in Japanese)

WB (2011). *World Development Indicators, (WDI). — 1993, The East Asian Miracle: Economic Growth and Public Policy*. Oxford: Oxford University Press.

CHAPTER 7

CAN SOUTH–SOUTH TRADE BE A DRIVING FORCE FOR FUTURE ECONOMIC GROWTH?

Shigesaburo Kabe

Japan Center for Economic Research
1-7-3, Otemachi, Chiyoda-ku, Tokyo 1008066, Japan
kabe@jcer.or.jp

1. Introduction

In the first decade of the twenty-first century, China has accomplished high economic growth and a huge trade surplus as a global manufacturer and export power. This rapid and substantial growth of the Chinese economy, compared with those of other advanced countries and developing countries, has led to a global issue — that is to say, global current account imbalances.

However, this is not the case only with China but with other Asian economies as well. Let us go back a few decades, to the latter half of the twentieth century, and examine major exporters to developed countries. At that time, Japan and Newly Industrialized Economies (NIEs), namely Hong Kong, Taiwan, South Korea and Singapore, tried to expand their exports around the world, including those to developed countries. They aimed at trading with these nations on the basis of having cost competitiveness and high-quality export goods. China followed the successful example of Japan and the NIEs in their process of rapid economic development. However, China was considerably more successful with its international trade strategy compared to its Asian forerunners and other developing countries.

The fact that the successful imitator, China, faced a trade issue that lead to global current account imbalances indicates that the previous Asian growth model based on their export-driven strategies had reached its limit. The developing Asian model attracted world-wide attention, being called the East Asian Miracle (World Bank, 1993). However, one of the lessons of the global imbalances is that this model either needs to be modified or we should explore a more adequately, well-balanced pathway to growth.

To understand why we need to find an alternative growth model, let us imagine that another developing country, other than China, is trying to adopt the same international trade nation strategy. If the attempt is successful, it will bring an economic growth to the developing country. In addition, if this endeavor leads to the type of success achieved by China, then this developing country could serve as an engine of the global economy. The world will welcome the new engine, however, at the same time, may wonder about the possibility of once again facing global imbalances. Therefore, to avoid current and future global imbalances, it is essential to revisit the growth path — that is, the successful Asian strategy — in both the medium and long terms.

A bird's eye view of the Asian economy provides a different perspective on the global imbalances that originated from China's huge trade surplus to a large extent; China's trade surplus may have had deep roots in the Asian economy. China is the world's factory, producing finished goods to be exported. However, as Li (2010) argues, a closer look reveals that the world's factory merely assembles intermediate goods, like components and materials imported from other countries, mainly Asian neighboring countries. Put another way, China is regarded as the final process in the production network spread across Asia. It is responsible for assembling finished goods by using intermediate goods that have been produced in the Asian network and exported to China. Thus, finished goods, such as domestic appliances and routine commodities, are exported from China to other countries, including developed countries, as goods that are *Made in China.*

For example, let us compare the Asian production network to an iceberg. Assembling finished goods in China and exporting them to developed countries is only the tip of the global-production iceberg. Finding a new pathway to growth, rather than continuing to merely export to developed countries, is important for China, as it is for other Asian countries embedded in the production network.

The growth model adopted by both China and its Asian precursors has lost a great deal of its much-vaunted magical power for economic growth. However, there still remains a refined and efficient production network in Asia. To utilize this production network, to repair the current global imbalances and to prevent future global imbalances, it seems realistic and feasible to find a new growth strategy by trading with or investing in developing countries.

In the long run, trade between developing countries is expected to play an important role in solving the global imbalances and creating a new growth strategy. Let us define developing countries in the broadest sense as "South", with trade between South countries known as "South–South trade". South–South trade should help to develop an alternative growth strategy. This will ultimately improve the balance of the global economy as well as solve global imbalance issues in the medium and long terms.

In this chapter, the author demonstrates the current status and future prospects of South–South trade and discusses the challenging issue of how to activate South–South trade. Given that investment has a close relationship with trade, issues related to investment are also discussed as necessary.

The remainder of this chapter is organized as follows. In the next section, the author discusses the reason why South–South trade is increasingly important as a means of driving the engine of economic growth. Section 3 provides a brief history of the status of South–South trade since the 1990s. Section 4 describes the key factors needed to expand South–South trade in the future, focusing on liberalization, regional cooperation, the service sector, and mutual understanding between trading partners. Finally, Sec. 5 wraps up this topic with concluding remarks.

For the purposes of this work, the South includes areas other than developed countries. Employing the definition of the Asia Development Bank (ADB) (2011), developed countries, or "North" area include North America, Europe, Russia, Japan, Australia and New Zealand. The South refers to Central Asia, South Asia, East Asia, Southeast Asia (including NIEs), the Middle East, the Pacific nations, Latin America (including Mexico) and Africa. As a point of clarification, although Japan, Australia and New Zealand geographically belong to the Asia-Pacific region, these three countries are considered belonging to the North, according to the definition of the ADB (2011).

2. Why is South–South Trade Important?

In the previous section, the author briefly explained the importance of South–South trade for the future. Readers, however, may still ask whether South–South trade is actually critical for encouraging worldwide economic growth. The question is fair because in the past, the advanced North countries have been perceived as having high living standards, advanced technology and sophisticated society, while the stereotyped image of the South has been of poor and developing countries with low per capita GDP, basic technology, and so on.

This preconceived image of the South may be still the case with readers. However, it is useful to note that the South is showing new promise, including latent expansibility and the potential to become a major economic power. This indicates that the South is emerging as a key player comparable to the North, attracting attention from traders, investors and manufacturers. Another counterstatement may be that the South had already come to world's attention in the twentieth century, although many South countries are still considered developing countries. However, the South has changed during recent decades, revealing South countries to be potential key economic players.

There are four main reasons why South–South trade is vital to realizing economic growth.

First, worldwide demographic changes will have a major impact on future world-trade trends, and this will increase the importance of South–South trade. Figure 1 shows that changes in the global population stem largely from increases in the South's population. While the North's population has stayed at around one billion over the last century and is not expected to change much, the South's population is projected to reach 7.9 billion by 2050. This population growth in the South is mainly attributed to Asia and Africa. Asia contains two major population centers: China (1.3 billion in 2050) and India (1.7 billion in 2050). In addition, Africa has a relatively higher fertility rate than the North.

As Fig. 1 shows, the South has continued its upward population trend since the latter half of the twentieth century, and it is projected to continue until the middle of this century. However, demographic structures like age structure have changed and will continue to change over the coming decades. Figure 2 shows the changes in the major index of

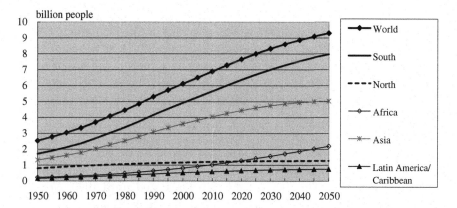

Fig. 1. Changes in population.

Source: United Nations (2010).

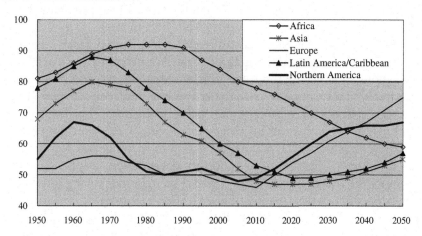

Fig. 2. Changes in the dependency ratio.

Source: United Nations (2010).

demographic structures, the dependency ratio,[1] which is a type of age-structure index.

The dependency ratio is equal to the burden of one earner (15 to 64 years old) sustaining non-earners — that is, children (less than 15 years old) and the elderly (65 years old and over). The higher this dependency

---

[1] Dependency ratio = (population of children (~14) & the elderly (65~)) / working-age (15~64) population.

ratio is, the higher the burden of sustaining children and the elderly by the working-age population (15 to 64 years old). In the past, many South countries faced the risk of a population explosion, which meant they would suffer from a heavy burden caused by a high dependency ratio. This left little capacity for economic development because feeding children in the present was more important than carrying out economic development for the future. This is one of the main reasons why many South countries have found it difficult to escape poverty.

The upward curve of the dependency rate in Africa during the 1960s and 1970s in Fig. 2 indicates that Africa was challenged by a high burden of rearing children. The peak of this burden lasted until 1990. Around 1990, this curve began a downward trend and had decreased to 78 by 2010, a level equivalent to that of Asia in 1975.

In this way, the demographic structure in Africa is rapidly changing. The dependency ratio is projected to fall to 59 in 2050, approximately the same as the level experienced by Asia from 1995 to 2000.

Other areas in the South have already experienced dramatic changes in terms of demographic structure. Latin America and the Caribbean have shown a substantial decline in their dependency ratio, from 87 in 1970 to 53 in 2010. Asia has also experienced a similar downward curve in its dependency ratio, from 80 in 1965 to 48 in 2010. This low level is highly significant if we recall that Asia contains two major population centers, China and India, making up one third of the global population.

Conversely, Fig. 2 indicates a disadvantaged demographic structure for the North. Europe and North America have been enjoying low levels of the dependency ratio, namely a low burden of supporting non-working generations. However, the dependency ratio of North America changed in 2005 and started to increase, inverse to Africa's trend. North America's dependency ratio is projected to reach 67 in 2050, returning to the same rate as that in 1960. Europe also changed direction in 2010 and is now projected to reach a dependency ratio of 57 in 2025, the same level as that in 1970. This trend is projected to continue increasing until 2050.[2]

---

[2]Such reverse trends found in the North countries result from low fertility rates and aging. Low fertility means a lower burden-to-dependency ratio, but at the same time, it indicates a lower working-age population in the future. Aging leads to an increased burden-to-dependency ratio. This is created by an increase in the number of elderly people in the population; this burden increases rapidly as life expectancy increases.

Thus, the South, currently and in the future, has an advantage from the viewpoint of demographic structure compared to the past. The large population size and projected growth, having conveyed a negative and impoverished image in the past, may now convey a positive image of latent growth ability in terms of both production and consumption, leading to economic growth.

As discussed above, the changing stages of the demographic structure are similar between South countries. Likewise, the relative closeness of economic development stages between South countries, compared with the closeness of those between the South and the North, is the second important factor to be discussed.

This closeness of development stages generates advantages in trade between South countries. For example, it makes it easier to provide merchandise that meets the needs of the designated export countries. Let us use the example of Japanese firms that tried to export high-quality goods to emerging markets.

Japanese goods are welcomed by developed countries in spite of their relatively expensive cost. However, that is not the case with emerging markets. In the South, major consumers prefer washing machines that remember which cycle they were on after a power outage (which frequently happens in South countries). Consumers require televisions with high volume in order to counteract noisy environments. There are many other examples. However, Japanese firms failed to provide goods that met consumers' real needs; instead, they supplied costly high-quality consumer electronics.

South countries are in a better position to understand the real needs of other South countries because of their own similar experience and ability to empathize with the circumstances of the South.

Similarly, South–South investment also has the potential to meet the host country's needs in terms of business knowledge and technology. Generally speaking, regardless of their level of development, countries are eager to attract or establish plants with the latest technology. North–South investment can provide the South with the North's advanced technology and business skills, which will attract the South side's interest. However, the latest technology does not always meet the real needs of the country. It is often difficult to fully utilize the most advanced technology after setting up a plant. Thus, the North's advanced technology does not always satisfy the South because the host country may not be able to assimilate and make full use of the advanced technology. This can be due to the low technology level of the host country or a lack of human resources.

On the other hand, South–South investment provides medium-level technology to the host country. This technology may be more easily accepted and transferred to a host country that has relatively low levels of technology and less-skilled human resources. In other words effective and appropriate technology transfer can be realized through South–South investment rather than through North–South investment.

Recently, Indian and Chinese firms have aggressively invested in Africa or have taken over African firms in order to cultivate African markets. Indian and Chinese firms have introduced a medium level of technology instead of a high level. By also bringing along their own knowledge and experience, they have helped African workers learn and master Indian and Chinese technology.

For example, mergers and acquisitions (M&A) by Indian firms target markets of consumer products such as personal-care products, mobile-phone services, steel, mining, and so on. Indian firms also apply their business expertise within African markets, including knowledge about low-cost marketing, revenue collection and credit management.

Third, technological developments, like information technology (IT), motivate countries in the developing stage to foster not only secondary industries (manufacturing) but also tertiary industries (service industries). Thus, looking closely at the recent economic development, a country may not always reflect the pattern of industrial development found in the past, in which the backbone of a nation's economy shifts from the primary sector (agriculture) to the secondary sector, and then to the tertiary sector, in step with economic development.

Modern humans take the benefits of technological development for granted, especially in service sectors. However, looking back only a few decades, it is amazing to witness the rate of technological development in communication and transport. In the mid 1980s, when the author studied abroad, the only available tools for international communication were letters, facsimile machines and expensive international telephone calls. As well, there was no affordable way to regularly return home. Today, we can use email, free Internet calls, Wi-Fi, and smart mobile phones for communication. Regarding transportation, low-cost carrier services enable frequent and low-cost travel across and within countries.

Thus, the technological developments in communication and transportation during the last decade have brought significant benefits to modern society, allowing tertiary industries to develop rapidly.

Assisted by technological developments, tertiary industries may be able to accomplish considerable development compared with earlier centuries. A typical example is in India, where the IT industry has rapidly developed. Technological development in the information field has caused a rapid development of information-related industries, one of the major service industries. In addition, it also promoted the service trade because traditionally service transactions across countries were difficult or expensive without the latest technology. Today, India is not only famous for its IT industry but also heavily depends on the service trade in IT fields as a driving force of its economy.

It is worth pointing out that another factor has contributed to the development of the Indian IT industry and to service trade in the IT field: human resources. India has a comparative advantage in the IT industry due to plentiful manpower resource — IT engineers who are English speakers.

Because many service industries, like retail, tourism, and medical care, as well as IT-related industries, have enough room to mediate service transactions through manpower, tertiary industries may take advantage of large-scale manpower if workers in service sectors are provided with training opportunities for learning essential skills. Thus, when a South country has a comparative advantage in a specific service industry, this country may have a chance to develop a service trade with other countries, especially other South countries.

Fourth, the growth of the middle class in the South can contribute to South–South trade. With economic development, the middle class population is expected to expand, which will also increase its spending power. According to the ADB (2010), the middle-class[3] population accounted for 56% of the total population in developing Asia[4] in 2008, which is a jump from 21% in 1990. Sub-Saharan Africa also extended its share of the middle-income population among the total population from 24% in 1990 to 33% in 2008.

---

[3] The ADB (2010) defined the middle class as those with consumption expenditures of $2 to $20 per person per day in 2005 PPP (purchasing power parity) $.
[4] Here, developing Asia refers to 22 countries in East, South, Southeast and Central Asia, excluding NIEs.

The Ministry of Economy, Trade and Industry (METI) (2010) defined a middle income in Asia as $5,000 to $35,000 of a household's disposable income. It stresses that the middle-income population in Asian countries increased from 220 million people in 2000 to 940 million people in 2010. This population is expected to expand to two billion people in 2020.

The amount of consumption expenditures or disposal income, above defined, for the middle class seem to be low when compared to the middle class in developed countries. However, in the context of large-scale populations, the purchasing power of this middle class is large enough to attract oversea firms' attention to this new and promising market, even though the unit price of merchandise may not be as high as in developed countries.

The emergence and rise of the middle class has also attracted the attention of lower-income classes, inspiring them to escape from deprivation into the middle class. For example, in India the income stratum pyramid consists of a rich class, a middle class, an aspirant class and a deprived class. The aspirant class is defined as "the new middle class" with an annual household income of 90,000 to 200,000 rupees[5] (approximately equivalent to U.S. $2,200 to U.S. $5,000). It sits between the deprived class, which has an annual household income of less than 90,000 rupees, and the middle class, which has an annual household income of 200,000 to 1,000,000 rupees (equivalent to approximately U.S. $5,000 to U.S. $25,000).

This aspirant class (new middle class) has attracted government attention because it is more likely than the aspirant class or deprived class to move up to the rich class. India's income-stratum pyramid shows that the base of the economic pyramid (BOP), which is comprised of the deprived class, was the largest layer in 2005. However, by 2015 the aspirant class is projected to be the largest layer of the income-stratum pyramid, consisting of 43% of households. The deprived class will become the second-largest class, falling to 30% from 49% in 2005. In 2025, the middle class is expected to become the largest class, with 46% of households, followed by the aspirant class (33%) and the deprived class (18%), (McKinsey Global Institute, 2007).

3. Current Status of South–South Trade

Since 1990, South–South trade has shown a rapid upward trend, and consequently, the share of South–South trade in world trade has also

---

[5] At 2001 fiscal year's prices.

jumped. According to the ADB (2011), South–South trade as a share of world trade has doubled from 6.9% in 1990–1991 to 16.9% in 2009 (Table 1). Looking at the top ten destinations of major Asian exporters and aggregating the share of North countries in the top ten destinations for all trade, the total share of the North decreased in the last half century. Conversely, the total share of South countries in the top destinations for all trade increased in last half century.

Figure 3 shows that South–South trade holds an important position in the South's merchandise trade. In 2009, the share of South–South exports in the Southern merchandise exports amounted to 45.9%, and its share of imports exceeded 50%.

Table 1. South–South trade as share of world trade.

	1990–1991	2000–2001	2006–2007	2008	2009
Exports	7.6	10.2	15	16.3	17.7
Imports	6.2	9.6	14.1	15.4	16.1
Trade	6.9	9.9	14.5	15.9	16.9

Unit: %
Note: Nonfuel merchandise trade.
Source: ADB (2011).

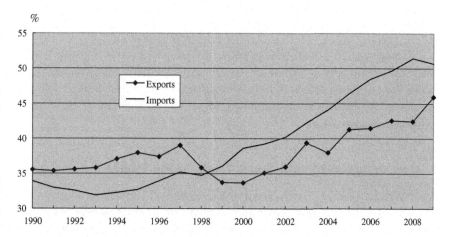

Fig. 3. Share of South–South trade in total southern merchandise trade.

Note: Nonfuel merchandise trade.
Source: ADB (2011).

Table 2. Inward and outward Foreign direct investment (FDI) stocks, by source and destination (2008).

	Inward stock from North	Outward stock to North	Inward stock from South	Outward stock to South
South Africa	0.13	0.02	0.21	0.05
Latin America	0.60	0.08	0.48	0.26
Middle East	0.09	0.03	0.29	0.12
Asia	0.18	0.14	1.40	1.40
North	9.12	9.53	1.49	3.84

Unit: trillions of dollars.
Source: ADB (2011).

What major factors increased South–South trade in recent years? The ADB (2011) argues that three main factors account for the expansion of South-South trade since the 1990s. The first factor is strong economic growth in emerging economies, such as China, India, Brazil and South Africa. The second factor is the spread of a fragmented production and trade network, especially that of the machinery, electronics and automobile industries. The third factor is the progressive elimination of trade barriers. The second and third factors are important for determining how to expand South–South trade further, and they are discussed in detail in Sec. 4.

Compared to South–South trade, investment between South countries still comprises a minor share of current global investments. The major investment pattern is North–North investment, as Table 2 shows. However, South–South investment within Asia is substantial compared with other South areas.

4. How to Expand South–South Trade in the Future

As shown in Table 1, South–South trade increased rapidly to account for one sixth of the world's merchandise trade in 2009. However, to boost further growth means that efforts must be made to arrange better and more effective environments for trade.

The historical evidence of the Maghribi and Genoese trades in the eleventh and twelfth centuries provides hints for how to expand

South–South trade in the future (Greif, 1994).[6] Genoese traders improved their inferior trade environment, compared with the Maghribis, by inventing effective and efficient mechanisms for increasing their trade in the Mediterranean Sea area.

Thus, building effective and efficient mechanisms may contribute to expanding South–South trade. First, this means promoting tariff reductions and facilitation of trade to improve current trade mechanisms in terms of their effectiveness and efficiency. Second, trade mechanisms need to be developed to include not only bilateral trade but also multilateral trade, especially region-based trade. Third, technological developments will help realize the growth potential of the service trade; the service trade had been only a minor trade type in the existing trade mechanism. Finally, the smooth functioning of trade mechanisms requires tolerance in the form of mutual understanding of socio-cultural differences with a trade partner. Without this tolerance, international trade often faces issues, such as trade imbalances, that can have a negative impact on future trade.

Put another way, the four factors are (1) tariff reduction and facilitation of trade, (2) the full usage of regional integration and cooperation, (3) the development of the service trade, and (4) a mutual understanding of socio-cultural aspects. These are all important for developing South–South trade. In the following section, these four factors are discussed in detail.

---

[6] The Genoese (from Italy) and the Maghribis (from Northwest Africa) were major traders in the Mediterranean Sea area in the eleventh and twelfth centuries. They adopted different approaches to expanding their trade area by hiring their agents in remote areas. The Maghribis made use of informal relationships among the Maghribis, investing money to find out whether agents had cheated trade partners in the past. The Genoese depended on formal relationships with non-Genoese for hiring agents, but without collecting information on the agent's trade history. The Maghribis had advantages over the Genoese in building credible relationships with agents in remote areas and in maintaining an effective punishment system because agents and traders all belonged to the society of Maghribis.

However, according to Greif (1994), the Genoese later developed formal legal and political enforcement organizations to facilitate trading activities: An extensive legal system for registration and enforcement of contracts, codification of customary contract law that governed the relations between Genoese traders. This strategy was much more effective and useful compared to that of the Maghribis.

4.1. Tariff reduction and facilitation of trade

Trade liberalization is a key factor in activating trade across countries. Above all, tariff reduction or elimination is one of the most fundamental methods for encouraging trade liberalization. Economic theory suggests that imposing tariffs to protect a domestic industry, especially an infant industry, does not promote a nation's welfare, but worsens it. Currently, the South imposes higher tariff on imported merchandise compared to the North (ADB, 2011), indicating that more effort by the South regarding trade liberalization is required.

Even though the reduction or elimination of tariffs is crucial to the development of trade, this is still not enough to promote trade liberalization. There remain Non-Tariff Barriers (NTBs) that inhibit smooth trade operations. NTBs include import-license procedures, import bans, quantitative restrictions of imported goods, the certification of standards, surcharges on imported goods, limitations on importers etc. The characteristics of NTBs are less transparent, consequently arbitrary, diminishing the effect of tariff reductions and making a nation's import policies murky. Given that NTBs easily discourage trade activities, NTBs should be eliminated as much as possible. In other words, conducting trade without these barriers is important to increasing the effectiveness of trade liberalization.

To achieve tariff reduction and facilitation of trade, regional cooperation, discussed in detail in Sec. 4.2, is both useful and realistic for South countries that may not have enough power to obtain desirable results through negotiation with trade partners.

It is worth noting that improving the trade infrastructure is also essential to encouraging trade. South countries have relatively poor infrastructure, such as a lack of trade ports at which large numbers of supertankers or container vessels can dock or poor accessibility to trade-by-land transport. Improving trade infrastructure can help exporters and importers experience a quick export process or a prompt delivery of import goods for domestic consumers. This leads to smooth trade processes and trader satisfaction.

4.2. Full usage of regional integration and cooperation

From the viewpoint of comprehensiveness and fairness, trade liberalization is initially expected to be achieved through World Trade Organization (WTO) negotiations. However, the multilateral trade negotiations presided by the WTO, namely by Doha Round, have been deadlocked, and it seems that it will be difficult to achieve a final settlement in the near future. Hence, in place of multilateral trade negotiations, many major trading countries have rushed into settling bilateral agreements, such as free-trade agreements (FTAs) or economic partnership agreements (EPAs). Bilateral negotiations to settle FTAs or EPAs contribute to trade liberalization between both parties.

However, in the case of bilateral negotiations between a major trading country and a minor trading country, the former can easily gain advantage, with the agreements and conditions being more favorable to the larger country's domestic industries and consumers compared to the latter's. If so, non-major trading countries may hesitate to agree to FTAs or EPAs to protect short-term interests, even though these countries understand the advantage of FTAs or EPAs in the longer term. For minor trade countries, an alternative is to join a framework of regional integration or cooperation in order to overcome these difficulties. A concrete example of a regional framework in the South is the ASEAN Economic Community (AEC). The Association of Southeast Asian Nations (ASEAN) aims to launch it by 2015 with the goal of encouraging regional economic integration.

What, then, are the merits of regional integration or cooperation? Here, let us focus on regional trade agreements (RTAs), which focus on regional cooperation and are a precursor to regional integration. Fernández (1997) mentions signaling, insurance and bargaining power as the goals of RTAs. Entering into an RTA signals an explicitly liberal attitude towards trade with non-RTA member countries as well as RTA member countries. An RTA also provides insurance against future events, such as trade wars and arbitrary impositions of standards (such as health standards).

One of the most attractive advantages of a RTA is the bargaining power that each member country can achieve compared with the reduced power they would have if they were to separately negotiate with major trading countries. Tariff reductions or the elimination of NTBs, discussed in Sec. 4.1, can be achieved because of the more favorable conditions for countries that are members of a RTA, compared with independent trade negotiations.

Looking at the example of ASEAN, in 2009 the top country's GDP was 96 times higher, its per capita GDP was 61 times higher, and its trade volume was 174 times higher than those of the bottom country. However, as a member of a RTA, the bottom country has a better advantage than it would if it were to negotiate on its own with major trading countries.

4.3. Development of service trade

In 2010, the global service export and import amounted to $3,695 billion and $3,510 billion, equivalent to one quarter of the global merchandise export and import, respectively. Of all world-service exports and imports, exports originating from the South amounted to 29%, and imports amounted to 35% (WTO, 2011).

The service trade is one step away from becoming a quasi-major trade pattern, and it is expected to extend further with the help of drastic price declines in transportation and communication due to technological developments. Based on an analysis of the liberalization of the service trade in Tunisia and Egypt, Konan and Kim (2004) argue that "the combined effect of goods and services liberalization are substantial" for both countries, and "services reform may provide an important new pathway to overall prosperity".

In addition to technological developments and increased liberalization in the service trade, if South countries develop service industries by providing training opportunities for learning essential skills, South countries may increase their service exports by taking advantage of their large numbers of workers.

Before discussing the development of the service trade in South countries, a brief explanation of the characteristics of the service trade should be provided. First of all, the service trade consists of four modes:

- Cross-border supply   (mode one)
- Consumption abroad   (mode two)
- Commercial presence   (mode three)
- Presence of natural persons (mode four)

Cross-border supply (mode one) does not require the cross-border movement of consumers or service providers. It consists of business-process outsourcing (BPO), such as outsourced call-center services to other counties. Advanced technology, like IT, which did not exist in the past, enables this type of service trade to develop. The South may also be able to take advantage of large worker numbers.

Consumption abroad (mode two) is that in which consumers go to other countries to consume. Overseas tourism is the most typical example. The development of transportation provides easier and safer access to tourist spots.

Commercial presence (mode three) includes moving suppliers (mostly commercial organizations) to a consumer's country of residence, leading to investments in service provisions. Setting up a hub for service in a host county and the presence of natural persons (mode four) refer to moving service providers from an export country to an import country.

Taking the example of medical-related services, the export of medical staff, such as doctors, nurses and care workers, is a service export (mode four) that began through EPAs. If a medical system is exported and a hub is established in the host country, this also is classified as a service export (mode three). Medical services can attract the attention of overseas patients who willingly visit the host country to be hospitalized for medical service (mode two). Medical tourism provided by South countries is expected to become popular among South countries in the future and is already popular among advanced countries. This is partly because the average income of people in South countries will increase with economic development and partly because principle of comparative advantage can be applicable to the service trade.

Modes two, three, and four demonstrate characteristics of the service trade: a close relationship with the flow of capital and also the flow of labor (or the flow of people, in a broader sense). If the cross-border movement of people is prohibited, modes two and four cannot occur. Likewise the limited flow of capital makes it difficult to realize mode three of the service trade. Therefore, Walley (2004) states that "to achieve meaningful trade liberalization in services may require modifications of factor mobility restrictions which may not be needed for goods liberalization". In other words, liberalization of the service trade itself does not necessary have a big impact unless it is accompanied by a liberalization of factor markets — that is, capital and labor markets. Services liberalization may bring larger gains if the obstacles to capital flow (FDIs) are removed (mode three) and if achieving a labor flow across countries is facilitated (mode four).

It is worth noting that the effects of liberalizing the service trade may differ among industries. El Khoury and Savvides (2006) studied the effects of the openness of telecommunication and financial services across higher-income countries and lower-income countries. They found that an openness of telecommunication services by lower-income countries triggered foreign direct investment, raising productivity growth of this sector in the host countries. On the contrary, liberalization of financial services in lower-income countries did not bring positive and significant results due to a lack of human capital and poor institutional and regulatory structures, while higher-income countries gained positive and significant results.

This subsection concludes by briefly mentioning the export of unskilled labor (mode four). Some countries have already started to export unskilled laborers, such as construction workers, maids etc. Although mode four of service trade includes such people, exports of unskilled workers do not seem to be sustainable or dominant in the long run. As mentioned earlier, the key factor that enabled India to develop its IT trade was its wealth of human resources with advanced skills in the IT field and who could speak English. Both of these are essential for obtaining requests for exports. Without these factors, South exports that are based only on low costs may not lead to subsequent orders.

4.4. Mutual understanding of socio-cultural aspects

In the process of developing South–South trade, current trade partners that have lower competitiveness may be crowded out by new trade partners that have more competitiveness. As international trade benefits both the exporting country and the importing country, it is natural that cheaper and better-quality import goods replace less-competitive domestic goods. However, the crowding-out effects caused by imports may evoke a sense of aversion against imported goods.

In other words, a flood of imported goods from a specific country may crowd out domestic goods and imported goods from other countries, leading to a heavy dependence on a specific country. Economically rational benefits, then, may not always be regarded as welcome news by people in the importing country. This may especially be the case in service trade (mode four) when foreign laborers from other countries flow in to provide their services.

To mitigate the latent negative effects of crowding out caused by the development of South–South trade (both merchandise and service trade), it is necessary for both sides of trade to have mutual understanding regarding each other's socio-cultural aspects. This may go a long way toward achieving the well-balanced development of South–South trade. However, past experience demonstrates that trade friction is embedded in the development process of trade, and frustration derived from trade friction often results in the exclusion of trade to some extent. Current trade mechanisms contain various procedures and tools to deal with trade friction, and socio-cultural understanding is expected to assume a role of backseat player by supporting trade mechanism to resolve issues.

5. Conclusion

In this chapter, the current status of South–South trade and its potential as an alternative growth strategy for the South are discussed. The expectation is that South–South trade can function as an alternative pathway to economic growth, avoiding future global imbalances. Of course, South–South trade is not currently strong enough to be a driving force for economic growth. However, if adequate and effective environments for trade are cultivated, South–South trade may develop and expand rapidly. Especially, the following four factors, which are tariff reduction and facilitation of trade, full use of regional integration/cooperation, development of trade in services and mutual understanding of socio-cultural aspects, are essential for environments to promote South–South trade.

Think of such a trade environment as a catalyst. South–South trade may experience a chemical reaction. Such a chemical reaction may take time to initiate and may seem fleeting at first, but once it occurs, its effects will continue to be seen everywhere in the South, to varying degrees. In this sense, the impacts of South–South trade will be achieved not in the short term but in the middle or long terms. Therefore, a continuous, accumulating effort to create a better environment for trade is important for developing South–South trade in the future.

Lastly, we need to realize that well-balanced economic growth through South–South trade requires a combination of trade, supporting human-resource development and infrastructure arrangements. An expansion of trade assumes the vigorous purchasing power of trade partners, which derive from sufficient income of consumers living in the trade partner countries. To gain sufficient income, consumers are required to supply labor with the requisite skills, based on human-resource development. In addition, making infrastructure arrangements regarding trade will lead to efficient and low-cost trading, which will encourage exporters and importers to further expand trade.

References

Asia Development Bank (ADB) (2010). Key Indicators for Asia and the Pacific 2010.

Asia Development Bank (ADB) (2011). Asian Development Outlook 2011: South–South Economic Links.

El Khoury, AC and A Savvides (2006). Openness in services trade and economic growth. *Economics Letters*, 92, 277–283.

Fernández, R (1997). Returns to regionalism: An evaluation of nontraditional gains from regional trade agreements. *World Bank Policy Research Working Paper* 1816, pp. 1–32.

Greif, A (1994). Cultural Beliefs and the Organization of Society: A Historical and Theoretical Reflection on Collectivist and Individualist Societies. *Journal of Political Economy*, 102(5), 912–950.

Konan, DE and KE Kim (2004). Beyond border barriers: The liberalisation of services trade in Tunisia and Egypt. *The World Economy*, 27(9), 1429–1447.

Li, X (2010). Global rebalancing and regional economic cooperation in Asia (Global rebalance to Asia chiiki keizai kyoryoku). *Ritsumeikan Journal of International Relations and Area Studies*, 32, 51–58. (in Japanese)

McKinsey Global Institute (2007). The 'Bird of Gold': The Rise of India's Consumer Market. Available at http://www.mckinsey.com/Insights/MGI/Research/Asia/The_bird_of_gold [accessed on 13 March 2012].

Ministry of Economy, Trade and Industry (METI) (2010). White Paper on International Economy and Trade. Available at http://www.meti.go.jp/english/report/data/gWT2010fe.html [accessed on 9 September 2012].

United Nations (UN) (2010). World Population Prospects, the 2010 Revision. http://esa.un.org/wpp/unpp/panel_population.htm [accessed on 13 March 2012].

Walley, J (2004). Assessing the benefits to developing countries of liberalisation in services trade. *The World Economy*, 27(8), 1223–1253.

World Bank (1993). *The East Asian Miracle: Economic Growth and Public Policy*. USA: Oxford University Press.

World Trade Organization (WTO) (2011). International Trade Statistics 2011. Available at http://www.wto.org/english/res_e/statis_e/its2011_e/its11_toc_e.htm [accessed on 13 March 2012].

CHAPTER 8

AN EMPIRICAL ANALYSIS OF THE DETERMINANTS OF HOUSEHOLD SAVING (CONSUMPTION) IN CHINA: A PANEL ANALYSIS OF PROVINCIAL DATA, 1995–2010

Guifu Chen

Center for Macroeconomics Research, Xiamen University
MOE Key Laboratory of Econometrics, Xiamen University
Fujian Key Laboratory of Statistical Sciences, Xiamen University
No. 422 Simingnan Road, Xiamen, Fujian, 361005 China
chenguifu@xmu.edu.cn

1. Introduction

China became the second largest economy in 2011 (at current exchange rates) and may overtake the U.S. as the largest economy in the future. Moreover, as the world's most populous nation, China has increasingly attracted attention in the world economy. As China integrates with the world economy, questions arise about the impact of the integration of this large country with the world economy. One noteworthy aspect of China's economy is its high saving rate. It is important to understand the determinants of and future trends in China's saving rate. This issue is, of course, important for China's policy makers who are currently aiming at rebalancing the composition of demand and the pattern of growth while facing the implications of the large

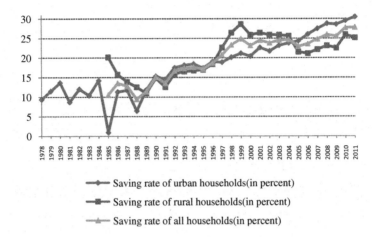

──── Saving rate of urban households(in percent)
──── Saving rate of rural households(in percent)
──── Saving rate of all households(in percent)

Fig. 1. Household saving rate in China, 1978–2011.

Source: Author's calculations based on *China Statistics Yearbook*, 1979–2012 editions.

external surplus for the monetary policy. This is also important for the world economy, because China is a large economy and is growing rapidly.

Figure 1 shows the data on the trends in the saving rates of urban households in 1978–2011 and that of rural and all households in 1985–2011, based on China's household survey.[1] From this figure, the saving rates of the three categories of households are roughly comparable not only with respect to their levels but also with respect to trends over time. The saving rates of urban, rural, and all households fluctuated in the 6.46%–30.49%, 11%–28.63% and 9.49%–27.83% ranges, respectively, and averaged 20.33%, 20.54% and 20.43%, respectively, in 1986–2011. The fact that the saving rate of rural households is slightly higher than that of urban households even though their income levels are much lower is surprising. Turning to trends over time in the saving rates of urban

---

[1] In this figure, the household saving rate is defined as the ratio of household per capita annual saving to household per capita annual disposable income (per capita annual net income in the case of rural households) and where household saving is calculated as household per capita annual disposable (or net) income minus household per capita annual consumption.

and all households, the saving rate of urban households showed an upward trend throughout the 1989–2011 period, while the saving rates of rural households showed an upward trend throughout the 1989–1999 period and showed a downward trend after 1999. Moreover, the saving rate of rural households is higher than that of urban households throughout the 1985–1988 and 1997–2004 periods. The level of the saving rate of all households showed an upward trend in 1986–2011, ranging from 9.49% to 27.83%. This sudden spurt in the saving ratio magnitude is called the "Chinese saving puzzle" by some economists.

What factors determine the household saving rate in China? Moreover, is the effect of these factors different on the saving rates of urban and rural households, considering the dual economic structure in China? This chapter tries to answer this interesting question using recent data and a superior estimation model. Further, after providing empirical results for urban, rural, and all households and a pool of urban and rural households, it attempts to provide some suggestions for studying China's saving patterns.

The rest of this chapter is structured as follows. Section 2 surveys some main findings that explain the determinants of China's saving rate using the Life Cycle and Permanent Income Hypothesis. Section 3 presents the estimation model and data. After the discussion on the empirical results, Sec. 4 provides a conclusion and some suggestions for studying China's saving patterns.

2. The Chinese Saving Puzzle and the Life-Cycle and Permanent Income Hypothesis

Kraay (2000) considers a variety of statistical issues that cloud the measurement of aggregate and household saving in China and provides new empirical evidence on the importance of intertemporal considerations in explaining inter-provincial variation in household saving in China. This study finds that the real per capita gross national disposable income positively and significantly affects cross-country saving rate (gross national saving/gross national disposable income); expectations of future income growth negatively and significantly affects current saving rates for rural households. However, this variable is insignificant in saving rate equation for urban households.

Modigliani and Cao (2004) compute the household saving rate in China in 1953–2000.[2] They find that this rate steadily increases from 2.02% in 1970 to 33.75% in 1994 and progressively decreases to 23.55% in 2000. They call this sudden spurt in the saving ratio magnitude the "Chinese saving puzzle". They explain that the key to the puzzle is provided by the LCH and its implication that the major systematic determinant of the rate of private saving is to be found in the rate of growth of income and the demographic structure of the economy, while per capita income, the traditional and commonsensical explanation counts little, if at all. Moreover, they suggest that the extraordinary behavior of the Chinese saving ratio is the result of two nearly coincidental sharp turns in two key policies. The first is the movement initiated in the late-1970s towards a market-oriented economy. This policy makes it possible for an explosive growth pattern that has never been seen before. The second turn regards demographic policies. Since the 1970s, the new population policy has been strictly enforced to limit the number of children per family (just one child in the cities). As noted, this policy has a double profound effect on the saving ratio. First, it is a drastic decline in the ratio of people under fifteen years to working population from 0.96 in the mid-70s to 0.41 at the turn of the century. Second, it undermines the traditional role of the family wherein children provide old-age support to the parents, thus encouraging provisions through individual accumulation.

Horioka and Wan (2007) carry out a dynamic panel analysis of the determinants of the household saving rate in China using a life cycle model. Their analysis is based on the panel data on Chinese provinces for the 1995–2004 period from China's household survey.[3] They find that

---

[2] Modigliani and Cao (2004) defined personal saving as follows. The personal saving consists of measuring the (annual) increase in personal wealth that results from personal saving. Their estimated calculations to show the increase in personal wealth are the sum of two components: The first is the increase in the holdings of a list of intangible assets, $A(t)-A(t-1)$. The second component is an estimate of the increase in the stock of some major tangibles (e.g., private residences). Then they measure the utilization of saving by the estimated flow of investment I. Thus, $S = [A(t)-A(t-1)] + I$.

[3] They defined the household saving rate as the ratio of household per capita annual saving to household per capita annual disposable income (per capita annual net income in the case of rural households) and where household saving is calculated as household per capita annual disposable (or net) income minus household per capita annual consumption.

China's household saving rate has been high and rising and that the main determinants of variations over time and over space therein are the lagged saving rate, the income growth rate, (in many cases) the real interest rate and (in some cases) the inflation rate. However, they find that the variables relating to the age structure of the population have the expected impact on the household saving rate in only one of the four samples. These results provide mixed support for the life cycle hypothesis as well as the permanent income hypothesis, and are consistent with the existence of inertia or persistence. They may imply that China's household saving rate will remain high for some time to come.

Chao *et al.* (2011) develop a structural model, which extends the model by Chamon and Prasad (2008) and includes all the components of the life cycle hypothesis introduced by Modigliani and Cao (2004). Their model identifies the respective contributions of the changes in the saving rates of the various age-cohorts and that in the weight of each cohort. They show that the changes of each of these variables have contributed to the surge of the household saving ratio during the period. Nonetheless, taken all together, they can reproduce no more than 35% of this rise. Moreover, they add a new feature to the model: After the opening of the housing market in the second half of the 1990s, parents have wanted to help their children buy homes and in the absence of a well-functioning mortgage market and have had to save for that. With this new assumption, the model can reproduce the saving ratio observed in the second half of the period. However, the model is unable to explain the big rise in the household saving rate in the 1980s. Finally, they find that about two-third of the rise generated by the model comes from the increase in the saving rate of the active population. The rest comes from changes in the sizes and incomes of the various age-cohorts of the population.

Yu and Li (2000) examine households' consumption behavior in China. They emphasize that the life cycle and permanent income hypothesis cannot properly explain Chinese households' consumption. They attempt to conceptualize the influence of cultural and institutional factors on the determination of households' consumption in China. They find that in China, the single most important factor determining consumption demand is households' inflation expectations. The second important factor is the price level. The real income and real wealth are the third and fourth important factors, respectively. The influence of the interest rate on consumption is found to be minimal.

Wan *et al.* (2003) explore the determinants of saving behavior in rural China, using a large set of household-level survey data. They find that the life cycle hypothesis is rejected since a "U-pattern" contrary to the commonly claimed "hump", is discovered; the permanent income hypothesis is not accepted as wealth is found to be negatively related to savings.

Other studies explain the household saving (consumption) rate in China based on liquidity restraints, precautionary saving, habit formation and income (expenditure) uncertainty hypotheses (Shi and Zhu, 2004; Li and Wen, 2005; Zhou, 2005; Hang and Guo, 2009; Man and Tong, 2009).

Some results are different in previous studies. Kraay (2000) finds that the real per capita gross national disposable income positively and significantly affects cross-country saving rate (gross national saving/gross national disposable income). Similarly, Horioka and Wan (2007) also show that China's household saving rate has been high and rising and has a positive relation with the per capita income growth rate. On the other hand, Modigliani and Cao (2004) explain that the rate of growth of income is a key factor in determining the higher saving rate in China, while per-capita income counts little, if at all.

Furthermore, some results are conflicting in the previous studies. Kraay (2000) finds that the expectations of future income growth negatively and significantly affect current saving rates for rural households. Similarly, Wan *et al.* (2003) find that wealth is negatively related to rural household savings, while Horioka and Wan (2007) find that the real growth rate of per capita disposable income positively relates to rural households saving rate. Further, Kraay (2000) shows that income variable is insignificant in the saving rate equation for urban households, while Horioka and Wan (2007) show that income variable is positive and significant for urban household saving rate.

This chapter tries to explore the determinants of household saving rate in China for urban, rural, and all households and a pool of urban and rural households, using recent data, panel provincial data of 1995–2010, and a superior estimation model — system Generalized Method of Moments (GMM). This chapter is similar to Horioka and Wan (2007) in that I can compare my results with those obtained by Horioka and Wan; however, the number of observations is greatly increased (457 versus 272).

3. Empirical Techniques and Data

Following the life cycle hypothesis (Modigliani, 1970; Deaton, 1992), I assume that the household saving rate will be a function of the real growth rate of per capita income and demographic structure. Moreover, following Modigliani and Cao (2004) and Horioka and Wan (2007), I use the following model to estimate the household saving rate in China.

$$SR_t^* = \beta_0 + \sum_{i=1}^{4} \beta_i X_{it} + \mu_t, \qquad (1)$$

where SR_t^* is permanent or is the long-run household saving rate, β_0 is constant term, X_{it} are variables that include the real growth rate of per capita income, the dependency rate, the real interest rate, and the change rate of the consumer price index, and μ_t is the disturbance term. The partial adjustment model (Nerlove, 1958) and the tedious but straightforward algebra transformation yield the short-run household saving rate function.

$$
\begin{aligned}
SR_t &= \gamma\beta_0 + \gamma\sum_{i=1}^{4} \beta_i X_{it} + (1-\gamma)SR_{t-1} + \gamma\mu_t, \\
&= \alpha_0 + \sum_{i=1}^{4} \alpha_i X_{it} + \alpha_5 SR_{t-1} + \nu_t,
\end{aligned}
\qquad (2)
$$

where $\alpha_{0-4} = \gamma\beta_{0-4}$, $\alpha_5 = 1-\gamma$, $\nu_t = [\mu_t - (1-\gamma)\mu_{t-1}]$.

I use a GMM model to estimate the short-run household saving rate function using dynamic provincial panel data in China, and I can obtain the long-run household saving rate function Eq. (1) using Eq. (2).

Following Loayza *et al.* (2000), Schrooten and Stephan (2005), and Horioka and Wan (2007), I use the alternative "system GMM estimator" (Arellano and Bover, 1995; Blundell and Bond, 1998), and I correct the standard errors using the method proposed by Windmeijer (2005), because the estimated asymptotic standard errors of the efficient two-step GMM estimator will be severely downward biased in small samples.[4]

In this chapter, the dependent variable is household saving rate (SR). SR is the ratio of household saving to urban household disposable income or net rural household income, and household saving is household disposable (or net) income minus household consumption. The household saving rate of urban, rural, and all households by province is shown in Table 1.

---

[4] All calculations were done using Stata/SE 10. I used Roodman's (2005, 2007) "xtabond2" program in Stata to correct the standard errors.

Table 1. Household saving rate by province (average in 1995–2010).

Province	Saving rate (in %)		
	Urban households	Rural households	All households
Anhui	22.6	23.1	22.8
Beijing	22.8	28.4	24.5
Chongqi	15.7	26.6	21.1
Fujian	24.9	24.9	25.0
Gansu	19.8	16.7	19.2
Guangdong	20.0	24.3	21.1
Guangxi	23.5	18.8	22.6
Guizhou	22.6	19.5	22.0
Hainan	24.0	33.5	26.6
Hebei	26.1	38.8	29.9
Heilongjiang	23.1	28.1	24.8
Henan	25.8	31.1	27.3
Hubei	20.3	23.1	21.1
Hunan	21.2	12.0	18.9
Inner Mongolia	22.6	17.8	21.2
Jiangsu	26.9	29.4	27.9
Jiangxi	27.3	23.7	26.3
Jilin	20.7	28.3	23.1
Liaoning	19.1	28.0	21.9
Ningxia	19.8	16.9	19.2
Qinghai	21.2	12.4	19.4
Shaanxi	17.9	8.6	16.0
Shandong	27.1	29.4	27.8
Shanghai	24.0	19.0	22.5
Shanxi	25.2	31.7	27.1
Sichuan	18.2	18.6	18.4
Tianjin	24.2	45.2	30.7
Tibet	23.0	25.6	24.3
Xinjiang	23.0	19.0	22.1
Yunnan	22.7	8.8	20.1
Zhejiang	24.8	22.0	24.1
Mean	22.6	23.6	23.2

Source: Author's calculations based on *China Statistics Yearbook*, 1996–2011 editions.

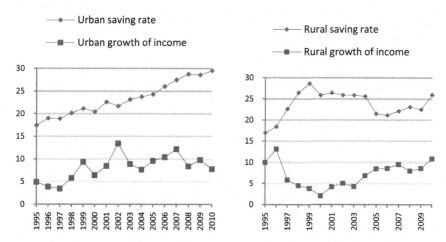

Fig. 2. Household saving rate and income growth rate, 1995–2010.

Source: Author's calculations based on *China Statistics Yearbook*, 1995–2011 editions.

The independent variables include the following variables. The first one is inertia or persistence variable, the one-year lag of the saving rate (SR(−1)). The second is income variable, the real growth rate of per capita income (CHY). Household saving rate and income growth rate for urban and rural households are shown in Fig. 2, where correlations of household saving rates and the real growth of per capita income is 0.57 in urban areas and −0.75 in rural areas. The third one is the financial variable, the real interest rate (RINT); the fourth one is demographic structure variable, the young dependency ratio (YOUNG) and the old dependency ratio (OLD), or the total dependency ratio (DEP). The age structure of the population in China is shown in Fig. 3, and the mean of these three variables for urban, rural and all households by province is shown in Table 2. The final one is the macroeconomic variable, the change rate of the consumer price index (INFL). The definitions of these variables are presented in Table 3.

Following Loayza *et al.* (2000), Schrooten and Stephan (2005), and Horioka and Wan (2007), I treat the demographic structure variables (YOUNG, OLD and DEP) as the only explanatory variables, that is, the strict exogenous, and I include them as instruments in the level equation as well as the first-difference equation. The other explanatory variables are treated as weakly exogenous and are included only in the first-difference equation. Finally, the one-period lag of the real growth rate of

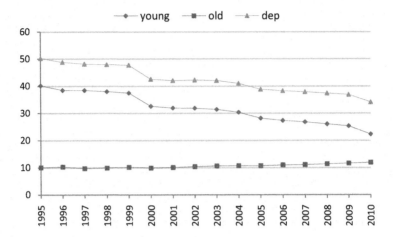

Fig. 3. Age structure of the population in China, 1995–2010.

Source: China Population Statistics Yearbook, 1996–2011 editions.

per capita gross provincial product was used as an instrument only in the level equation.

All provincial data are obtained from *China Statistic Yearbook* 1995–2011 editions, except the provincial data of demographic structure that is obtained from *China Population Statistic Yearbook* 1995–2011 editions. All provincial data are available for urban, rural and all households, with the exception of the real interest rate (RINT), which is available only for the country as a whole, and the real growth rate of per capita gross provincial product, which is available only for the province as a whole. Data for Chongqing, which became independent of Sichuan province in 1997, are available for 1997–2010, that for Tibet are available for 1999–2010, and that for other 29 provinces are available for 1994–2010. Thus, the total number of samples is 519. However, the income growth rate is used as an explanatory variable, and this reduces the number of samples to 488. Finally, the one-year lag term is used as explanatory variables in Eq. (2), reducing the number of samples to 457. The descriptive statistics on the variables is presented in Table 4.

4. Empirical Results

In this section, I describe my estimation results. The results of the determinants of the household saving rate for urban households, rural

Table 2. Age structure of the population by province (average in 1995–2010).

Province	Urban households			Rural households			All households		
	Young dependency ratio	Old dependency ratio	Total dependency ratio	Young dependency ratio	Old dependency ratio	Total dependency ratio	Young dependency ratio	Old dependency ratio	Total dependency ratio
Anhui	32.5	11.8	44.4	36.7	13.1	49.8	34.6	12.5	47.1
Beijing	11.4	12.3	23.7	22.8	12.7	35.5	17.1	12.5	29.6
Chongqi	23.9	14.1	38.0	34.1	15.3	49.4	29.0	14.7	43.7
Fujian	29.8	10.5	40.3	36.4	13.1	49.4	33.1	11.8	44.9
Gansu	32.5	9.6	42.1	38.0	8.6	46.6	35.3	9.1	44.4
Guangdong	29.5	8.9	38.3	45.2	13.3	58.6	37.4	11.1	48.5
Guangxi	35.0	12.0	47.0	39.6	12.6	52.2	37.3	12.3	49.6
Guizhou	39.3	10.5	49.8	45.8	10.5	56.3	42.5	10.5	53.0
Hainan	36.3	10.2	46.5	43.1	12.5	55.6	39.7	11.3	51.0
Hebei	29.0	10.6	39.6	30.8	10.7	41.4	29.9	10.6	40.5
Heilongjiang	20.8	9.7	30.5	25.3	7.4	32.8	23.1	8.6	31.6
Henan	33.3	10.9	44.1	36.5	11.1	47.6	34.9	11.0	45.9
Hubei	27.5	10.5	38.1	34.3	12.1	46.3	30.9	11.3	42.2
Hunan	28.3	11.9	40.3	32.4	13.1	45.5	30.3	12.5	42.9
Inner Mongolia	26.3	8.6	34.9	28.0	9.5	37.6	27.1	9.1	36.2
Jiangsu	23.5	12.6	36.1	27.1	15.5	42.6	25.3	14.1	39.3
Jiangxi	34.3	10.4	44.7	40.5	11.0	51.5	37.4	10.7	48.1

(*Continued*)

Table 2. (*Continued*)

Province	Urban households			Rural households			All households		
	Young dependency ratio	Old dependency ratio	Total dependency ratio	Young dependency ratio	Old dependency ratio	Total dependency ratio	Young dependency ratio	Old dependency ratio	Total dependency ratio
Jilin	19.3	10.1	29.4	24.4	8.3	32.7	21.8	9.2	31.1
Liaoning	18.4	13.1	31.5	24.7	10.8	35.5	21.6	12.0	33.5
Ningxia	34.3	7.9	42.2	45.0	7.3	52.3	39.7	7.6	47.3
Qinghai	32.3	8.4	40.8	41.6	7.5	49.1	36.9	8.0	44.9
Shaanxi	30.1	11.1	41.2	35.2	10.6	45.8	32.6	10.8	43.5
Shandong	26.1	11.1	37.1	28.3	13.1	41.4	27.2	12.1	39.3
Shanghai	14.4	18.1	32.4	16.5	17.5	34.0	15.4	17.8	33.2
Shanxi	31.5	9.4	40.9	36.1	10.3	46.4	33.8	9.8	43.7
Sichuan	27.2	13.4	40.5	33.1	13.6	46.8	30.1	13.5	43.6
Tianjin	13.7	15.5	29.1	29.1	10.7	39.8	21.4	13.1	34.5
Tibet	33.9	9.3	43.2	37.8	9.0	46.8	35.9	9.2	45.0
Xinjiang	35.4	23.6	24.5	42.8	7.5	50.3	39.1	15.6	37.4
Yunnan	34.9	10.6	45.5	39.3	10.0	49.3	37.1	10.3	47.4
Zhejiang	21.9	12.0	33.8	25.3	15.3	40.7	23.6	13.6	37.3
Mean	27.9	11.6	38.3	34.0	11.4	45.4	31.0	11.5	41.9

Notes: The young dependency ratio is defined as the ratio of the population aged 0–14 to the population aged 15–64; the old dependency ratio is defined as the ratio of the population aged 65 or older to the population aged 15–64; the total dependency ratio is defined as the ratio of the population aged 0–14 or 65 or older to the population aged 15–64.

Source: Author's calculations based on *China Population Statistics Yearbook*, 1996–2011 editions.

Table 3. Definition of variables.

Variable	Definition
SR(–1)	The one-year lag of the saving rate
CHY	The real rate of growth of per urban household disposable income or per rural household net income
RINT	The difference between nominal interest rate on 1-year bank and the rate of change of the consumer price index (The real interest rate)
YOUNG	The ratio of the population aged 0–14 to the population aged 15–64 (the young dependency rate)
OLD	The ratio of the population aged 65 or older to the population aged 15–64 (the old dependency rate)
DEP	The ratio of the population aged 0–14 or 65 or older to the population aged 15–64 (the total dependency rate)
INFL	The change rate of the consumer price index
RURAL	1 for rural households and 0 for urban households
Dependent variable	
SR	The household saving rate is the ratio of household saving to urban household disposable income or net rural household income (Household saving: Household disposable (or net) income minus household consumption).

households, all households and a pooled sample of urban households and rural households are presented in Tables 5 and 6, respectively.

First, I describe Table 5, which shows the results of the determinants of the household saving rate for urban households and rural households. The coefficient of SR(–1) (one-year lagged household saving rate) is positive and significant at 1% for four cases, which indicates inertia or persistence. Its coefficient is 0.792 and 0.793 for urban households and 0.738 and 0.545 for rural households, respectively. This indicates that γ of Eq. (2) is 0.208 and 0.207 for urban households and 0.262 and 0.455 for rural households, respectively. Thus, the long-run effect is 4.81 and 4.83 time short-run effect, for urban households, 3.82 and 2.20 time short-run effect, for rural households, respectively. The coefficient of CHY (the real rate of growth of per urban household

Table 4. Descriptive statistics.

Variable	Obs.	Mean	Std. Dev.	Minimum	Maximum
SR(all)	457	23.48	5.17	9.99	37.45
SR(urban)	457	22.88	5.46	7.66	37.43
SR(rural)	457	23.99	10.00	−6.45	51.64
YOUNG(all)	457	30.37	9.24	9.65	53.41
YOUNG(urban)	457	27.33	10.70	4.35	81.41
YOUNG(rural)	457	33.41	9.83	11.13	59.55
OLD(all)	457	11.52	3.35	5.25	46.41
OLD(urban)	457	11.51	5.38	4.22	87.46
OLD(rural)	457	11.53	3.19	5.13	22.97
DEP(all)	457	41.52	8.31	7.00	65.47
DEP(urban)	457	38.10	10.62	−48.60	78.72
DEP(rural)	457	44.95	9.10	26.22	73.29
NINT(all)	457	3.81	2.67	1.98	10.98
INFL(all)	457	3.07	4.57	−3.30	21.40
INFL(urban)	457	3.00	4.56	−3.40	20.30
INFL(rural)	457	3.25	4.67	−3.70	24.70
RINT(all)	457	0.75	3.17	−10.42	10.12
RINT(urban)	457	0.81	3.11	−9.32	10.02
RINT(rural)	457	0.56	3.42	−13.72	10.52
CHGDP(all)	457	10.93	4.99	−5.13	27.90
INCOME(all)	457	5895.22	3226.54	2021.75	21024.00
INCOME(urban)	457	9300.44	5039.74	2863.00	31838.00
INCOME(rural)	457	3336.78	2030.70	880.34	13978.00
CONS(all)	457	4745.84	2433.03	1766.48	16705.00
CONS(urban)	457	7001.68	3451.04	2482.20	23200.00
CONS(rural)	457	2490.00	1498.28	880.65	10210.00
CPI(all)	457	103.07	4.57	96.70	121.40
CPI(urban)	457	103.00	4.56	96.60	120.30
CPI(rural)	457	103.25	4.67	96.30	124.70
CHY(all)	457	7.37	3.69	−5.83	18.70
CHY(urban)	457	7.70	4.06	−6.93	22.77
CHY(rural)	457	7.16	4.83	−10.17	31.40

Notes: All income and consumption in this table are calculated at current prices.
Source: Author's calculations based on *China Statistics Yearbook* and *China Population Statistics Yearbook*, 1995–2011 editions.

disposable income or per rural household net income) is positive and significant in the sample of urban households; however, it is negative and significant for rural households. This indicates that a percentage point increase in the real rate of growth of per urban household disposable income causes 0.227 and 0.239 percentage points increase in the household saving rate, while a percentage point increase in the real rate of growth of per rural household net income causes 0.277 percentage and 0.285 percentage points decrease in the household saving rate. The long-run income effect is 2.20–4.83 times these short-run effects. The coefficient of RINT (the real interest rate) is not significant for urban households, whereas it is positive and significant in the sample of rural households. The real interest elasticity of saving rate is 0.520 and 0.665 for rural households. This indicates that a percentage point increase in the real interest rate causes 0.520 percentage and 0.665 percentage points increase in the short-run rural household saving rate. The coefficient of dependency ratio is negative in three out of four cases; however, it is insignificant in four cases. The coefficient of INFL (the change rate of the consumer price index) is positive and significant in three out of four cases. The coefficient of constant term, which shows a time trend, is positive and significant only in the last equation in Table 5, which suggests that there is an upward trend in rural household saving rate. All the instruments I used passed the Hansen test of over-identification in all four cases.

Second, I analyze Table 6, which shows the results of the determinants of the household saving rate for all households and a pooled sample of urban and rural households. The coefficient of SR(−1) is positive and significant at 1% level for four cases, which indicates inertia or persistence. Its coefficient is 0.492 and 0.891 for all households and 0.741 and 0.766 for a pooled sample of urban and rural households, respectively. This indicates that γ of Eq. (2) is 0.508 and 0.101 for all households and 0.259 and 0.234 for a pooled sample of urban and rural households, respectively. Thus, the long-run effect is 1.97 and 9.90 times the short-run effect for all households and 3.86 and 4.27 times the short-run effect for a pooled sample of urban households and rural households, respectively. The coefficient of CHY is insignificant for all four cases. The coefficient of RINT (the real interest rate) is not significant for all households, whereas it is positive and significant in a pooled sample of urban households and rural households. The real interest elasticity of saving rate is 0.556 and 0.599 for a pooled sample

Table 5. Results of the determinants of the household saving rate in China (Urban households and Rural households).

	Urban households		Rural households	
SR(−1)	0.792***	0.793***	0.738***	0.545***
	(0.079)	(0.075)	(0.123)	(0.136)
CHY	0.227*	0.239*	−0.277*	−0.285**
	(0.127)	(0.125)	(0.161)	(0.128)
RINT	0.042	0.043	0.520*	0.665*
	(0.176)	(0.181)	(0.276)	(0.358)
YOUNG	−0.012		−0.150	
	(0.026)		(0.122)	
OLD	0.044		−0.344	
	(0.032)		(0.307)	
DEP		−0.013		−0.101
		(0.017)		(0.088)
INFL	0.427**	0.450***	0.653*	0.546
	(0.168)	(0.171)	(0.285)	(0.333)
CONSTANT	2.472	2.946	16.125	16.406**
	(2.093)	(1.892)	(10.252)	(6.852)
Number of observations	457	457	457	457
Number of groups	31	31	31	31
Hansen test of over-identification (p-value)	0.371	0.359	0.399	0.998
Transformation used	First differences			
Instruments only for first difference equation	GMM (SR(−1), CHY, RINT, INFL,(4 4) YOUNG, OLD	GMM (SR(−1), CHY, RINT, INFL, (4 4) collapse) DEP	GMM (SR(−1), CHY, RINT, INFL, (4 4) collapse) YOUNG, OLD	GMM (SR(−1), CHY, RINT, INFL, (4 .) collapse) DEP
Instruments for both first difference and level equations				
Instruments only for level equation	CHGDP(−1)			

Note: Numbers in parentheses are standard errors. ***, **, * are statistically significant at the 1%, 5% and 10% levels, respectively.

Table 6. Results of the determinants of the household saving rate in China (all households and pooled sample of urban and rural households).

	All households		Pooled sample of urban and rural households	
SR(−1)	0.492***	0.891***	0.741***	0.766***
	(0.133)	(0.063)	(0.063)	(0.060)
CHY	0.109	−0.038	0.004	0.023
	(0.099)	(0.069)	(0.063)	(0.056)
RINT	0.155	0.099	0.556***	0.599***
	(0.208)	(0.164)	(0.197)	(0.186)
YOUNG	−0.111*		−0.076**	
	(0.047)		(0.032)	
OLD	0.101		−0.000	
	(0.120)		(0.059)	
DEP		0.000		−0.077**
		(0.044)		(0.035)
INFL	0.403**	0.367**	0.521***	0.577***
	(0.187)	(0.148)	(0.160)	(0.151)
RURAL			0.962*	1.028*
			(0.521)	(0.526)
CONSTANT	12.705***	2.725	6.693***	6.717***
	(3.774)	(2.420)	(2.033)	(2.167)

(Continued)

Table 6. (*Continued*)

	All households		Pooled sample of urban and rural households	
Number of observations	457	457	914	914
Number of groups	31	31	62	62
Hansen test of over-identification (p-value)	0.150	0.999	1.000	1.000
Transformation used		First differences		
Instruments only for first difference Equation	GMM (SR(−1), CHY, RINT, INFL, (4 4) collapse)	GMM (SR(−1), CHY, RINT, INFL,(4 4) collapse)	GMM (SR(−1), CHY, RINT, INFL,(4 4))	GMM (SR(−1), CHY, RINT, INFL, (4.))
Instruments for both first difference and level equations	YOUNG, OLD	DEP	YOUNG, OLD	DEP
Instruments only for level equation		CHGDP(−1)		

Note: Numbers in parentheses are standard errors. ***, **, * are statistically significant at the 1%, 5%, and 10% levels, respectively.

of urban households and rural households. This indicates that a percentage point increase in the real interest rate causes 0.556 and 0.599 percentage points increase in the pooled short-run household saving rate. The coefficient of young dependency ratio is negative and significant in the two cases; the total dependency ratio is negative and significant in one out of two cases. The coefficient of the RURAL dummy in the pooled sample of urban and rural households is positive and significant in two cases, which suggests that the saving rate of rural households has a more pronounced upward trend than that of urban households after controlling for other factors. The coefficient of INFL is positive and significant in four cases. The coefficient of constant term is positive and significant in three out of four cases, which suggests that there is an upward trend in household saving rate in China. All the instruments I used passed the Hansen test of over-identification in these four cases.

Finally, I compare my empirical results with that of previous studies. The coefficient of SR(−1) (one-year lagged household saving rate) is positive and significant at 1% level for all cases. This result is similar to Horioka and Wan (2007). Moreover, the coefficient of CHY is positive and significant in the sample of urban households, and this result is also similar to that of Horioka and Wan (2007). Coefficients of CHY for rural households are inverse, that is, my result is negative, which is similar to Kraay (2000) and Wan *et al.* (2003); however, it is positive in Horioka and Wan (2007). In particular, the coefficient of CHY is insignificant for four cases in all households and a pooled sample of urban and rural households, while it is positive and significant in Kraay (2000), Modigliani and Cao (2004) and Horioka and Wan (2007). The insignificance of the coefficient of CHY in this study may be caused by the offset effect of the inverse income effect on household saving rate for urban and rural households. The effect of other variables on household saving rate is similar to that in Horioka and Wan (2007).

5. Conclusion

This chapter explores the determinants of household saving rate in China for urban, rural, and all types of households and a pool of urban and rural households, using recent data, panel provincial data of 1995–2010, and a superior estimation model — system GMM.

I find that the coefficient of SR(−1) is positive and significant at 1% level for all cases; this indicates inertia or persistence. The coefficient of CHY is positive and significant in the sample of urban households; however, it is negative for rural households; moreover, it is insignificant in all four cases for all households and a pooled sample of urban and rural households. The coefficient of RINT is positive and significant in two cases for rural households and a pooled sample. The expected effect of dependency ratio on household saving rate is insignificant for urban and rural households, whereas the young dependency ratio is negative and significant in two cases for all households and a pooled sample, while the old dependency ratio is negative and significant for a pooled sample. The coefficient of INFL is positive and significant in seven cases out of all nine cases. The coefficient of the RURAL dummy in the pooled sample of urban and rural households is positive and significant in all cases. In summary, my study in part supports the life cycle and permanent income hypothesis.

The effect of CHY on household saving rate for urban households is positive and significant, perhaps because of uncertain expenditure that includes education, medical expenditure, buying a home and expenditure after retirement. On the other hand, the effect of CHY on household saving rate for rural households is negative and significant, perhaps because of the implementation of many policies since 2004 favoring rural residents, including exemption from all agricultural taxes, agricultural subsidies and the New Cooperative Medical System for rural residents implemented in 2003.

This research mainly recommends the introduction of a policy to further improve the level of social security system and to increase the income of residents, in particular, rural residents. Such a policy could reduce the income disparity between rural and urban residents and be expected to increase household consumption, thereby supporting the sustainable growth of the Chinese economy in the future.

Acknowledgments

This research was supported by a grant-in-aid from Project of Young Foundation for Humanities and Social Sciences of the Ministry of Education of China (Grant No. 09YJC790166) and Major Project for Humanities and Social Sciences Key Research Institutes of Ministry of Education of China (Grant No. 12JJD790001).

References

Arellano, M and O Bover (1995). Another look at the instrumental variable estimation of error-components models. *Journal of Econometrics*, 68, 29–51.

Blundell, R and S Bond (1998). Initial conditions and moment restrictions in dynamic panel data models. *Journal of Econometrics*, 87, 115–143.

Chao, CC, JP Laffargue and E Yu (2011). The Chinese saving puzzle and the life-cycle hypothesis: A revaluation. *China Economic Review*, 22, 108–120.

Chamon, M and E Prasad (2008). Why are saving rates of urban households in China rising? *IMF Working Paper* WP/08/145.

Deaton, A (1992). *Understanding Consumption*. Oxford: Clarendon Press.

Hang, B and X Guo (2009). Precautionary saving under habit formation: An empirical study of Chinese urban population consumption behavior. *Statistical Research*, 26(3), 38–43. (in Chinese)

Horioka, CY and J Wan (2007). The determinants of household saving in China: A dynamic panel analysis of provincial data. *Journal of Money, Credit and Banking*, 39(8), 2077–2096.

Kraay, A (2000). Household saving in China. *World Bank Economic Review*, 14, 545–570.

Li, Y and J Wen (2005). An analysis on relation between precautionary saving behaviors of urban residents and uncertainty of consumption in China. *Management World*, 5, 14–18. (in Chinese)

Loayza, N, K Schmidt-Hebbel and L Serven (2000). What drives private saving across the world? *Review of Economics and Statistics*, 82, 165–181.

Man, J and Y Tong (2009). An empirical analysis of liquidity restraints' effect on urban residents' consumption in China. *Mathematics in Practice and Theory*, 39, 16–21. (in Chinese)

Modigliani, F (1970). The life cycle hypothesis of saving and intercountry differences in the saving ratio. In *Induction, Growth and Trade: Essays in Honour of Sir Roy Harrod*, WA Eltis, MFG Scott and JN Wolfe (eds.), pp. 197–225. Oxford: Clarendon Press.

Modigliani, F and SL Cao (2004). The Chinese saving puzzle and the life-cycle hypothesis. *Journal of Economic Literature*, 42, 145–170.

Nerlove, M (1958). Distributed lags and demand analysis for agricultural and other commodities. In *Agricultural Handbook*, N.141. Washington: US Dept. of Agriculture.

Roodman, D (2005). *Xtabond2: Stata Module to Extend Xtabond Dynamic Panel Data Estimator.* Washington DC: Center for Global Development. Available at http://econpapers.repec.org/software/bocbocode/s435901.htm.

Roodman, D (2007). How to do xtabond2: An introduction to 'difference' and 'system' GMM in Stata. *Working Paper* 103, Center for Global Development, Washington, DC. Available at http://www.cgdev.org/content/publications/detail/11619.

Schrooten, M and S Stephan (2005). Private savings and transition: Dynamic panel data evidence from accession countries. *Economics of Transition*, 13, 287–309.

Shi, J and H Zhu (2004). Household precautionary saving and strength of the precautionary motive in China: 1999–2003. *Economic Research Journal*, 10, 66–74. (in Chinese)

Wan, G, Q Shi and S Tang (2003). Saving behavior in a transition economy: An empirical case study of rural China. *Economic Research Journal*, 5, 3–12. (in Chinese)

Windmeijer, F (2005). A finite sample correction for the variance of linear efficient two-step GMM estimators. *Journal of Econometrics*, 126, 25–51.

Yu, Y and J Li (2000). The theory of consumption functions of Chinese residents and its verification. *Social Sciences in China*, 1, 123–133. (in Chinese)

Zhou, J (2005). An analysis on precautionary saving behaviors of Chinese rural people. *Statistical Research*, 9, 45–50. (in Chinese)

CHAPTER 9[1]

FINANCING INFRASTRUCTURE CONSTRUCTION IN CHINA

Long Ke

Senior Fellow, Fujitsu Research Institute (FRI)
New Pier Takeshiba South Tower
16-1, Kaigan 1-chome, Minato-ku, Tokyo 105-0022, Japan

1. Introduction

The Chinese government launched a reform of the economic system thirty four years ago and decided to build a real market-oriented economic system instead of a central planning system about twenty years ago. Deng Xiaoping was the architect of the so called "open door policy". He proposed the liberalization of economic control by the government. Deng himself is a reformer, but at the same time he is also a realist. He knew that China could not maintain social stability and economic development without the flag of socialism post-Mao Zedong thirty years ago. In short, Deng Xiaoping's reform aims to improve economic development through liberalization and deregulation while maintaining the monopoly status of the communist party.

Deng Xiaoping's reform is called "gradualism", which is different from the shock therapy of East European countries. In fact, Deng Xiaoping never mentioned the privatization of state-owned enterprises (SOEs). The gradualism reform aims to allow private companies to enter into market

---

[1] This chapter owes much to Demigruc-Kunt and Levine (2004), Faure (2006), Gao (2007), Lardy (2007), NDRC comprehensive Transportation Institute (2009), Nolan (2001), and Walter and Howei (2011).

competition. To strengthen SOE competitiveness, the Chinese government tried to clarify ownership and responsibility. In 1990 and 1991, stock exchange markets were established in Shanghai and Shenzhen. Thousands of SOEs are listed in these two markets. It is expected that stock listing will contribute to the ownership reform of SOEs.

But Deng Xiaoping's reform faced some difficulties, i.e., lack of funding and technology. This presented a big challenge for Deng Xiaoping to reform the economic system because the political system was still ideologically communist. In the 1980s, building a market economy was still taboo in the public media. It was said of the reform that "a commercial economy will play a complimentary role in Chinese society", so the central planning economy was still the main part of China's economy.

For Deng Xiaoping the real challenge was enforcing the open door policy to allow foreign companies to invest in China freely. There were many critics of the open door policy within the government. Their main concern, which was a reasonable one, was that a free market economy would require a trade-off with socialism. As a result, the SOEs lost their shares in market competition. However, the Chinese economy is benefitting from the open door policy. First of all, market competition improved the efficiency of the economy. Second, Chinese local companies acquired many advanced technologies from foreign companies. Third, foreign companies generated much liquidity in China. These are all key points for Chinese economy and industry to catch up with the global economy.

In this chapter, I focus on how the Chinese government financed infrastructure construction, especially in the early stages of the open door policy, since at that time it was almost impossible to finance in the domestic market. As a result, some government officials wanted to open the door to foreign companies. But due to security concerns, the Chinese government only allowed domestic infrastructure companies to borrow money from foreign commercial banks and companies. This strategy of infrastructure construction is an example of China's gradualism over the past decades. It seems to me that this gradualism strategy is both a choice by the government and a result of the Chinese social situation.

2. The Constraints of Economic Development and Infrastructure Projects

For any emerging economy it is important to first build a good infrastructure, including roads, bridges, dams, railways, water processing and

Table 1.   Construction of transportation routes (10,000 km).

	Railways in operation	Electric railways	Roads	Highways	Civil aviation routes	Petroleum and gas pipelines
1980	5.33	0.17	88.83	—	19.53	0.87
1985	5.52	0.41	94.24	—	27.72	1.17
1990	5.79	0.69	102.83	0.05	50.68	1.59
1995	6.24	0.97	115.70	0.21	112.90	1.72
2000	6.87	1.49	140.27	1.63	150.29	2.47
2005	7.54	1.94	334.52	4.10	199.85	4.40
2009	8.55	3.02	386.08	6.51	234.51	6.91

Source: National Bureau of Statistics of China.

supply systems, and power plants. Table 1 shows the progress of communication and transportation infrastructure construction. In the early days of the open door policy, the lack of infrastructure was a serious bottleneck for economic development. The policy makers knew how important infrastructure was for the economy to catch up to other countries, but the problem was a shortage of money. Unlike other emerging economies, China is still a socialist country; ownership of land has not been liberalized and private investors are not allowed to invest their capital in infrastructure building.

Another issue was that the level of technology was too low. The state-run power generators needed to develop their technology, and even the technology to build roads, railways and bridges was lacking and needed to be improved.

To overcome the constraints imposed by lack of infrastructure-building technology, the Chinese government decided to allow foreign companies to form alliances with state-run companies in order to invest in China partially. For example, a foreign company could invest in power generation, but the power plant's operation would still be regulated by the government. Foreign companies were not allowed to operate power plants in China.

China's national strategy was to improve domestic companies to be able to pick up high level technology from top global companies. Infrastructure like power plants, roads, railways, dams, water processing and supply plants are all capital-concentrated industries. In China almost all of these projects are national projects. The government, including central and local governments, generated a huge amount of fiscal liquidity and poured it into infrastructure development. In the 1980s, many local governments began to use the slogan *Yao Zhi Fu, Xian Xiu Lu*, which means "If you want to be rich, you must build the road". Compared to other emerging economies, the Chinese people paid much more attention to infrastructure development. Although China's per capita GDP is still about $5,000, its highway network in urban areas is complete. Last year, there was a serious express railway accident in Wenzhou, Zhejiang province, but the express railway has developed rapidly nonetheless.

Compared with infrastructure development in India, the biggest difference is that China has ensured that its water supply is safe. Although environmental pollution has become more serious day by day and China is facing a serious shortage of clean water, in urban areas the water supply is not the bottleneck of economic development.

What about electric power generation in today's China? Basically, power supply and demand is balanced, but the first problem is how to adjust the load of peak power demand. Second is how to stabilize the supply of power resources. Third is how to increase the efficiency of power usage.

Over the past decades the government has made great efforts to reform the state-run enterprises into commercial-based companies. The only organization which has not been reformed is the Ministry of Railways (MOR). MOR is still a government sector, and also a player. It is easy for MOR to finance within the government and formal financial government, but the problem is that its operations are not transparent enough. It is important to strengthen the governance on the operations of infrastructure developers.

It is doubtless that China's infrastructure development over the past decades has contributed a lot to its economic development. About twenty years ago in a closed international meeting about the urban re-development in Shanghai sponsored by the World Bank and the Chinese government, there was much discussion about infrastructure development. One of the Chinese officials commented as follows: "Developing infrastructure in a developing country is just like making clothes for a baby; just as the clothes must be made not in the baby's current size but big enough for the baby to grow into, so too must infrastructure be targeted at the future size of the economy." This philosophy is applicable even to China's current situation.

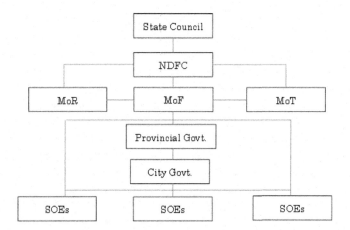

Fig. 1. The administration of infrastructure development in China.

Note: MoF = Ministry of Finance; MoR = Ministry of Railways; MoT = Ministry of Transport. *Source*: Interviews with government think tanks.

3. The Role of Government in Infrastructure Development

As with most of the other emerging economies, the Chinese government recognized the importance of infrastructure development in the early 1980s. But the key point of an economic development strategy is to sustain the economic development; priority for developing infrastructure was given to roads, railways and power station construction. This strategy played a very important role in accelerating China's economic catch-up.

Under the central planning economy, infrastructure development and operation was controlled by the government. Figure 1 simply shows us the administrative system related to infrastructure in China. In the first step of the reform, the developers and operators became market-based bodies, although most of these companies are still state-run or state-owned. As a result, infrastructure development was given an important place in the economic development strategy. However, if the government only cares about economic development in the short term, some projects, such as environmental protection, will be very difficult to realize, and the current economic development will become unsustainable.

Chinese politics is still a monopolistic system. It is hard to imagine the Chinese government relinquishing control of infrastructure development at all. Even under the Jiang Zemin administration, Premier Zhu

Rongji made progress in deregulation and liberalization, but this was limited to small businesses only; this was called *"Zhua Da Fang Xiao"*, which means "keep the big ones, throw the small ones back". In other words, the government will not allow the privatization of big state-owned enterprises. Delays in liberalization, deregulation and privatization of SOEs are causing an imbalance in infrastructure development in China. For example, there are a lot of big projects, like the three gorges dam, but fewer necessary small projects, like peak load power stations. The big SOEs only care about big projects and never turn their attention to small business. In most cases, infrastructure will not function without small projects complementing larger ones.

4. The New Stage of Infrastructure Development

It seems that the Chinese government has recognized the importance of advancing the liberalization of infrastructure investment by private companies. This means that China cannot rely on the SOEs' investment to develop infrastructure anymore. China needs to allow private companies to play a much more important and active role in infrastructure. In its twelfth five-year plan, which covers the period from 2011 to 2015, the government announced that it would allow more and more private companies to invest in infrastructure development. This could be an important turning point for China in opening its infrastructure market.

But in the early 1990s, China experienced serious shortages of electricity in coastal industrial areas. To overcome this difficulty, the Chinese government allowed foreign capital to flow into the power generation market. In Guangdong and Guangxi provinces several BOT projects (build-operation-transfer) were established. It was a pioneer case in China, and a globally unique case at that. Foreign banks organized a consortium to generate liquidity for Chinese power stations, which then used the money to buy advanced machinery from foreign heavy electric makers. It was considered a win–win situation for China and industrialized countries. But the Chinese government did not seem to be generally encouraging of domestic companies forming alliances with foreign firms anymore, whether through BOTs or joint ventures. One of the reasons for this may have been that the government was concerned that domestic infrastructure would be controlled by foreign companies. Therefore, China needed new technologies and money, but refused to be controlled by the foreign companies.

Since the mid-1990s, Chinese heavy electric industries have succeeded in catching up rapidly. As a result, China, in essence succeeded in overcoming its shortage of electricity supply. Nowadays, Chinese heavy electric manufactures are powerful enough to compete globally. Such a movement happened not only in heavy electric industries, but in highways, express railways and container port terminals as well.

However, China cannot simply expect the infrastructure to be developed by big SOEs alone. China needs to improve deregulation and allow more and more private capital inflow into the market. There is in fact great concern about Chinese provincial and municipal fiscal balance sheets. Most of the local governments financed huge amounts of money to build up their cities, for example by constructing a subway system. And it is clear that in many cities local government officials were corrupted because of the lack of governance. Therefore, the problem here is figuring out the best mix for developing infrastructure. We need to make clear what the role of government is and what the role of private companies is. For example, Zhang Weiying, a professor at Beijing University, raised his voice at an international forum held in Beijing recently, saying: "China needs to privatize all of its SOEs". Although there are still many conservative officials inside the government, the citizenry have reached a consensus on privatization. The problem now is only the speed and timing of privatization's progress. The China of today has no other option but to privatize its SOEs. The monopoly in infrastructure development is reducing the efficiency of infrastructure construction and operation.

According to the new five-year plan, the government will allow private companies to compete with SOEs to construct infrastructure. Such reform means that China is about to step up to a new stage of constructing and developing infrastructure, although there is still a long way to go. For example, China needs to undertake the creation of a transparent and fair bidding system, and it also needs to strengthen governance of construction and operation.

5. PFI-Based Infrastructure Development

On July 23, 2011, a serious express railway accident occurred and an estimated 50 people lost their lives. One of the lessons to be learned from this is that the MoR is only concerned with realizing speed and did not pay enough attention to safety. Since then the MoR has been faced with a shortage of liquidity because investors have refused to invest in railway bonds. At the same time, the state council forced the MoR to reform its management and recapitalize its express business. As a result, the MoR had to slow down express railway construction and operation. Until now, the MoR has financed from the formal financial market, which includes state-owned commercial banks, and the domestic bond market. It seems now that this is not enough. The state council has decided to push the MoR to partially open the railway construction to private companies. Although the scheme has not been confirmed, this could be a real PFI (private finance initiative)-based infrastructure development model in railway construction.

In China, highway and bridge construction and operation are regulated by the MoT. But early on, a part of highways at the local level was opened to private capital, even overseas Chinese capital. The typical BOT and TOT models were tested in China's southern coastal area, and until now there were few reports of trouble within the operation.

On the other hand, airport terminals and container terminals are basically constructed and operated by state-owned special companies. These SPCs can finance from domestic banks while also accepting ODA from foreign governments, but they must be licensed by the government (SDRC and MoF).

Furthermore, China reformed the administrative system of its electricity supply. First, China divided the national grid into five regional base sub-grids, e.g., the East China Electric Grid. Electric power generation is basically separated at the provincial level; a state-owned electricity company was established in each province. But since the electricity companies only generate and sell the electricity to the grid, the power stations can of course be state-owned, but they can also be BOT, TOT or Joint Ventures with private or foreign capital.

Finally, China decided to try accepting foreign capital to construct its waterworks system. The waterworks system in China is still under development and the water pollution is very serious. First, the water business cannot be commercially based, so local governments want to construct a new water supply system, but they do not have enough resources to repay their debts. Second, water supply infrastructure development is not a strong enough driving force to support economic development, and therefore local governments do not attribute high priority to the construction of waterworks.

The conclusion here is that in China, the government is the main player in the construction of infrastructure. China's political monopoly system will not likely change in the near future, but China needs to liberalize control and allow private companies to participate in the construction of infrastructure.

6. Privatization, Liberalization and Deregulation

The Chinese government implemented a 4 trillion yuan stimulation policy in 2009 and 2010 to encourage economic development. Most of the planned projects were infrastructure construction, including railways, highways and electricity grids and distribution systems. But the government never made it clear how it would finance such a huge budget. In China most big projects like express railways are managed and constructed by the central government and companies under government control. Such national companies borrow money from state-owned commercial banks and raise bond in the market, which is supported by the government directly or indirectly. In the bond market, infrastructure bonds are considered to be almost the same as sovereign bonds, because infrastructure cannot go bankrupt. According to official data, developers are raising much more money by themselves than they receive from state budgets and state bank loans (Table 2).

However, infrastructure cannot be constructed by the government and state-owned companies alone. The government needs to promote deregulation in order to allow private companies to invest more in infrastructure construction. In the past two decades, road and bridge construction has been opened to private companies through BOT and TOT

Table 2.   The finance of fixed-assets investment in China.

	1990	1995	2000	2009	2010
State budget	393.0	621.1	2,109.5	12,685.7	14,672.7
Bank loans	885.5	4,1987	6,727.3	39,302.8	47,022.8
Foreign investment	284.6	2,295.9	1,696.2	4,623.7	5,025.3
Self-raising funds	2,954.4	13,409.2	22,577.1	153,514.8	197,552.1
Others	—	—	—	40,102.6	46,060.8
Total	**4,517.0**	**20,019.3**	**32,917.7**	**224,598.8**	**278,139.8**

Source: National Bureau of Statistics of China.

models. Electric power plants have also allowed some private companies to invest, including foreign companies, but non-state-owned companies are not allowed to take the majority share of capital.

On the other hand, railway construction is still controlled by the Ministry of Railways. There have been many recommendations to increase deregulation and liberalization in railway construction and operation, but the Hu Jingtao administration does not have strong enough leadership to reform the railway administration system, which yet remains a monopoly system. In 2011, Liu Zhijun, the Minister of Railways, was arrested by the Central Commission for Discipline Inspection of the Communist Party. This case brought the corruption in the railway administration into focus. Similarly, bad service and inefficiency are also major problems. Regardless of the kind of financing, the key here is to strengthen the transparency of operation and administration and to improve the disclosure of information in order to keep corruption under control.

7. Conclusion

In conclusion, improving infrastructure construction is still a main engine for driving Chinese economic development. The government and state-owned companies are still the main players in infrastructure construction. State-owned commercial banks and national policy banks will play an important role in helping to finance the state-owned companies. Finally, the fiscal budget is still an important source of funds for infrastructure construction.

In addition to public funds, it is becoming increasingly important to introduce private capital investment into infrastructure construction. There have been some successful cases of using BOT and TOT models to construct roads and power plants. China can extend such models to other infrastructure, such as railway construction.

At present, there are over five hundred cities in China which have decided to build "smart cities". Smart cities are much friendlier to the environment and more efficient in energy utilization. In the future, infrastructure construction will shift from hardware to software. Many new concepts of infrastructure construction will be created.

However, there are still some difficulties and problems which need to be solved. First of all, the infrastructure administration system needs to be reformed to be more transparent. Second, the bidding system must be more fair and just. Third, it is necessary to privatize state-owned companies so that they can compete with private companies in the same market and under the same conditions. Fourth, the key point here is not only to construct new infrastructure, but also to increase the efficiency of its operation as well. There is still a long way to go for China to improve its infrastructure construction.

References

Demirguc-Kunt, A and R Levine (2004). *Financial Structure and Economic Growth.* Cambridge, MA and London: MIT Press.

Faure, D (2006). *China and Capitalism: A History of Business Enterprise in Modern China.* Hong Kong: Hong Kong University Press.

Gao, J (2007). *China's Debt Capital Market.* Hoboken, NJ: John Wiley & Son.

Lardy, NR (2002). *Integrating China into the Global Economy.* Washington DC: Brookings Institution Press.

NDRC Comprehensive Transportation Research Institute (2009). *The Road of China's Communication and Transportation Development and Reform.* China Railway Publishing House.

Nolan, P (2001). *China and the Global Economy: National Champions, Industrial Policy and the Big Business Revolution.* Houndmills, Basingstoke, Hampshire and New York: Palgrave MacMillan.

Walter, CE and FJT Howei (2011). *Red Capitalism: The Fragile Financial Foundation of China's Extraordinary Rise.* Singapore: John Wiley & Sons (Asia) Pte. Ltd.

CHAPTER 10

IS THE RENMINBI
APPRECIATING FAST ENOUGH?

Takuji Kinkyo

Faculty of Economics, Kobe University
2-1, Rokkodai, Nada-Ku, Kobe 657-8501, Japan
Kinkyo@econ.kobe-u.ac.jp

1. Introduction

China has long been accused of keeping the renminbi undervalued so
that its export competitiveness can be maintained (IMF, 2004; Goldstein
and Mussa, 2005; Bergsten *et al.*, 2009). In response to the international
pressures to increase flexibility in the exchange rate regime, the Chinese
government introduced a new exchange rate regime in July 2005. Under
this regime, the renminbi would be managed with reference to a basket
of currencies rather than being pegged to the U.S. dollar. However, the
renminbi-dollar rate is kept within a narrow band and its central rate
has been allowed to appreciate only slowly. Although China's current
account surplus has declined sharply from the peak level, it continues to
run large trade surplus and accumulate huge foreign reserves. These
observations naturally raise the following question: Is the renminbi
appreciating fast enough to match the pace of changes in underlying
economic fundamentals, notably the growth of productivity and the
accumulation of net foreign assets?

This chapter addresses this question by estimating the equilibrium
exchange rate of the renminbi using the Clark and MacDonald's (1999)
behavioral equilibrium exchange rate (BEER) approach. The BEER

approach posits that the real exchange rate varies according to changes in underlying fundamentals and explicitly models the real exchange rate as a function of a set of fundamental variables. Estimates of the BEER are derived from the equilibrium relation between the real exchange rate and the fundamental variables. The exchange rate is considered to be in equilibrium when it coincides with the BEER.

To test and estimate the long-run relationship between the real exchange rate and fundamentals, we employ the autoregressive distributed-lag (ARDL) procedure developed by Pesaran *et al.* (1996) and Pesaran and Shin (1999). The ARDL procedure has the advantage that it can be applied irrespective of whether the underlying regressors are integrated of order zero $I(0)$ or one $I(1)$.[1] Accordingly, it can circumvent the pre-testing problems associated with standard co-integration analysis which requires the classification of the variables into $I(0)$ and $I(1)$.

The rest of the paper is organized as follows. Section 2 provides a brief review of existing studies that apply the BEER approach to the renminbi. Section 3 describes the econometric methodology and presents the results of the estimation. Section 4 provides the evaluation of the magnitude of the undervaluation and examines the underlying causes. Section 5 concludes.

2. Review of BEER Approach

The BEER approach has been extensively used in the estimation of equilibrium exchange rates.[2] However, there are not many studies that apply the BEER approach to the renminbi. One major obstacle to applying the BEER approach is the limited availability of Chinese statistical data. Many of the key data on fundamental variables are available at best on annual basis. Accordingly, the existing studies tend to use a smaller set

---

[1] If a variable must be differenced d times before it becomes stationary, then it is said to be integrated of order d, or $I(d)$. $I(0)$ is stationary in levels, while $I(1)$ becomes stationary after differencing once.

[2] The empirical work that applies the BEER approach includes Maeso-Fernandez *et al.* (2001), MacDonald (2002), MacDonald and Ricci (2003), Egert (2005), Iimi (2006), and Kinkyo (2008).

of fundamental variables. Moreover, when the quarterly data are not available, the interpolation technique is applied to convert annual data to quarterly data.

In addition to data constraints, there is a potential structural break in the official data on exchange rates. Prior to the unification in 1994, two types of exchange rates coexisted: The official rate and the swap market rate.[3] The official rate had been higher than the then prevailing swap market rate and the official rate was devalued by more than 30% when the two rates were unified.[4] This indicates that there is a potential structural break in the exchange rate data measured by the official rate.

In fact, Funke and Rahn (2005) apply the unit-root test suggested by Perron (1997) and find a structural break in China's real exchange rate data at 1993Q4. The data on nominal exchange rates are based on official rates, which are derived from the IMF's International Financial Statistics. They also estimate a threshold model using Hansen's (2000) estimation procedure and find a significant structural break at 1993Q4. Given the significant evidence of structural break, they estimate the final model for the period from 1994Q1 to 2002Q4.

Table 1 summarizes the main results of recent studies that apply the BEER approach to the renminbi. As can be seen from the table, the magnitude of undervaluation differs significantly from one study to another. One major source of difference seems to be whether time series or panel data are used for estimation. While Funke and Rahn (2005) and Wang (2004) use the time series data of China, Benassy-Quere *et al.* (2006), Coudert and Couharde (2007) and MacDonald and Dias (2007) use the panel data composed of a group of countries. The latter set of studies tends to find greater amount of undervaluation for the renminbi. It should, however, be noted that panel estimates can be sensitive to the country sample. This is particularly so when there is a large degree of heterogeneity in the long-run relationship between the real exchange rate and fundamentals across the sample countries. This appears to be a major drawback of panel estimation.

---

[3] Goldstein and Lardy (2009) provide detailed descriptions on the evolution of China's exchange rate regimes.

[4] The official rate was devalued from 5.8 RMB/U.S. dollar to 8.7 RMB/U.S. dollar in January 1997 (Goldstein and Lardy, 2009, p. 6).

Table 1. BEER estimation of the Renminbi.

	Country sample	Estimation period	Fundamentals variables	Estimated undervaluation	Others
Benassy-Quere et al. (2006)	15 countries and regions including China	1980Q1–2004Q3	*pro, nfa*	31~45% in 2004 (real effective rate)	
Coudert and Couharde (2007)	23 emerging market economies	1980Q1–2005Q2	*pro*	16~29% in 2005 (bilateral dollar rate)	The coefficient on *pro* not significant for China
Funke and Rahn (2005)	China	1994Q1–2002Q4	*pro, nfa*	6% in 2002 (real effective rate)	Significant evidence of structural break
MacDonald and Dias (2007)	15 countries and regions including China	1988Q1–2006Q1	*pro*, terms of trade, *nfa, ird*	17% appreciation in real effective terms needed to reduce global imbalances substantially	The coefficient on *ird* not significant
Wang (2004)	China	1980–2003 (annual)	*pro, nfa*, openness	5% in 2003 (real effective rate)	

Note: pro; productivity differential, *nfa*; net foreign assets, *ird*; interest rate differential.

3. Econometric Methodology and Results

Given the potential drawback of using panel data, we use the time series data of China for the estimation. We also explicitly take into account a potential structural break around 1994 by including a dummy variable. Following the existing studies, we assume that the BEER for the renminbi is a function of three variables such that

$$q = f(pro, nfa, tot), \tag{1}$$

where q denotes the real effective exchange rate expressed as the foreign currency price of a unit of home currency and *pro* denotes the productivity differential capturing the Balassa–Samuelson effect (Balassa, 1964; Samuelson, 1964), which is measured by China's purchasing power parity (PPP)-based per-capita GDP relative those of major trading partners. This variable is expected to be positively related to q. The net foreign asset (*nfa*) position is defined as the stock of net foreign assets to GDP. As predicted by a stock-flow consistent exchange rate model such as the one developed by Obstfeld and Rogoff (1995), *nfa* is expected to be positively related to q. Due to data constraints, the accumulated value of trade balance is used as a proxy for measuring the stock of net foreign assets.

The variable denoted by *tot* refers to terms of trade, which is measured by the export unit value to the import unit value. The effect of terms of trade on q cannot be signed *a priori*. For example, a worsening of the terms of trade may lower real income and, thus, lower the demand for all goods, leading to a fall in q (Harberger, 1950; Laurenson and Metzler, 1950). However, this income effect can be exceeded by the substitution effect (Edwards, 1989; Cashin and McDermott, 1998). A rise in the relative price of imported goods may induce a shift in demand towards non-traded goods, which leads to an increase in the prices of non-traded goods (intratemporal substitution). Moreover, a higher import price may lead to an increase in overall price levels, inducing a shift in demand from the current consumption to the future consumption (intertemporal substitution). When these substitution effects are stronger than the income effect, the terms of trade will be negatively related to q.

The model also includes a constant, trend and a dummy variable. The dummy variable, which is denoted by $D94$, is added to adjust for the divergence between the official rate and the swap market rate before 1994. The effective exchange rate faced by exporters and importers can be considered to be some weighted average of the official rate and the swap market rate. *D94* takes the value of one until 1993Q4 and zero afterwards. The positive coefficient for *D94* implies that the official rate was higher than the implied effective exchange rate.

In our model, the interest rate differential is not included in the set of fundamental variables. This is due to the assumption that the uncovered interest parity condition will not hold under the stringent capital controls and interest rate regulations in China. This assumption is consistent with the estimation result of MacDonald and Dias (2007) in which the coefficient on the interest rate differential is not statistically significant (see Table 1).

Equation (1) is estimated using quarterly data for the period 1990Q1 to 2009Q4. The definitions of the variables are described in the Appendix. The econometric method used for the test and estimation of the long-run relationship is the ARDL procedure developed Pesaran *et al.* (1996) and Pesaran and Shin (1999). The ARDL procedure has the advantage that it can be applied irrespective of whether the underlying regressors are $I(0)$ or $I(1)$ and thus, it can circumvent the pre-testing problems associated with standard co-integration analysis.

The estimation results of the ARDL procedure are shown in Tables 2–6. The ARDL model is estimated using the ordinary least square (OLS) method for all possible orders of lags between 0 and 4. An order of 4 was chosen as the maximum lag because the observations are quarterly. Using the Schwarz Bayesian criterion (SBC), the ARDL (2, 2, 2, 2) was selected. Table 2 shows the estimates of the selected ARDL model. With the exception of the coefficient of *tot* (–1), all other coefficients are statistically significant.

Table 3 shows the residual diagnostic statistics, which suggest that the selected model satisfies the assumption of non-autocorrelation, homoscedasticity and normality.

Table 4 shows the estimates of the error correction model based on the selected ARDL (2, 2, 2, 2) model. All coefficients are statistically significant. As expected, the coefficient of error correction term (*EC*) is negative, implying that the real exchange rate has a tendency to revert to the equilibrium value consistent with underlying fundamentals.

The existence of the long-run relationship between the variables is tested by computing the *F* statistic or the Wald statistic for testing the significance of the lagged levels of the variables in the error correction form of the underlying ARDL model. As shown in Table 5, both *F* and Wald statistics exceed the upper bounds of the critical value bands, and thus, the null of no long-run relation between the variables can be rejected at the 95% level.

Table 2. Estimates of ARDL model.

	Coefficient	*t*-value
q(−1)	0.491	4.830
q(−2)	−0.253	−2.809
pro	9.310	2.414
pro(−1)	−18.500	−2.562
pro(−2)	10.604	2.988
nfa	2.873	3.589
nfa(−1)	−3.963	−3.184
nfa(−2)	2.467	2.968
tot	0.687	2.689
tot(−1)	−0.588	−1.528
tot(−2)	0.871	3.367
const	7.903	7.770
trend	−0.026	−6.467
D94	0.154	5.855
R^2	0.906	—
Adjusted R^2	0.887	—
DW-statistics	1.751	—

Table 3. Residual diagnostic statistics.

	Lagrange multiplier (LM) statistics		*F*-statistics	
		P-value		*P*-value
Serial correlation[a]	7.583	[0.186]	1.607	[0.185]
Normality[b]	2.381	[0.304]	—	
Heteroscedasticity[c]	1.750	[0.108]	1.744	[0.191]

a. Godfrey's (1978a, 1978b) test of residual serial correlation.
b. Jarque and Bera's (1980) test of the normality of residuals.
c. Based on the regression of squared residuals on squared fitted values.

Table 6 shows the estimates of the long-run coefficients. All of the estimates are correctly signed and statistically significant. The coefficient of *tot* is positive, indicating that the income effect exceeds the substitution effect. The negative coefficient of the trend variable appears to capture the

Table 4. Estimates of error correction model.

	Coefficient	t-value
$\Delta q(-1)$	0.253	2.809
Δpro	9.310	2.414
$\Delta pro(-1)$	−10.604	−2.988
Δnfa	2.873	3.589
$\Delta nfa(-1)$	−2.467	−2.968
Δtot	0.687	2.689
$\Delta tot(-1)$	−0.871	−3.367
$\Delta trend$	−0.026	−6.467
$\Delta D94$	0.154	5.855
$EC(-1)$	−0.763	−8.025

Table 5. Testing for the existence of long-run relationship.

		95% critical values	
	Test statistics	Lower bound	Upper bound
F-statistics	17.295	4.719	5.817
Wald statistics	69.180	18.876	23.269

Table 6. Estimates of long-run coefficients.

	Coefficient	*t*-value
pro	1.853	8.122
nfa	1.805	5.244
tot	1.270	6.424
constant	10.360	15.010
trend	−0.035	−9.428
D94	0.202	5.625

effect of a continuous rise in the degree of openness, for example, the reduction in trade restrictions, which help to lower the price of traded goods. The positive coefficient of the dummy variable indicates that the official rate was higher than the effective rate.

Using the estimated long-run coefficients, the equilibrium relationship between the real exchange rate and the fundamentals can be expressed as follows:

$$q = 1.853\ pro + 1.805nfa + 1.270tot + 10.360 - 0.035trend$$
$$+ 0.202D94. \qquad (2)$$

The estimate of the BEER is given by inserting the current values of the fundamental variables into Eq. (2).

4. Exchange Rate Regimes and Undervaluation

The deviation in the real exchange rate from the estimated BEER can be considered as a misalignment in the sense that the real exchange rate is not in line with the underlying fundamentals. However, the fundamentals can also depart from their sustainable values as a result of cyclical factors and disturbances. In this case, the BEER deviates from its long-run equilibrium value which corresponds to the sustainable values of the fundamentals.

Following Clark and MacDonald (1999), we distinguish between the current and the total misalignment. The current refers to the deviation of the real exchange rate from the BEER; the total misalignment refers to the deviation of the real exchange rate from the long-run equilibrium or sustainable value of the BEER given by calibrating the fundamentals at their sustainable values (long-run BEER, hereafter). The sustainable values of the fundamentals are derived by applying the Hodrick–Prescott filter to the data.

The estimates of the BEER and the long-run BEER are plotted against the actual real exchange rate in Fig. 1. There are five points worth noting.

First, the renminbi was substantially overvalued under the dual exchange rates before 1994. The size of the overvaluation exceeds 16% in 1993Q4. The overvaluation was eliminated after the exchange rates were unified by devaluing the official rate in early 1994. However, the magnitude of the devaluation was so large that it caused overshooting in the BEER. As a result, the renminbi became substantially undervalued.

Second, while the renminbi remained undervalued for the majority of the period after 1994, the size of undervaluation was reduced

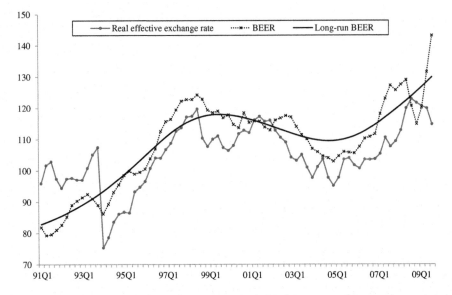

Fig. 1. BEER and long-run BEER of the renminbi.

Note: The values are expressed in the original number by reversing the operation of logarithm.

significantly and was almost eliminated during the period between the late 1990s and the early 2000s. After the unification of the exchange rates, the renminbi was effectively pegged to the U.S. dollar until mid-2005. Consequently, the size of undervaluation was reduced as the U.S. dollar appreciated against other currencies; conversely, it increased as the U.S. dollar depreciated.

Third, the long-run BEER has an increasing trend for most of the sample period. The major factors that have consistently contributed to the increase in the long-run BEER are the Balassa–Samuelson effect and the accumulation of net foreign assets. There was a reversal in this trend due to the worsening of terms of trade in the first half of 2000s (see Fig. 2). However, the long-run BEER returned to an increasing trend after 2005 as the accumulation of net foreign assets accelerated its pace due to large trade surplus.

Fourth, the size of undervaluation remains large even after a new exchange rate regime was introduced in July 2005. The Chinese government officially claims to have moved to managed floating exchange rates, under which the renminbi is managed with reference to a basket of currencies. However, this regime can be best characterized as an adjustable

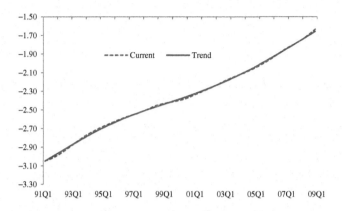

Fig. 2. (a)   Productivity differential.

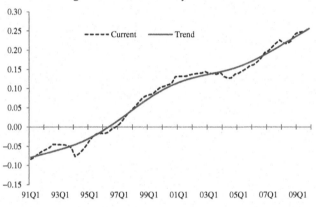

Fig. 2. (b)   Net foreign assets.

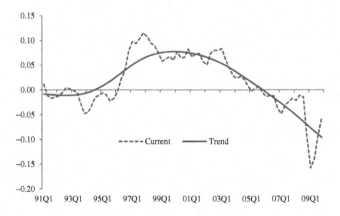

Fig. 2. (c)   Terms of trade.

dollar peg. The renminbi–dollar rate is kept within a narrow band by official market interventions.[5] Although central rate of the band is allowed to appreciate in response to market pressures, the pace of appreciation is very slow.

Despite the continued appreciation, the renminbi remains substantially undervalued due to an increase in the BEER. An increase in the BEER reflects the acceleration of net foreign asset accumulation as well as the Balassa–Samuelson effect. Apparently, the renminbi is not appreciating fast enough to match the pace of changes in underlying fundamentals.

Finally, there was a sharp reduction in the BEER and, as a result, in the degree of undervaluation in 2008Q3. This was due to a sudden drop in China's exports to the United States in the wake of the Lehman shock in September 2008. However, the reduction in the undervaluation proved to be temporary as the BEER increased again as China's exports recovered in 2009. The size of undervaluation reached 20% and 12% relative to the BEER and the long-run BEER, respectively, in 2009Q4.

The above findings suggest that the fundamental cause of the renminbi's persistent undervaluation is the lack of flexibility in China's exchange rate regime. The *de facto* dollar peg kept the renminbi undervalued relative to the BEER, which had an increasing trend. The size of the undervaluation decreased as the U.S. dollar appreciated. However, the undervaluation increased again as the U.S. dollar depreciated.

The Chinese government officially claims to have moved to managed floating exchange rates in mid-2005. However, the renminbi–dollar rate is kept within a narrow band by official market interventions and the central rate has been allowed to appreciate only slowly. The pace of renminbi's appreciation is not fast enough to offset the increase in the BEER due to the Balassa–Samuelson effect and the accumulation of net foreign assets. Consequently, the renminbi remained substantially undervalued despite the continued appreciation.

5. Conclusion

This chapter has examined whether the renminbi is appreciating fast enough to match the pace of changes in underlying fundamentals. To address this question, the renminbi's equilibrium exchange rate is

---

[5] The width of the band was set at ±0.3% for the renminbi–dollar rate at the beginning and was subsequently widened to ±1.0%.

estimated using the Clark and MacDonald's (1999) BEER approach. The econometric method used for the test and estimation of the long-run relationship is the ARDL procedure developed by Pesaran *et al.* (1996) and Pesaran and Shin (1999).

The main findings of the analysis can be summarized as follows. Under the *de facto* dollar peg after 1994, the renminbi was kept undervalued relative to the BEER, which had an increasing trend. The Chinese government officially claims to have moved to managed floating exchange rates in mid-2005. However, the renminbi–dollar rate is kept within a narrow band and has been allowed to appreciate only slowly. Despite the continued appreciation, the renminbi remains undervalued relative to the BEER. The renminbi is not appreciating fast enough to match the pace of changes in underlying fundamentals, notably the Balassa–Samuelson effect and net foreign asset accumulation. These findings suggest that the fundamental cause of the renminbi's persistent undervaluation is the lack of flexibility in China's exchange rate regime.

The fundamental solution to the renminbi's chronic problem of undervaluation is to introduce a more flexible exchange rate regime under which the exchange rate is, in principle, determined by market supply and demand. By doing so, the exchange rate will converge to the equilibrium value consistent with underlying fundamentals over the medium term, thereby preventing large and persistent misalignments.

Given the prospect of slower economic growth in the United States and Europe after the global financial crisis, for sustainable growth in China, it is important to rebalance demand away from external sources and towards domestic sources. Greater flexibility in the exchange rate regime would help China to promote economic rebalancing for two reasons. First, exchange rate flexibility would contribute to narrowing external imbalances by allowing real exchange rates to appreciate in line with underlying fundamentals. It would also contribute to reducing price distortions causing imbalances in China's production and investment structures. The undervaluation of the renminbi effectively provides manufacturing sectors with subsidies by increasing the relative price of tradable goods to non-tradable goods. The real exchange rate appreciation would contribute to shifting investment towards services and away from manufacturing, thereby slowing the growth of manufacturing exports. Second, greater flexibility would contribute to increasing household consumption by allowing the real interest rates of bank deposits to rise. Currently, bank deposit rates are kept low by the central bank to create profit margins for commercial banks. In return, commercial banks are required to purchase bills issued by the central bank to sterilize massive foreign exchange market interventions. In this regard, greater exchange rate flexibility would be a prerequisite for further interest rate liberalization. Interest rate liberalization would allow deposit rates to rise, which would increase household income and, other things being equal, increase consumption.[6] In these important ways, greater exchange rate flexibility would help China to promote economic rebalancing and achieve sustainable growth.

Appendix

Real effective exchange rate, q: The consumer price index (CPI)-based real effective exchange rate relative to the weighted geometrical average of China's major trading partners. The weights are based on 1993–1995 trade data, which are derived from the BIS effective exchange rate indices. China's quarterly CPI is estimated from the year-on-year percentage changes using 1986 as the base year. For 1986, interpolation technique is used to convert the annual CPI data to the quarterly one. This variable is expressed in logarithmic terms.

Productivity differential, pro: The PPP-based per capita GDP relative to the weighted average of major trading partners (the weights are same as above). Interpolation technique is used to convert the annual data to the quarterly one for China. This variable is expressed in logarithmic terms.

Net foreign assets, nfa: The ratio of accumulated sum of quarterly trade balance to the nominal GDP. Interpolation technique is used to convert the annual GDP data to the quarterly one.

Terms of trade, tot: The ratio of the export unit value to the import unit value relative to the weighted ratio of the major trading partner (the weights are same as above). Interpolation technique is used to convert the

---

[6] The response of household saving rates to changes in interest rates will depend on the relative strength of substitute and income effects. Lardy (2012) argues that the primary motivation of Chinese household to save is to achieve a target level of savings in an environment of underdeveloped social security systems. Under such circumstances, the income effect is likely to dominate the substitute effect; thus, household saving rates will increase in response to an increase in deposit rates.

annual data to the quarterly one for China and India. This variable is expressed in logarithmic terms.

Sources: BIS, Effective exchange rate indices; IMF International Financial Statistics (IFS), World Economic Outlook Database; World Bank, World Development Indicators.

References

Balassa, B (1964). The purchasing-power parity doctrine: A reappraisal. *Journal of Political Economy*, 72, 584–596.

Benassy-Quere, A, A Lahreche-Revil and V Mignon (2006). World consistent equilibrium exchange rates. *CEPII Working Paper, 2006–20*, Centre D'Etudes Prospectives et D'Informations Internationales, Paris.

Bergsten, CF, C Freeman, NR Lardy and DJ Mitchell (2009). *China's Rise: Challenges and Opportunities*. Washington DC: Peterson Institute for International economics and Center for Strategic and International Studies.

Cashin, P and C-J McDermott (1998). Terms of trade shocks and the current account. *IMF Working Paper* WP/98/177, IMF, Washington DC.

Clark, P and R MacDonald (1999). Exchange rates and economic fundamentals: A methodological comparison of BEERs and FEERs. In *Equilibrium Exchange Rates*, J Stein and R MacDonald (eds.), pp. 285–322. Boston: Kluwer.

Coudert, V and C Couharde (2007). Real equilibrium exchange rate in China: Is the renminbi undervalued? *Journal of Asian Economics*, 18, 568–594.

Edwards, S (1989). Temporary terms-of-trade disturbances, the real exchange rate and the current account. *Economica*, 56, 343–357.

Egert, B (2005). Equilibrium exchange rates in south eastern Europe, Russia, Ukraine and Turkey: Healthy or (Dutch) diseased? *Economic Systems*, 29, 205–241.

Funke, M and J Rahn (2005). Just how undervalued is the Chinese renminbi? *World Economy*, 28, 465–489.

Godfrey, LG (1978a). A note on the use of Durbin's h test when the equation is estimated by instrumental variables. *Econometrica*, 46, 225–228.

Godfrey, LG (1978b). Testing against general autoregressive and moving average error models when the regressors include lagged dependent variables. *Econometrica*, 46, 1293–1301.

Goldstein, M and M Mussa (2005). The fund appears to be sleeping at the wheel (3 October 2005). *Financial Times*.

Goldstein, M and NR Lardy (2009). The future of China's exchange rate policy. In *Policy Analyses in International Economics*, Vol. 87. Washington DC: Peterson Institute for International Economics.

Hansen, BE (2000). Sample splitting and threshold estimation. *Econometrica*, 68, 575–603.

Harberger, A-C (1950). Currency depreciation, income and the balance of trade. *Journal of Political Economy*, 58, 47–60.

Iimi, A (2006). Exchange rate misalignment: An application of the behavioral equilibrium exchange rate (Beer) to Botswana. *IMF Working Paper* WP/06/140, IMF, Washington DC.

IMF (2004). People's Republic of China: 2004 article IV consultation. *IMF Country Report* 064/351, IMF, Washington DC.

Jarque, CM and AK Bera (1980). Efficient tests for normality, homoscedasticity and serial independence of regression residuals. *Economics Letters*, 6, 255–259.

Kinkyo, T (2008). Disorderly adjustments to the misalignments in the Korean won. *Cambridge Journal of Economics*, 32, 111–124.

Lardy, NR (2012). *Sustaining China's Economic Growth*. Washington DC: Peterson Institute for International Economics.

Laurenson, S and L-A Metzler (1950). Flexible exchange rates and the theory of employment. *Review of Economics and Statistics*, 32, 281–299.

MacDonald, R (2002). Modeling the long-run real effective exchange rate of the New Zealand dollar. *Australian Economic Papers*, 41, 519–537.

MacDonald, R and P Dias (2007). Behavioral equilibrium exchange rate estimates and implied exchange rate adjustments for ten countries. *Paper prepared for the workshop on Global Imbalances*, February 8–9, Peterson Institute of International Economics, Washington DC.

MacDonald, R and L Ricci (2003). Estimation of the equilibrium real exchange rate for South Africa. *IMF Working Paper* WP/03/44, IMF, Washington DC.

Maeso-Fernandez, F, C Osbat and B Schnatz (2001). Determinants of the euro real effective exchange rate: A Beer/Peer approach. *European Central Bank Working Paper* No. 85, European Central Bank, Frankfurt.

Obstfeld, M and K Rogoff (1995). Exchange rate dynamics redux. *Journal of Political Economy*, 103, 624–660.

Perron, P (1997). Further evidence on breaking trend functions in macroeconomic variables, *Journal of Econometrics*, 80, 355–385.

Pesaran, MH and Y Shin (1999). An autoregressive distributed lag modeling approach to cointegration analysis. In *Econometrics and Economic Theory in 20th Century: The Ragnar Frisch Centennial Symposium*, S Strom (ed.), pp. 371–413. Cambridge: Cambridge University Press.

Pesaran, MH, Y Shin and RJ Smith (1996). Testing for the existence of a long run relationship. DAE Working Paper, No. 9622, University of Cambridge.

Samuelson, PA (1964). Theoretical notes on trade problems. *Review of Economics and Statistics*, 46, 145–154.

Wang, T (2004). Exchange Rate Dynamics. In *China's Growth and Integration into the World Economy: Prospects and Challenges*. IMF Occasional Paper 232, E Prasad (ed.), pp. 21–28. Washington DC: IMF.

Index

211

Printed in the United States
By Bookmasters